ACCOUNTING
IRREGULARITIES
AND
FINANCIAL
FRAUD

ACCOUNTING IRREGULARITIES AND FINANCIAL FRAUD

A Corporate Governance Guide

Second Edition

Edited by

MICHAEL R. YOUNG

ASPEN LAW & BUSINESS
A Division of Aspen Publishers, Inc.
New York   Gaithersburg
(Formerly published by Harcourt Professional Publishing)

Copyright © 2002 by Aspen Law & Business
A Division of Aspen Publishers, Inc.
A Wolters Kluwer Company
www.aspenpublishers.com

Printed in the United States of America

Library of Congress Cataloging-in-Publication Data

Accounting irregularities and financial fraud: a corporate governance guide / edited by Michael R. Young; [Jack H. Nusbaum ... et al., contributors].–2nd ed.
    p. cm.
Includes bibliographical references (p.) and index.
ISBN 0-7355-2691-5
    1.Corporations–United States–Accounting–Corrupt practices. 2. Fraud. 3. Internal audit. 4. Corporate governance. 5. Audit committees. 6. Class action (Civil procedure)–United States. I. Young, Michael R. II. Nusbaum, Jack H.

HF5686.C7 A3194 2001
658.4'73–dc21

                                                                            2001045886

About Aspen Law & Business

Aspen Law & Business is a leading publisher of authoritative treatises, practice manuals, services, and journals for attorneys, corporate and bank directors, accountants, auditors, environmental compliance professionals, financial and tax advisors, and other business professionals. Our mission is to provide practical solution-based how-to information keyed to the latest original pronouncements, as well as the latest legislative, judicial, and regulatory developments.

We offer publications in the areas of accounting and auditing; antitrust; banking and finance; bankruptcy; business and commercial law; construction law; corporate law; criminal law; environmental compliance; government and administrative law; health law; insurance law; intellectual property; international law; legal practice and litigation; matrimonial and family law; pensions, benefits, and labor; real estate law; securities; and taxation.

Other Aspen Law & Business products treating accounting and auditing and corporate governance issues include:

    A Practical Guide to SEC Proxy and Compensation Rules

    A Practical Guide to Section 16: Reporting and Compliance

    Audit Committees: A Guide for Directors, Management, and Consultants

    Business Judgment Rule: Fiduciary Duties of Corporate Directors

    Construction Accounting Deskbook

    CPA's Guide to Developing Effective Business Plans

    CPA's Guide to Effective Engagement Letters

    CPA's Guide to E-Business

    EDGAR and Electronic Filing

    Federal Government Contractor's Manual

    How to Manage Your Accounting Practice

    Medical Practice Management Handbook

    Meetings of Stockholders

    Miller Audit Procedures

    Miller Compilations and Reviews

    Miller European Accounting Guide

    Miller GAAP Financial Statement Disclosures Manual

Miller GAAP Guide
Miller GAAP Practice Manual
Miller GAAS Guide
Miller GAAS Practice Manual
Miller Governmental GAAP Guide
Miller International Accounting Standards Guide
Miller Local Government Audits
Miller Not-for-Profit Organization Audits
Miller Not-for-Profit Reporting
Miller Single Audits
Professional's Guide to Value Pricing
Regulation of Corporate Disclosure
The Corporate Governance Advisor
Takeover Defense

ASPEN LAW & BUSINESS
A Division of Aspen Publishers, Inc.
A Wolters Kluwer Company
www.aspenpublishers.com

SUBSCRIPTION NOTICE

This Aspen Law & Business product is updated on a periodic basis with supplements to reflect important changes in the subject matter. If you purchased this product directly from Aspen Law & Business, we have already recorded your subscription for the update service.

If, however, you purchased this product from a bookstore and wish to receive future updates and revised or related volumes billed separately with a 30-day examination review, please contact our Customer Service Department at 1-800-234-1660, or send your name, company name (if applicable), address, and the title of the product to:

ASPEN LAW & BUSINESS
A Division of Aspen Publishers, Inc.
7201 McKinney Circle
Frederick, MD 21704

CONTRIBUTORS

Jack H. Nusbaum, Chairman
Willkie Farr & Gallagher

Stephen Greiner, Litigation Partner
Willkie Farr & Gallagher

Joseph T. Baio, Litigation Partner
Willkie Farr & Gallagher

Benito Romano, Litigation Partner
Willkie Farr & Gallagher

John Oller, Litigation Partner
Willkie Farr & Gallagher

Harvey R. Kelly, Partner
PricewaterhouseCoopers LLP

Ty R. Sagalow, Chief Operating Officer
AIG eBusiness Risk Solutions

CONTENTS

Foreword xi

Preface xiii

Acknowledgments xiv

About the Authors xv

Detailed Table of Contents xix

Table of Exhibits xxvii

Chapter 1: The Origin of Financial Fraud 1

Chapter 2: So Who Gets the Blame? 23

Chapter 3: The Immediate Aftermath 45

Chapter 4: Getting New Audited Financial Statements 61

Chapter 5: Digging Out the Fraud: The Lawyers 81

Chapter 6: Digging Out the Fraud: The Forensic
            Accountants 97

Chapter 7: Class Action Lawsuits 119

Chapter 8: Dealing with the D&O Insurer 141

Chapter 9: Dealing with the Regulators 167

Chapter 10: Criminal Investigations 191

Chapter 11: What's an Audit Committee to Do? 227

Chapter 12: Due Diligence 281

Chapter 13: Accounting Irregularities and the Future of
            Financial Reporting 305

Index 319

by Mario M. Cuomo

The unprecedented era of spectacular growth over the last decade has unleashed cascading new wealth in the financial industry and created a new American world of glorious possibilities and challenges. One of the challenges is the disconcerting outbreak of "accounting irregularities," a nice euphemism for what amounts to the deliberate manipulation of bookkeeping to disguise regrettable realities with desirable illusions. In my old neighborhood that was usually called "fraud."

In the pages that follow, you will learn about the corporate environment that causes it, how it spreads, the kind of crises it can create for the company, and the best ways to deal with them. Experts will offer advice on the conduct of the initial investigation and the first meeting of the board of directors. They will give insights dealing with insurance, indemnity, and the possibility of class action lawsuits, and demonstrate how to restore corporate and individual credibility after the event.

There are also helpful ideas about how to strengthen the company against a recurrence of lapses in judgments and ethics. To do that we have to understand the dynamics and temptations that help spawn the manipulations: the corporate pressure that can push honest people into doing dishonest things, how an executive can be trapped by what seems an easy escape from the embarrassment of disillusioned earnings expectations. Business people with firsthand experience show how, in the process, the executive overlooks the possible cost in dollars and reputation and marketability, not just to the offending company and all those implicated by the company, but even to honest competitors in the rest of the industry whose reputations suffer by association.

All of that is described, clearly and vividly, from the cumulative experience of knowledgeable professionals, making this volume the first authentic "how to" book on dealing with accounting irregularities.

It can also prompt some badly needed reflection on the larger economic and fiscal context in which we find ourselves.

A lot has happened to economics and business in the last 30 years. So much so that a new language is being developed to describe our changing world. Words like "transparency" are suddenly and obviously recurrent in the pages of financial journals, on paper and on the computer screen. Thirty years ago the word "transparency" was used only infrequently and almost never by economists. Today that word means that if you want help from the IMF or the World Bank, or if you want credibility in your fiscal practice here at home, your books and accounting records ought to be clean, honest, and comprehensible.

Most dictionaries still don't list that particular meaning. But it is found in almost every speech by former Treasury Secretary Robert Rubin and current Chairman of the Federal Reserve Board Alan Greenspan.

And only a few years ahead of "transparency," the words "interconnectedness" and "interdependence" resurfaced. Wendell Willkie, who ran against FDR in 1941, had used those words over a half a century ago in his book *One World*, while predicting the inevitable emergence of another new word, "globalization." Four decades later, Mikhail Gorbachev and Vaclav Havel resuscitated Willkie's words and now they regularly appear when the point is being made that the financial world and the rest of the planet are intensifying dealings with one another all over the globe. Horizons have broadened, borders have become infinitely elastic. Mergers and mega-mergers, joint ventures and affiliations, stretching the reach of companies across seas and over continents, have created tremendous new opportunities and fearsome new competition at the same time.

The message in this book is that, in this world of exciting new options and intense new competition, financial regularity and transparency will be a *sine qua non* to success. Only the enterprise that can be believed and depended upon will survive. Our hope is that the contributions we offer will make that case clearly enough that, before much longer, this kind of fraud will become so rare we won't need clumsy euphemisms like "accounting irregularities" at all.

It only takes a phone call. One moment you're a titan of corporate management. You are, among other things, an outside director of a company that has, yet again, reported stellar results. The stock price is up. Senior management is happy with their well-deserved bonuses. And you're basking in the glow of a favorable article that has just appeared in *Business Week*.

Then, with a single phone call, everything changes. You're told that accounting irregularities have surfaced at the company. Inexplicably, the CFO has confessed. An emergency board of directors meeting is being called for the next day. There will be one item on the agenda: How to deal with a crisis.

Increasingly, boards of directors, audit committee members, and senior executives are finding themselves in precisely this situation. For virtually all of them, it will be the first time that they will go through it. For that matter, it will probably be the first time for their outside law firm, the certified public accountants who serve as their outside auditors, and almost everybody else involved. Some will choose the proper course of action almost as a matter of instinct. But, experience teaches, many will not.

This book is intended to provide a step-by-step guide to the crises enveloping a company in the wake of fraudulent financial reporting—and how to prevent it from happening in the first place. It is directed to almost everybody involved: outside directors, audit committee members, senior executives, CFOs, CPAs, in-house lawyers, and outside law firms. Experience teaches that, where fraudulent financial reporting surfaces, the root causes and effects are almost always the same. Also the same are the strategies for dealing with them.

Michael R. Young

ACKNOWLEDGMENTS

The authors would like to thank the following for their invaluable contributions to this book:

Laila Abou-Rahme, Willkie Farr & Gallagher

William T. Allen, Independence Standards Board

Joseph G. Davis, Willkie Farr & Gallagher

Paul A. Ferrillo, American International Group, Inc.

Alan S. Fox, PricewaterhouseCoopers LLP

Paul V. Gerlach, Securities and Exchange Commission

Vinita M. Juneja, National Economic Research Associates, Inc.

Alison M. Scarpaci, BDO Seidman, LLP

Michael G. Marks, Willkie Farr & Gallagher (retired)

D. Edward Martin, Richard A. Eisner & Company, LLP

Scott S. Rose, Reboul, Mac Murray, Hewitt, Maynard & Kristol

Diane M. Tokarz, Willkie Farr & Gallagher

Lynn E. Turner, formerly of the Securities and Exchange Commission

William U. Westerfield, Price Waterhouse LLP (retired)

John O. Whitney, Columbia University Graduate School of Business

ABOUT THE AUTHORS

Editor

Michael R. Young is a litigation partner of Willkie Farr & Gallagher where he heads the firm's Accounting Irregularities Practice Group. For more than a decade, Mr. Young has served as a counsel to the American Institute of Certified Public Accountants, and he has accordingly assisted in such matters as the formulation of the federal securities tort reform legislation of the mid-1990s, the drafting of generally accepted auditing standards, the enactment of the Uniform Accountancy Act, and the submission to the United States Supreme Court and Courts of Appeal of *amicus curiae* briefs on matters of importance to financial reporting. Mr. Young also actively investigates and defends companies, officers and directors, accounting firms, and others in matters involving financial reporting and liability, and he has been involved in some of the most significant accounting irregularities matters of the past twenty years. He is a member of the American Bar Association's Committee on Law and Accounting and writes and lectures frequently on financial reporting and liability issues.

Foreword

Mario M. Cuomo, before he entered public service, had been a law clerk to the Honorable Adrian P. Burke of the New York State Court of Appeals, an Adjunct Professor of Law, and a practicing attorney who had appeared in every level of the New York State courts and before the Supreme Court of the United States. As Secretary of State and then Governor of New York for 12 years, he took a leading role in the enhancement of the laws of public disclosure and integrity in public reporting. As Secretary of State, Mr. Cuomo helped write the first public disclosure laws in New York State and drafted the first reform of New York's lobbying laws in over 70 years. As Governor, he proposed and signed the first ethics law for public officials; the law requiring the application of generally accepted accounting principles to the state budget; and the first state statute requiring regular and independent audits of all executive agencies, including the Comptroller's Office, the State Inspector xvi Accounting Irregularities and Financial Fraud

General's Office, and his own Office of the Governor. As a partner of Willkie Farr & Gallagher, Mr. Cuomo has played an active role in advising public companies, boards of directors, and audit committees on issues of corporate governance and financial reporting, and he has engaged in a broader practice specializing in national and international corporate law. Mr. Cuomo is the author or editor of more than a half-dozen books, including *The Blue Spruce, Reason to Believe, The New York Idea: An Experiment in Democracy, More Than Words, Lincoln on Democracy, Diaries of Mario Cuomo,* and *Forest Hills Diary.*

Contributing Authors

Jack H. Nusbaum is Chairman of Willkie Farr & Gallagher and leads the firm's Mergers and Acquisitions Practice Group. Mr. Nusbaum also actively advises public companies, senior executives, and professionals in matters relating to financial reporting and accounting irregularities, and he headed the team responsible for the 1998 Report to the Audit Committee of the Board of Directors of Cendant Corporation. Mr. Nusbaum is also a director of a number of publicly held corporations, including W.R. Berkley Corporation; Pioneer Companies, Inc.; Prime Hospitality Corp.; Neuberger Berman, LLC; Strategic Distribution, Inc.; and The Topps Company, Inc. He also serves on the board of directors of Hirschl & Adler Galleries, Inc. Mr. Nusbaum is a trustee of The Robert Steel Foundation, Prep for Prep, and The Joseph Collins Foundation.

Stephen Greiner is a litigation partner of Willkie Farr & Gallagher specializing in securities litigation. Throughout his career, he has represented officers and directors, financial services organizations, accounting firms, and other businesses in a broad variety of securities matters, including litigation and investigations initiated by the Securities and Exchange Commission and other regulatory agencies. He has also specialized in conducting internal investigations, including matters involving accounting irregularities and other financial reporting issues.

Joseph T. Baio is a litigation partner of Willkie Farr & Gallagher and a member of the firm's Executive Committee. Although his practice is not limited to any area, he regularly represents individuals and companies involved in litigations arising out of large commercial or securities transactions. He has defended companies and corporate officers in connection with Securities and Exchange Commission, Department of Justice, and FBI investigations and in proceedings before the New York Stock Exchange and the National Association of Securities Dealers. Mr. Baio is a frequent lecturer on business law at the Columbia University School of Business and is a regular speaker for the Directors' Network, an organization that instructs members of boards of directors about their responsibilities and potential liabilities under state and federal law.

Benito Romano has been a litigation partner of Willkie Farr & Gallagher and head of its white collar crime practice group since November 1989. Mr. Romano has represented numerous companies and individuals in criminal investigations involving allegations of financial fraud, fraud against the government, and regulatory offenses. Before his return to private practice, Mr. Romano served as United States Attorney for the Southern District of New York. Before assuming the position of United States Attorney, Mr. Romano served in a variety of supervisory and executive positions in that office, including Chief Appellate Attorney for the Criminal Division, Executive Assistant United States Attorney and Chief of the Public Corruption Unit, and Associate United States Attorney.

John Oller is a litigation partner of Willkie Farr & Gallagher. Since joining the firm in 1982, Mr. Oller has specialized in complex commercial litigation with particular emphases on federal securities litigation and internal and independent corporate investigations. He was a principal author of the 1998 Cendant Report, based on the internal investigation of Cendant Corporation on behalf of its audit committee, which the *New York Times* called a definitive case study in the area of accounting irregularities and fraud.

Harvey R. Kelly is a certified public accountant and a partner in the Financial Advisory Services practice of PricewaterhouseCoopers LLP. Mr. Kelly specializes in forensic accounting investigations and litigation consulting and has conducted forensic investigations into alleged accounting errors and irregularities on behalf of companies, directors, creditors, and shareholders. Mr. Kelly has also been called upon to provide litigation consulting services and expert witness testimony in related securities litigation and regulatory investigation proceedings and has served as a court-appointed examiner charged with investigating fraud allegations. He is an experienced financial statement auditor and has audited the financial statements of public and private companies in a wide range of industries. Mr. Kelly is a frequent lecturer on the topics of forensic accounting investigations and securities litigation.

Ty R. Sagalow is Chief Operating Officer and Executive Vice President of AIG eBusiness Risk Solutions, a member company of American International Group, Inc. Mr. Sagalow, who has authored AIG director and officer insurance policies since 1987, is on the faculty of the National Association of Corporate Directors and has spoken before numerous legal and insurance forums throughout the nation on issues affecting directors' and officers' (D&O) liability and corporate governance, including Stanford University's *Director's College*, Watson Wyatt's *D&O Symposium*, and the American and New York Bar Associations. Mr. Sagalow has also written a number of articles on director and officer liability which have appeared in such publications as *Bank Director* and *Director's Monthly*. He was both guest editor and a contributing author for the *Special Issue on D&O Liability, Indemnification and Insurance* appearing in *Director's Monthly*. Most recently, he co-authored the chapter "Directors and Officers Insurance" appearing in *Directors & Officers Liability: Indemnification and Insurance*. Mr. Sagalow is vice chairman of the American Bar Association's standing committee on Directors, Officers and Professional Liability for the Tort & Insurance Professional Liability section.

DETAILED TABLE OF CONTENTS

Chapter 1: The Origin of Financial Fraud 1

Let's Step Back 2

What Is an "Accounting Irregularity?" 3

So How Do Accounting Irregularities Come About? 6

    Example 6

Isolating the Elements 11

The Danger of "Managed Earnings" 14

The Audit Committee, the Internal Audit Department, and the
    Outside Auditor 16

    The Audit Committee 16

    Internal Audit 17

    The Outside Auditor 18

The Fraud Surfaces 20

A Crisis for the Board 20

Chapter 2: So Who Gets the Blame? 23

Blaming the Outside Auditor 23

The Treadway Commission 25

Consequences of the Treadway Commission Report 28

Further Developments 30

The Levitt Initiatives 32

So Who Gets the Blame? 40

Chapter 3: The Immediate Aftermath 45

The Preliminary Investigation 45

The Initial Board Meeting 46

A Race Against Time 51

Action Plan 53

The Initial Press Release 54

Other Issues 56

The Auditor's Upper Hand 60

Chapter 4: Getting New Audited Financial Statements 61

Initial Involvement of the Outside Auditor 61

Effect on Previously Issued Audit Reports 62

The Element of Mistrust 64

Benefits of Continuing the Audit Relationship 65

The Independent Forensic Accounting Team 68

Responsibility for Restated Financial Statements 68

Restatement Requirements 69

Restatements and Materiality 72

The Audit Process 74

Representations to the Auditor 76

Effect of Lawsuits on Auditor Independence 78

The Bottom Line 79

Chapter 5: Digging Out the Fraud: The Lawyers 81

Purposes of the Investigation 81

Who Conducts the Investigation? 83

Time Frame of the Investigation 84

Tasks to Perform 85

Lack of Subpoena Power and the Interview Process 87

Unresolved Questions 91

The Report 92

Can the Report Remain Privileged? 94

Is the Investigators' Work Product Privileged? 95

Chapter 6: Digging Out the Fraud: The Forensic
    Accountants 97

What Is a Forensic Accountant? 97

Why Hire a Forensic Accountant? 97

The Difference between a Forensic Investigation and
    an Audit 102

Immediate Objectives 105

Framing the Issues 107

Revenue Recognition 109

Reserves 110

Inventory 111

Expenses 112

Conducting the Investigation 113

Interacting with the Lawyers and the Attorney-Client
     Privilege 114

Coordination with the Outside Auditor 116

Knowing When to Stop 118

Chapter 7: Class Action Lawsuits 119

What Is a Class Action? 119

The Commencement of Class Action Litigation 120

The Likely Defendants 121

Sorting Out Parties and Counsel...123

The Consolidated Complaint 124

Liability Implications of the Initial Press Release 127

The Motion to Dismiss 130

The Prospects of an Early Settlement 131

The Process of Discovery 132

    The Production of Documents 132

    Addition of the Outside Auditor 134

    The Taking of Depositions...136

Dynamics Favoring Settlement..136

Securities Law Damages 138

Ultimately a Settlement 139

Chapter 8: Dealing with the D&O Insurer 141

The Structure of a Typical Policy 142

Analysis of a D&O Policy 144

    A Claim Must Have Been Made During the
         Policy Period...144

The Claim Must Be Made Against an Insured 146

The Claim Must Be for a Wrongful Act 147

The Insured Must Have Incurred a Loss 148

The Claim Must Not Be Excluded 149

    Conduct Exclusions 150

    Exclusions Due to Other Policies 151

    The Insured v. Insured Exclusion 152

    Endorsements 153

The Insurer Must Be Timely Notified 154

The Loss Must Be in Excess of the Retention Amount
    and Not Within Any Applicable Coinsurance
    Percentage 156

The D&O Policy and Accounting Irregularities 156

    The Deliberate Fraudulent Act Exclusion 157

    Imputation from One Insured to Another 158

    The Need for a Factual Determination 159

    The Problem of "Loose Cannons on the Deck" 160

    The Application Process 162

So How Does All This End Up? 163

The Best Approach 164

Chapter 9: Dealing with the Regulators 167

The SEC: The Power to Investigate, Correct, and Punish 167

    Disclosure Requirements 168

    Additional Provisions 170

    Financial Fraud Investigations 170

    Formal Orders of Investigation and Subpoena Powers 171

    Penalties and Sanctions 172

    Regaining Credibility with the SEC: Fight or
        Acquiesce? 173

    Cooperating with the SEC 174

    Initial Contact with the SEC 175

Early Communication with the SEC 175

Responding to SEC Subpoenas and the Representation
of Witnesses 176

Turning Over an Investigative Report to the SEC 177

Making Peace with the SEC 178

Dealing with Self-Regulatory Organizations 181

What "SROs" Are and What They Do 181

SROs and the SEC 182

Listing Requirements 183

Enhanced Exchange Requirements 184

Preventing and Handling Delisting Proceedings 186

Early Dialogue and Suspension of Trading 187

Corrective Measures 188

A Two-Pronged Approach to Delisting Proceedings 188

Chapter 10: Criminal Investigations 191

The Initial Grand Jury Phase 195

Producing Documents to the Prosecutor 198

Initial Contacts with Counsel for Individual Employees 200

Employee Interviews 202

The Testimonial Grand Jury Phase 205

The Fifth Amendment Privilege 206

The Attorney-Client Privilege 208

The Attorney Work-Product Doctrine 208

The Joint-Defense Privilege 209

Prosecutorial Status and Immunity 210

Corporate Criminal Liability for Employee Actions 213

Corporate Indemnification for Counsel Fees 214

Separate Counsel for Targets and Subjects 216

Plea Discussions and Sentencing Considerations 217

Other Responsibilities of Counsel for a Target Company 221

Parallel Proceedings 224

Chapter 11: What's an Audit Committee to Do? **227**

Financial Reporting and the Audit Committee 228

    Checklists, Checklists, Checklists 229

An Approach to Audit Committee Oversight 230

    The Tone at the Top 231

    Logistical Capability 233

    Immediate Detection of Financial Misreporting 233

A Properly Configured Audit Committee 234

    Independence 237

    Financial Sophistication 241

    Willingness to Work 242

The Biggest Challenge: Information...247

Getting Information from Senior Management....................................248

Getting Information from the Outside Auditor 249

    Environmental Information 251

    Logistical Capabilities of the Financial Reporting
        System 252

    Managerial Bias in the Application of GAAP 253

    The Level of Cooperation and Difficulties Encountered..............253

    Unusual Revenue or Reserve Activity..255

    Nonmaterial PAJEs 256

    Thoroughness of the Audit..258

    SAS-61 Items 259

    Auditor Independence 260

Getting Information from the Internal Audit 269

Making the Tools Work..271

    More on the Tone at the Top 271

    Minimize Reliance on Paper 273

    Learn the Business..274

    Meet with Others and Alone 275

Meet When Necessary 276

Use Good Judgment 276

Chapter 12: Due Diligence **281**

Looking at the Numbers 281

Looking at the Environment...285

The Chief Executive Officer 289

The Chief Financial Officer 290

The Effectiveness of the Audit Committee 292

A New Industry 297

An Aggressive Growth Program 300

An Industry Downturn 303

Chapter 13: Accounting Irregularities and the Future of

Financial Reporting 305

A Real-Time World 306

A 1930s Financial Reporting System 307

So Enter the Analysts 309

A Consequence Is Accounting Irregularities 310

Other Capital Market Inefficiencies......................................311

There's Another Way 315

TABLE OF EXHIBITS

Chapter 1: The Origin of Financial Fraud 1

Exhibit 1-1. A Word About Nomenclature 4

Exhibit 1-2. Statement on Auditing Standards No. 53's
Definition of "Errors and Irregularities" 5

Exhibit 1-3. The Treadmill Effect 10

Chapter 2: So Who Gets the Blame? **23**

Exhibit 2-1. The Evolution of Financial Reporting 24

Exhibit 2-2. Key Recommendations of the Treadway
Commission for Public Companies 29

Exhibit 2-3. Evolving Perceptions of Auditor Responsibility 33

Exhibit 2-4. Arthur Levitt's Speech: "The Numbers Game" 35

Chapter 3: The Immediate Aftermath **45**

Exhibit 3-1. Restoring Crediblity 52

Exhibit 3-2. Implementation Checklist 53

Chapter 4: Getting New Audited Financial Statements **61**

Exhibit 4-1. Selecting an Auditor 66

Exhibit 4-2. Restatement Guidance 70

Exhibit 4-3. What to Expect from Auditors Auditing Fraud-
Related Restatements 75

Chapter 5: Digging Out the Fraud: The Lawyers **81**

Exhibit 5-1. Investigative Tasks 85

Exhibit 5-2. Pros and Cons of a Written Report 93

**Chapter 6: Digging Out the Fraud:
The Forensic Accountants** **97**

Exhibit 6-1. Key Benefits of Using Outside Forensic
Accountants 100

Exhibit 6-2. Typical Approach of Forensic Accountants 105

Exhibit 6-3. Common Accounting Fraud Areas 108

Chapter 7: Class Action Lawsuits 119

Exhibit 7-1. Typical Stages of a Securities Class Action 120

Chapter 8: Dealing with the D&O Insurer 141

Exhibit 8-1. D&O Insurance Issues 144

Chapter 9: Dealing with the Regulators 167

Exhibit 9-1. SEC Objectives 168

Exhibit 9-2. SEC Penalties 180

Exhibit 9-3. New York Stock Exchange Delisting
Procedures 185

Exhibit 9-4. Nasdaq Delisting Procedures 186

Chapter 10: Criminal Investigations 191

Exhibit 10-1. Securities Act of 1933 192

Exhibit 10-2. Securities Exchange Act of 1934 192

Exhibit 10-3. Criminal Sentences 194

Exhibit 10-4. Phases of a Criminal Investigation 195

Exhibit 10-5. Federal Sentencing Guidelines: An Effective
Program to Prevent and Detect Violations of Law 223

Chapter 11: What's an Audit Committee To Do? 227

Exhibit 11-1. New NYSE Rules: Audit Committee
Composition 235

Exhibit 11-2. New NASD Rules: Audit Committee
Composition 236

Exhibit 11-3. New NYSE Rules: Audit Committee
Independence 238

Exhibit 11-4. New NASD Rules: Audit Committee
Independence 239

Exhibit 11-5. New NYSE Rules: Audit Committee Charter 243

Exhibit 11-6. New NASD Rules: Audit Committee Charter 244

Exhibit 11-7. New SEC Rules to Implement the Recommendations
of the Blue Ribbon Committee 245

Exhibit 11-8. Delaware Law 246

Exhibit 11-9. Foreign Corrupt Practices Act 252

Exhibit 11-10. SEC Rule: Book and Records 253

Exhibit 11-11. New Amendments to Statement on Auditing
Standards No. 61 (Communication with
Audit Committees) 254

Exhibit 11-12. New Amendments to Statement on Auditing
Standards No. 71 (Interim Financial Information) 255

Exhibit 11-13. SEC Staff Accounting Bulletin No. 99
(Materiality) 257

Exhibit 11-14. SAS-61 Communications 259

Exhibit 11-15. Auditor Independence 263

Exhibit 11-16. Independence Standards Board Standard No. 1
(Independence Discussions with Audit Committees) 265

Exhibit 11-17. New SEC Rules on Auditor Independence 266

Exhibit 11-18. A Five-Step Approach to Audit Committee
Assessment of Auditor Independence 268

Exhibit 11-19. Sample Audit Committee Charter 277

Chapter 12: Due Diligence 281

Exhibit 12-1. An Effective Audit Committee 293

Exhibit 12-2. Public Sources to Evaluate Audit Committee
Effectiveness 297

Exhibit 12-3. "New Industry" Problems 298

Exhibit 12-4. A Petri Dish for Accounting Irregularities 303

ACCOUNTING IRREGULARITIES AND FINANCIAL FRAUD

CHAPTER 1

THE ORIGIN OF FINANCIAL FRAUD

Michael R. Young

On top of everything else, today's senior executive, outside director, and (in particular) audit committee member now face a growing problem that seems to have appeared in the financial headlines almost overnight. It is the problem of so-called accounting irregularities. That is to say, it is the problem of deliberately misreported financial results.

The accounting irregularities to attract the most public attention were those that surfaced at Cendant Corporation in April 1998, where the announcement of misstated financial results at Cendant's newly acquired CUC International unit led to a $14 billion loss in market capital in just a few hours. But Cendant is far from alone. Highly publicized financial misreporting problems have also surfaced at Lucent, Microstrategy, Xerox, Lernout & Hauspie, Anicom, Rent-Way, McKesson, Livent, Mercury Finance, Donnkenny, Rite Aid, Boston Scientific, Informix, Sunbeam, Micro Warehouse, Northstar Health Services, Paracelsus Healthcare, Penguin, Photran, Sensormatic, Thor Industries, BT Office Products, Guildford Mills, Bankers Trust, and Physician Computer Network. And that's just to name a few.

Evidence of an increase in accounting irregularities is more than anecdotal. A series of surveys conducted by PricewaterhouseCoopers shows that claims based on alleged accounting irregularities increased from 25% of securities claims in 1997 to 49% just two years later. A similar study concluded that, between 1992 and 1998, the number of securities lawsuits based on the need to restate audited financial statements increased by 750%. Meanwhile, the number of companies needing to correct or "restate" earlier financial statements has increased at an accelerated pace: 116 in 1997, 158 in 1998, 216 in 1999, and 233 in 2000. Separately, a survey of chief financial officers, conducted on a strictly anonymous basis, found that fully two-thirds had been subjected to pressure within their companies to misrepresent financial results. According to the survey, 55% had successfully resisted. At the same time, 12% had not.

The Securities and Exchange Commission (SEC) is understandably up in arms. At a seminal speech at New York University on September 28, 1998, then-SEC Chairman Arthur Levitt threw down the gauntlet to the financial community and announced a series of initiatives to combat accounting fraud. These included heightened SEC scrutiny of certain types of reporting practices, the formation of a Blue Ribbon Committee to study the effectiveness of corporate audit committees, and an effort to reexamine the outside audit function. In the ten months following that September 28 speech, the topic of accounting irregularities was the subject of no fewer than 21 speeches by the SEC's Chairman, the Chief Accountant, the Director of Enforcement, or others within either the Office of the Chief Accountant or the Division of Enforcement.

Under prodding from the SEC, others within the financial community have taken action. The New York Stock Exchange (NYSE) and the National Association of Securities Dealers (NASD), based on the recommendations of a newly formed Blue Ribbon Committee on Improving the Effectiveness of Corporate Audit Committees, have adopted a new set of rules to combat financial fraud. The Committee of Sponsoring Organizations of the Treadway Commission (COSO) has published the results of an extensive study on the underlying causes of fraudulent financial reporting. The Public Oversight Board—a collection of elder statesmen charged with oversight of the audit profession—has completed a new initiative directed to a revamping of the audit function. And the Financial Accounting Standards Board (FASB) is subjecting technical pronouncements to new scrutiny. Even entirely private groups, such as sponsors of seminars, law firms, and bar associations, have convened conferences and programs to explore why a wholesale breakdown in financial reporting systems seems to be taking place.

Let's Step Back

At one point, someone is bound to ask: Are we witnessing a collapse of honesty and morality in financial America? Have we finally reached the point in the evolution of business practice where dishonesty has become the norm rather than the exception? If not, how do we explain a statistic that tells us that two-thirds of corporate America is putting pressure on its accounting departments to commit fraud?

These questions can be answered. But first we need to step back and take an objective look at what is really going on.

To begin, there is little question that reported instances of accounting irregularities are on the rise. The evidence is anecdotal, statistical, and convincing. More and more companies are experiencing some level of financial misreporting, and the evidence suggests that the misreporting is not always innocent.

But that does not mean that corporate America is slipping into an abyss of dissembling and dishonesty. On the contrary, ample evidence exists that the individual integrity of those running public companies today has never been at a higher level. Never before have we seen such attentiveness to the welfare of employees and their families, the effect of corporate activity on the environment, or the need for a corporation to act, in the words of one recent book, like "a good corporation citizen." Those who would argue that corporate managers behave less responsibly and with a greater level of dishonesty than their predecessors have a tough argument to make.

So how can these seemingly inconsistent trends be reconciled? How do we reconcile an increase in financial misreporting with increasing executive interest in proper corporate behavior? The answer lies in an understanding of the root causes of financial misreporting. In particular, it lies in the recognition that financial misreporting—even deliberate financial misreporting—does not, at root, start with dishonesty. Rather, financial misreporting stems from a certain type of corporate environment. Where that kind of environment exists, accounting irregularities can develop and grow undetected at companies whose senior executives are ostensibly of unimpeachable integrity.

What Is an "Accounting Irregularity?"

Before we go further in dissecting the origin of financial fraud, we need to establish some basics. In particular, we need to make sure we have a common vocabulary as to exactly what financial writers mean when they refer to an "accounting irregularity."

The term has its origin in the obscure (and, ironically, now superseded) authoritative literature of the accounting profession. (See Exhib-

---

Exhibit 1–1. A Word about Nomenclature

The now ubiquitous term *accounting irregularities* comes from one of the standards explicating generally accepted auditing standards—Statement on Auditing Standards (SAS) No. 53 (The Auditor's Responsibility to Detect and Report Errors and Irregularities). SAS-53 defines *irregularities* as "*intentional* misstatements or omissions of amounts or disclosures in financial statements."

Ironically, just as the term *irregularities* has come into vogue, SAS-53 has been superseded by a new standard on the same subject—SAS-82 (Consideration of Fraud in a Financial Statement Audit). Although SAS-82 does not seek to alter the auditor's responsibility for detecting fraud, it does serve to heighten auditor awareness of that responsibility and, in the process, completely drops the reference to irregularities and adopts the term *fraud*.

Technically, a distinction can be drawn between an irregularity and fraud insofar as an irregularity consists of an intentional misstatement in financial statements, whereas an irregularity evolves into fraud only when those financial statements are shown to another who then justifiably relies on them to his or her detriment. In common parlance, though, the terms are being used interchangeably and they will largely be used interchangeably in this book.

---

its 1–1 and 1–2.) Perhaps out of a belief that the word *fraud* was too rude for its authoritative literature, accountants have historically avoided the term *fraud* altogether and, instead, divided financial statement misstatements into two categories: errors and irregularities.

The difference between the two has nothing to do with the accuracy of the reported numbers—one or the other may apply even where numbers are equally wrong. The difference has to do with the intent of the individual by whom the incorrect numbers have been provided. *Errors* are defined to be accidental inaccuracies. *Irregularities* are defined to be inaccuracies that are deliberate.

Why does the literature distinguish between the two? Because the distinction between an accounting *error* and an accounting *irregularity*

Exhibit 1–2. Statement on Auditing Standards No. 53's Definition of "Errors and Irregularities"

The term *errors* refers to unintentional misstatements or omissions of amounts or disclosures in financial statements. Errors may involve:

- Mistakes in gathering or processing accounting data from which financial statements are prepared
- Incorrect accounting estimates arising from oversight or misinterpretation of facts
- Mistakes in the application of accounting principles relating to amount, classification, manner of presentation, or disclosure

The term *irregularities* refers to intentional misstatements or omissions of amounts or disclosures in financial statements. Irregularities may include fraudulent financial reporting undertaken to render financial statements misleading and misappropriation of assets. Irregularities may involve:

- Manipulation, falsification, or alteration of accounting records or supporting documents from which financial statements are prepared
- Misrepresentation or intentional omission of events, transactions, or other significant information
- Intentional misapplication of accounting principles relating to amounts, classification, manner of presentation, or disclosure

---

is comparable (to paraphrase one American jurist) to the difference between a dog that has been stumbled over and a dog that has been kicked. Where a company finds an accounting error, it does its best to fix it and move on. If the accounting misstatement has truly been accidental, in many cases the federal securities laws will not even allow shareholders to sue.

Where the misstatement is an irregularity, the situation is completely different. When financial statements are misstated because of an irregularity, someone has not made an innocent mistake. Someone has deliberately lied. And the resulting concern is that somebody (best scenario) or a group of people (worst scenario) is dishonest and is lying to everyone about financial performance. So the company is not in a position in which it can just fix the numbers and move on. Some level of corporate housecleaning is going to be involved.

None of this means that an irregularity implies that everyone in an organization was in on the fraud or even that executives were in on the fraud. Unfortunately, an irregularity can be brought about by just one bad apple. But, when we see the label "accounting irregularity," we know that someone within the organization has deliberately misstated some aspect of financial performance, and that misstatement has seeped its way into the company's publicly reported results.

So How Do Accounting Irregularities Come About?

Accounting irregularities start and grow within a certain type of corporate environment. The key to understanding this kind of financial fraud—and the key to its prevention—is to understand that environment and the way it influences individual conduct.

Example

To illustrate, let's consider a situation that many will recognize as all too familiar. Hypothesize a manufacturing company that went public not too long ago at a time when the market was hitting new highs and an economic expansion was surpassing all records. Accordingly, management has been able to announce a series of record-breaking quarters. In the meantime, management has struggled to attract the attention of Wall Street analysts whose attention is, management believes, necessary if the company's laudable earnings history is to be fairly reflected in the stock price. Several analysts are following the company's stock and, in fact, among the company's stockholders are momentum investors who are investing based on an anticipation of a continuing upward trajectory to ever-increasing heights.

There is, though, a problem. The company's industry—which, quarter after quarter, had enabled continued expansion and double-digit earnings growth—is starting to slow down. Management perceives this slowdown in growth, moreover, before its potential effects are fully appreciated by the investment community. In particular, the slowdown largely seems to escape the notice of the Wall Street analysts following the stock.

Therefore a mismatch exists. Wall Street is expecting a new record quarter (and the analysts have got it nailed down to the exact penny). But management sees that a new record quarter is not likely to happen. For the first time, the company is facing the specter of a failure to attain analyst expectations.

The more seasoned members of the business community might recognize that it's time for the company to take its lumps and move on. But this company is somewhat lacking in seasoned managers—it's only been public for a few years. For management, the thought of missing analyst expectations—and the specter of momentum investors fleeing the stock—is more terrifying than it can endure. So what happens? Executives' feet are to be held to the fire. The word goes out to all division heads: Pull out the stops. Specific earnings targets are distributed to various divisions. Along with the targets comes an admonition: There is to be no slippage. A failure to attain the target will be viewed as unforgivable.

So now key elements of a certain kind of corporate environment are in place. There is pressure. There is an aggressive earnings target. And there is a vivid recognition that, one way or another, that earnings target must be attained.

Let's now shift our attention to someone who's on the receiving end of all this—a division president, a graduate of the finest schools, and an individual whose personal integrity has heretofore been unchallenged. He is now facing the most difficult crisis of his career.

For it is plain to our division president that, excruciating pressure or no, he cannot meet his earnings target. The business simply isn't there. He has already cut expenses to the bone. He has already admonished his sales force to make every effort. But, as he comes to the end of the quarter, he's just not going to make it.

Our division president has one of two choices. One, of course, is that he can report up the chain-of-command that he has failed. Admitting failure, though, is never an attractive option, especially in an environment in which failure is viewed as unforgivable. Our division president, though, sees another alternative. He can take a hard look at his numbers and see if there's enough flexibility in his division's financial reporting system to find a way to come up with the specified earnings.

What can he do? Because the president works for a manufacturing company, he sees a simple solution. He realizes that during the last few days of the quarter he can bring in overtime help and accelerate shipments. He does the math and sees that shipment acceleration would give him a couple of extra pennies in earnings. By the way, he doesn't think he's planning to do anything wrong. His understanding is that, under generally accepted accounting principles (GAAP), if you ship the goods, you are actually entitled to recognize the revenue. (He views it as sort of a hazy area of financial reporting.) And he figures that this is only going to be a one-quarter thing. He's confident that next quarter he'll have enough business to more than make up for what he is borrowing for this quarter.

So that's what he chooses to do. As the quarter comes to a close, he brings in overtime help. He accelerates shipments. He generates a couple of extra pennies in earnings. He meets his earnings target. And in the company he's a big hero.

But—now he's got a new quarter. And with the new quarter comes a new earnings target. And he finds that the business has not bounced back the way he hoped it would. Now the president has twice the problem. First, he's got to meet his earnings target for this new quarter. Second, he has to make up for what he borrowed out of the new quarter for the previous quarter.

So what does he do? Again, he decides to accelerate shipments. This time, though, he sees that shipment acceleration by itself won't be enough. So he thinks this might be a good time to take a look at some of his reserves. His gut tells him that his reserve, say, for returns is too big, and if he can reduce his reserve for returns, that can translate into a couple of extra pennies in earnings.

So that's what he does. In addition to again accelerating shipments, he reduces his reserve for returns. And, again, he meets his earnings target.

But—now he's got a new quarter. Now the problem is three times as bad. He's got a new earnings target, plus he's got to make up for what he's borrowed out of this quarter for the previous two quarters. And what makes it a little worse is that this happens to be the fourth quarter. For soon the auditors of the financial statements are going to show up.

Still, the division president isn't overly concerned. First of all, it's far from clear to him that he's done anything wrong. He figures you're allowed to second-guess reserves. He figures you're allowed to ship early. Besides, at this point everything is so small, and the real issue isn't asset values as much as quarterly timing, so there is very little likelihood that the outside auditors are going to pick it up. He's pretty confident of that, by the way, because he used to be a manager at the Big Five accounting firm that audits his company's financial statements. He basically knows how the firm goes about its audit. More than that, audit fees have been under some pressure lately, and there is no reason to think that this year the auditors will undertake more than their standard audit steps.

So he makes it through the audit without a problem. And, in fact, reported earnings for the year are terrific. Stock analyst expectations have been met. The stock price is up. He gets a nice bonus. And a complimentary article appears in *Business Week.*

But—now he's got a new quarter. Now he's got a bunch of quarters from the previous year to make up for, and it's becoming increasingly clear that the business is not going to bounce back. Now little beads of sweat appear. Soon he is creating charts with earnings on one side and Wall Street expectations on the other. For the president, the preoccupation of financial reporting is no longer accurately reflecting the operations of the business. It has become: How are we going to meet this quarter's street expectations?

So he goes through the year. As the quarters proceed, he finds himself keeping bad accounts receivables, delaying the recognition of expenses, and altering inventory levels. At one point, dispensing with all formality, he finds himself directing his accounting staff to cross out real numbers and insert false ones. More and more he feels like he's on a treadmill on which he has to run faster and faster just to stay in place. (See Exhibit 1–3.)

Now it's audit season again. Now there's reason to be a little nervous. The word goes out to others within the division who have to deal with the auditors: Extra caution is to be used in providing the auditors with certain kinds of information. Supporting documentation for questionable entries comes to be manufactured by people within the accounting department to try to respond to questions that the auditors will inevitably raise. Members of the accounting department convene meetings for the sole purpose of talking about how to survive the audit.

Exhibit 1–3. The Treadmill Effect

- Shipments accelerated
- Quarters kept open
- Reserves reduced
- Revenue recognized on anticipated orders
- Consignment sales improperly recognized
- Bill-and-hold sales improperly recognized
- Accounts receivable manipulated
- Expense recognition delayed
- Intercompany credits used
- Acquisition reserves adjusted
- False inventory "in transit" recorded
- Phantom inventory created
- Phony shipments recorded
- Unsupportable general ledger revisions made
- Unsupportable top-side adjustments made

Now a fair question would be: What's the president's exit strategy? The answer is: He hasn't got one. He didn't intend for this to happen. This was supposed to be a little glitch in the numbers that came and went away in a single quarter. But somehow it got away from him. And now, quarter to quarter, the president is basically scrambling for his life.

And let's pause to look at what's happened. At this point, the physical implementation of what's going on, and in particular the need to deal with the outside auditors, has broadened participation beyond one or two people. By the time a fraud surfaces, it's not unusual to have a large percentage of the entire accounting department involved. It's not that these people are fundamentally dishonest or evil. In fact, typically, very few people actually see the whole picture.

But as the quarters proceed, ostensibly innocent people within the accounting department know that they've been asked to make entries without understanding why. They know they've watched numbers on their computer screens change for reasons they don't completely understand.

They know they've been asked to second-guess reserves without understanding the underlying reason. They don't know that they are now participants in a fraud. But they suspect it. And it begins to eat at them. And it eats at their conscience. And they worry.

And at one point, they see it. They see that they are up to their eyeballs in a massive financial fraud. The problem is that, by the time that light bulb has gone on, it's too late. They are participants.

Isolating the Elements

Even though the example is hypothetical, those knowledgeable of fraudulent financial reporting will recognize a pattern. Let's break out the key elements and focus on each one.

1. *It doesn't start with dishonesty.* The starting point is the recognition that fraudulent financial reporting ordinarily does not start with dishonesty. It does not start because the CEO is dishonest. It does not start because the CFO is dishonest. It does not start because the company has had the misfortune of hiring a group of dishonest people in its accounting department. In fact, the level of honesty of the individual participants has very little to do with it.

2. *It starts with pressure.* Rather than starting with dishonesty, fraudulent financial reporting starts with a certain kind of environment. In particular, it starts with an environment in which two things are present. The first is an aggressive target of financial performance. The second is a vivid realization that a failure to attain that target will be viewed as unforgivable. In other words, fraudulent financial reporting starts with pressure.

   Now the example described above assumes—as is very much the case in today's volatile stock market—pressure created by the market expectations created by Wall Street analysts. But that's not the only potential source of pressure. The pressure can come from almost anywhere. It may come from a hard-driving CEO who wants to make a name for himself by attaining a certain return on equity. The pressure may come from the need to satisfy the performance demands of one or more large shareholders. For a bank, the pressure may come from an unwillingness to report increased loan loss reserves to the FDIC. For some, the pressure may come from a senior executive who simply is not a very good manager.

But whatever the source, deliberate financial misreporting starts with pressure. It starts with pressure to attain an aggressive performance target and with a vivid realization that a failure to attain that target will be viewed as unforgivable.

3. *It starts out small.* Massive financial fraud does not start with a grand plan or conspiracy. It does not start with a group of executives in a conference room in which someone volunteers, "Let's perpetrate a massive fraud." In fact, its origin typically is precisely the opposite. It starts out very small—so small that the one or two participants don't even appreciate that they are stepping over the line. Then, as the need to disguise past performance inadequacies is compounded by the need to make up for new ones, the problem starts to grow.

4. *It starts with hazy areas of financial reporting.* Rarely does even a lone participant in a large-scale financial fraud start with a deliberate decision to do something dishonest. Now it is true, of course, that some people are dishonest and that they make deliberate decisions to lie, cheat, and steal. But rarely do those kinds of individuals survive long in a company, and they almost never make their way up the ranks to the senior levels.

So when we're talking about massive financial fraud, we're talking about a fraud that is being perpetrated by people who are not by nature or training the type to step over the line. What do they do? They exploit what they perceive to be ambiguities in the rules. They exploit ambiguities with regard to revenue recognition. They exploit the need to exercise judgment in the establishment and adjustment of reserves. They exploit areas where the dictates of GAAP do not lead inexorably to any particular number. Then, as the fraud grows deeper, they end up taking positions that should have objectively been viewed as indefensible.

5. *The fraud grows over time.* If the financial misreporting came and went away in a single quarter, that would be the end of it,

and no one would be the wiser. That wouldn't make it right, but it wouldn't make it a massive financial fraud.

The problem is that the nature of financial misreporting makes it difficult to create and correct the misreporting in one quarter. By its nature, financial misreporting typically starts out in the form of borrowing from future quarters. Whether it be through changes in revenue recognition practices, the adjustment of reserves, the delay of expenses, or whatever, the nature of the fraud at its origin is such that the participants are almost always borrowing from Peter to pay Paul.

As the quarters progress, therefore, the problem is mathematically incapable of staying the same. Insofar as the perpetrator is always borrowing from future quarters to meet the present one, the fraud mathematically has got to get worse—in the absence of a dramatic business upturn. The fraud grows, moreover, not only in terms of its numerical significance, but also in terms of the number of people needed to perpetrate it. As the fraud numerically grows larger, the efforts of increasing numbers of individuals are needed simply to keep up with its implementation. Thus, the fraud grows beyond the original one or two perpetrators and, by the time it surfaces, may have, in one way or another, involved close to everyone in the accounting department.

6. *There's no way out.* In a sense, getting caught up in accounting irregularities is a one-way street. It's easy to start down the road, but it's almost impossible to turn back.

That's not to say that the participants will not be looking for a way out. As fear turns to desperation, those involved may dream of some kind of extraordinary event—a massive restructuring, a corporate acquisition, a divestiture—that will create enough smoke around the company's accounting that the improper entries may be removed from the books.

Indeed, it may be that the dream of such an extraordinary event—combined with the lack of any other alternative—is what keeps the fraud going. All the while, though, it keeps getting larger and larger, and the hoped-for event remains like a mirage on the horizon.

The Danger of "Managed Earnings"

Such an understanding of the origin and growth of fraudulent financial reporting points to the underlying weakness in the argument of those who would seek to defend the practice of what has become known as "managed earnings." Now in talking about managed earnings, one has got to be careful. There are two types of managed earnings. One type is simply conducting the business of the enterprise in order to attain controlled, disciplined growth. The other type involves deliberate manipulation of the accounting in order to create the *appearance* of growth—when, in fact, all that is happening is that accounting entries are being manipulated.

The topic at hand, of course, is the latter—the manipulation of accounting entries in order to create the appearance of growth. Still, the practice of even this kind of managed earnings has its defenders. The argument goes like this. In today's volatile stock market, precise reporting of the sharp edges of business upticks and downturns can turn a stock price into a roller coaster. That kind of volatility serves no one. It is far better, therefore, for management to use its judgment in the application of GAAP to take a longer-term view and smooth out earnings as they are reported. Such smoothing can be attained, for example, by putting away extra reserves (i.e., overestimating expenses and establishing concurrent liabilities) when times are good and tapping into them during temporary business downturns by acknowledging previous periods' expense overstatements and reversing them in the current period. According to one publication, some financial officers of public companies "see it as their duty to take the rough edges off operating results." *Business Week* has reported "a tolerance bordering on a thirst for earnings management." *The Wall Street Journal*, in a much-discussed editorial, came close to accepting just this kind of approach.

Certainly some can argue that aspects of the objectives of this kind of managed earnings are to an extent laudable. A long-term approach is obviously better than an approach that is limited only to the present quarter. And the volatility in many companies' stock prices has genuinely reached the point where it can seem almost unbearable.

A major fallacy in the argument for managed earnings, however, lies in its implicit premise that the practice can be neatly packaged and controlled. The problem is that it cannot be. True, establishing cookie-jar reserves in good times is easy enough and, in a different era, might have even been defended as good, conservative financial reporting. However, when downturns arrive, it can be more difficult for management to make the decision that investors should be permitted to see the truth. Nor can a normal manager be expected to forecast accurately which downturns are only the result of the normal ebb and flow of the business, and therefore theoretically appropriate for use of the cookie-jar reserves, and which signify a more serious reversal in the company's prospects. More than that, once any cookie-jar reserves were exhausted, the temptation to exploit other reserves—ones that had been *appropriately* estimated—would have to be almost irresistible. It is easy to see how even such well-meaning management would find itself on a treadmill.

That is not to ignore other problems with the defense of accounting adjustments to smooth out earnings. Probably a more obvious one is its advocacy of distortion of a company's true operations in order to accommodate the investment expectations of financial analysts and the public. The fulfillment of expectations can be rewarding, but when it is achieved through distortion, it rarely works out in the long run.

Still another problem with a managed-earnings approach to financial reporting is the effect it can have on a company's financial reporting culture. Managerial acceptance of managed earnings, and in particular the use of such cookie-jar reserves, can send an extraordinarily dangerous message to the troops: "Where it is for the good of the corporate enterprise, it is all right to camouflage the truth." Once that genie is out of the bottle, it will never go back. Managers at all levels will perceive themselves as having license, if not encouragement, to do what they have internally tried to resist all along—camouflage their own dismal inadequacies by subtle rearrangement of the numbers. Where that should happen, investors, creditors, and suppliers will never be in a position to trust the numbers again. Not even management itself will be certain it is getting the truth. Under such a circumstance, lack of rigor in financial reporting can be expected to infect every fiber of the enterprise and become part of the corporate culture. If a company should get to that point, probably the best move is to sell the stock short. It is only a matter of time.

The Audit Committee, the Internal Audit Department, and the Outside Auditor

Any public company, of course, is supposed to have in place systems of corporate governance and internal control that keep any of this from happening. In particular, modern scholars of corporate governance would point to a triumvirate of internal control elements whose principal objectives would include the prevention of financial fraud: the audit committee, the internal audit department, and the outside auditor. To understand the origin of accounting irregularities, therefore, we have to consider how accounting irregularities are able to get by each of them.

The Audit Committee

Let's start with the audit committee. Under modern systems of internal control and corporate governance, it is the audit committee that is to be at the vanguard in the prevention and detection of financial fraud. What kinds of failures do we typically see at the audit committee level when financial fraud is given an opportunity to develop and grow undetected?

There is no single answer, but several audit committee inadequacies are candidates. One inadequacy potentially stems from the fact that the members of the audit committee are not always genuinely independent. A typical audit committee will have three members, and it may be that those members in substance, if not in form, have ties to the CEO or others that make any meaningful degree of independence awkward if not impossible.

Another inadequacy is that audit committee members are not always terribly sophisticated. Frequently, companies that are most susceptible to the demands of analyst earnings expectations are new, entrepreneurial companies that have recently gone public and that have engaged in a heroic struggle to get outside analysts to notice them in the first place. Such a newly hatched public company is unlikely to have exceedingly sophisticated or experienced financial management, let alone the luxury of sophisticated and mature outside directors on its audit committee. Rather, the audit committee members may have been added to the board in the first place because of industry expertise, because they were friends or even relatives of management, or simply because they were available.

A third inadequacy is that audit committee members are not always clear on exactly what they're supposed to do. Historically, the rules of the NYSE, as well as the NASD, in this regard have been somewhat vague. Even the new rules, while providing some detail as to the proper configuration of audit committees, decline to explicate all the specifics of audit committee activity, and instead implicitly assume that the audit committee will correctly exercise some level of oversight of the financial reporting function. For many audit committee members, however, that "oversight" will translate into listening to the outside auditor once a year. The concept of active oversight of the financial reporting process and establishing broad objectives for the outside auditor would strike many audit committee members as completely backward.

Some or all of the above audit committee inadequacies may be found in companies that have experienced accounting irregularities. Almost always there will be an additional one. That is that the audit committee— no matter how independent, sophisticated, or active—will have functioned largely in ignorance. It will not have had a clue as to what was happening within the organization. The reason is that a typical audit committee (and the problem here is much broader than newly public startups) will get most of its information from management and from the outside auditor. Rarely is management going to reveal financial manipulations. And, for reasons explained later, reliance on the outside auditor for the discovery of the accounting irregularities is hazardous at best. Even the most sophisticated and attentive of audit committee members have had the misfortune of accounting irregularities that have unexpectedly surfaced on their watch.

The unfortunate lack of access to candid information on the part of the audit committee directs attention to the second in the triumvirate of fraud preventers: the internal audit department.

Internal Audit

It may be that the internal audit department is one of the least understood, and most ineffectively used, of all vehicles to combat financial fraud. Theoretically, internal audit is perfectly positioned to nip in the bud an accounting irregularity problem. The internal auditors are theoretically trained in financial reporting and accounting. The internal auditors theoretically have a vivid understanding as to how financial fraud begins and grows. Unlike the outside auditor, internal auditors do not merely appear once a year: they work at the company full time. And, theoretically, the internal auditors should be able to plug themselves into the financial reporting environment and report directly to the audit committee what they have seen and heard.

The reason all of these theoretical vehicles for the detection and prevention of financial fraud have not been effective is that, where massive fraud has surfaced, the internal audit department has been somewhere between nonfunctional and nonexistent. In part, this may be the result of an unfortunate cultural tradition in which, as one business leader has put it, internal auditors are viewed as the Rodney Dangerfields of corporate governance—they get no respect. Whatever the explanation, where massive financial fraud has surfaced, a viable internal audit function is typically nowhere to be found.

The Outside Auditor

That, of course, leaves the outside auditor which, for most public companies, means some of the largest accounting firms in the world. Indeed, it is frequently the inclination of those learning of an accounting irregularity problem to point to a failure by the outside auditor as the principal explanation. Recent criticisms made against the accounting profession have included compromised independence, a transformation in the audit function away from data assurance, the use of immature and inexperienced audit staff for important audit functions, and the perceived use by the large accounting firms of audit as a loss leader rather than a viable professional engagement in its own right.

Each of these is certainly worthy of consideration and inquiry, but the fundamental explanation for the failure of the outside auditor to detect financial fraud lies in the way that fraudulent financial reporting typically begins and grows. Most important is the fact that, as discussed earlier, the fraud almost inevitably starts out very small—well beneath the radar screen of the materiality thresholds of a normal audit pursuant to generally accepted auditing standards (GAAS)—and almost inevitably begins with issues of quarterly timing. Quarterly timing has not historically been a subject of intense audit scrutiny; the auditor, rather, has been concerned with financial performance for the entire year. The combined effect of the small size of an accounting irregularity at its origin and the fact that it begins with an allocation of financial results over quarters almost guarantees that, at least at the outset, the fraud will escape outside auditor detection.

These two attributes of financial fraud at the outset are compounded by another problem that enables it to escape auditor detection. That problem is that, at root, massive financial fraud stems from a certain type of corporate environment. Of those involved, perhaps no one is worse positioned to detect that type of environment than the outside accountants conducting the annual audit. The typical audit may involve fieldwork at the company once a year. That once-a-year period may only last for 8 or 12 weeks. During the fieldwork, the individual accountants are typically secreted by themselves in a conference room. In dealing with these accountants, moreover, employees are frequently on their guard. There exists, accordingly, little opportunity for the outside accountants to get plugged into the all-important corporate environment and culture, which is where financial fraud has its origins.

As the fraud inevitably grows, of course, its materiality increases as does the number of individuals involved. Correspondingly, also increasing is the susceptibility of the fraud to outside auditor detection. However, at the point where the fraud approaches the thresholds at which outside auditor detection becomes a realistic possibility, deception of the auditor becomes one of the preoccupations of the perpetrators. False schedules, forged documents, manipulated accounting entries, fabrications and lies at all levels—each of these becomes a vehicle for perpetrating the fraud during the annual interlude of audit testing. Ultimately, the fraud almost inevitably becomes too large to continue to escape discovery, and auditor detection at some point is by no means unusual. The problem is that, by the time the fraud is sufficiently large, it has probably gone on for years.

That is not to exonerate the audit profession, and certainly profession-wide improvements should be considered. These might include greater involvement of the outside auditor in quarterly data, the reduction of materiality thresholds, and a greater effort on the part of the profession to assess the corporate culture and environment. Nonetheless, compared to, say, the potential for early fraud detection possessed by the internal audit department, the once-a-year outside auditor is at a noticeable disadvantage.

The Fraud Surfaces

So, having been missed for so long by so many, how does the fraud typically surface? One of several ways. Sometimes there's a change in personnel, either from a corporate acquisition or a change in management, and the new hires stumble onto the problems. Sometimes the fraud—which quarter to quarter is mathematically incapable of staying the same—grows to the point where it can no longer be hidden from the outside auditor. Sometimes detection results when the conscience of one of the accounting department people gets the better of him. All along he wanted to tell somebody. And it gets to the point where he can't stand it anymore and he does. Then you have a whistle-blower.

Now there are exceptions to all of this. But in almost any big accounting irregularity problem, one will almost inevitably see some or all of these elements. We need just change the names of the companies and the people and the industry.

A Crisis for the Board

So that's the origin of an accounting irregularity. And when it surfaces, problems will come out of the woodwork like nothing the board of directors has ever seen. Those problems will involve crises of corporate governance; of disclosure; and with creditors, employees, insurers, and shareholders. And that's just in the first two hours.

Before we get to this myriad of corporate problems, though, it is worth pausing to take stock of the plight of an unfortunate outside director who suddenly learns of an accounting irregularities problem on an otherwise uneventful afternoon. He didn't have a clue of any financial misreporting. He knew nothing of undue pressure for financial performance or that the company was not doing as well as it said. Now he's being told of massive financial fraud and asked to report for an emergency board meeting the next morning. The urgency of the request makes clear to him that he had better put aside everything else and oblige.

Such a director could hardly be blamed, however, if he momentarily turned away from critical issues of corporate operations and financial reporting to consider just briefly his own vulnerability: Will he get sued? Did he do everything he was supposed to? Is responsibility for this problem in part his? Or will the blame go entirely to the outside auditor and to the director of internal audit? (Actually, our director is not even sure who the director of internal audit is.)

All of the director's questions are valid. So before turning to the immediate crises engulfing a corporation in the wake of a massive financial fraud, let's take on some of this director's questions. When accounting irregularities surface, who is going to get the blame?

CHAPTER 2

SO WHO GETS
THE BLAME?

Michael R. Young

Pausing to think about who will get the blame is not a frivolous exercise by any means. Once an irregularity has been exposed, class action litigation is only days away. That litigation is sure to include as defendants almost anyone within the vicinity of the accounting irregularity or the company's financial reporting function. Beyond that, investigations by the Securities and Exchange Commission (SEC) and the National Association of Securities Dealers (NASD) (or, for larger companies, the New York Stock Exchange [NYSE]) will quickly follow. The targets of investigation and inquiry will quickly fall into three categories. One is those who will be viewed as guilty. The second is those who will be viewed as not guilty. The third is those who could go either way.

Focusing on the allocation of responsibility for the financial misstatements, therefore, is a natural first step. However, determining that allocation is not easy. At bottom, it requires an understanding of an evolution of responsibility for financial reporting that has taken place over roughly the last 15 years (see Exhibit 2–1). Spurred in part by privately commissioned groups, the SEC, and the accounting profession, the principal theme of the evolution has been a shift in responsibility for financial reporting. In particular, the prevalent theme has been a shift in responsibility for financial reporting to those within the reporting entity itself. That is not to suggest the evolution is complete. With the advent of an entire set of new initiatives and rules by the SEC, the evolution continues to this day.

Blaming the Outside Auditor

To begin, let's go back about 20 years—to the early part of the 1980s. Back then, things were not quite so complex and the target of blame for financial

Exhibit 2–1. The Evolution of Financial Reporting

- Treadway Commission Report (1987)

- Expectation Gap revision of Statements on Auditing Standards (1989)

- Private Securities Litigation Reform Act (1995)

- Independence Standards Board (1997)

- Levitt Speech at New York University (1998)

- Securities Litigation Uniform Standards Act (1998)

- Report of Blue Ribbon Committee on Improving the Effectiveness of Corporate Audit Committees (1999)

- New rules of the SEC, NYSE, NASD, and American Stock Exchange (1999)

- Report of the O'Malley Panel on Audit Effectiveness (2000)

misreporting was fairly straightforward. It would be blamed on the outside auditor. There were several reasons, but most of them revolved around the fact that the auditor had money. In the inevitable litigation, a typical outside director, or for that matter senior executive, might simply testify, "I was relying on the outside auditor," to the general satisfaction of all.

All, that is, except the auditor. For its part, the auditor quickly came to realize that it was in a no-win position. Given the way that financial fraud develops, by the time an accounting irregularity had surfaced the auditor would typically be in the unenviable position of having missed it for years. Subsequent scrutiny of the auditor's workpapers would by definition show that, sure enough, had the auditor undertaken this or that additional task, the fraud would have been exposed.

Once the auditor actually entered the courtroom, the situation only became more difficult. There, the contention of fraud detection as an auditor's responsibility fed into a jury's normal inclination to view the auditor as providing a "guarantee" of accuracy or "a clean bill of health," which was accompanied by only a hazy understanding of what generally accepted auditing standards (GAAS) actually required the auditor to do. The common courtroom scenario would involve the auditor getting blamed from all sides. The auditor's defensive-sounding response that it should be viewed as a fellow victim of the fraud, rather than a participant, could be a tough sell.

In this context, the law was no help at all. To the contrary, courts came to view the accounting profession almost as a vehicle for risk diversification. Thus, one state supreme court justified an expansion of audit liability through an observation that "independent auditors have apparently been able to obtain liability insurance . . . to satisfy their financial obligations." Other courts similarly expanded the categories of plaintiffs who, when accounting problems surfaced, were entitled to sue. Federal courts, interpreting the federal securities laws, came to the conclusion that investors could be found to have relied upon audit reports they had never even seen.

Within the accounting firms during the first half of the 1980s, therefore, two things grew. One was their in-house legal departments. The other was their exposure to liability. Data collected by the then Big Six firms showed that those firms by themselves would ultimately end up facing legal liability of around $30 billion—roughly $3.8 million per partner.

It was thus somewhat understandable that, by the mid-1980s, the accounting profession had come to view the liability landscape with a blend of frustration and terror. On the one hand, its exposure to liability seemed to be increasing almost exponentially as financial community frustration intensified over the profession's seemingly inexplicable inability to detect fraudulent financial reporting before it got out of hand. On the other hand, the ability of a typical outside auditor to discover fraud at the outset was limited. Key members of the financial community came to the fairly vivid realization that it was time to rethink, and to rationalize, the allocation of responsibility for fraudulent financial reporting between the outside auditor and others. The question was how to do it.

The Treadway Commission

The stage was thus set for what would prove to be a watershed in the evolution of financial reporting and corporate governance: The formation of the National Commission on Fraudulent Financial Reporting, later known as the Treadway Commission after its chairman, former SEC Commissioner James Treadway. The task to be undertaken by the Treadway Commission went to the crux of the matter. The Commission's task was to investigate the underlying causes of fraudulent financial reporting, to examine the role of the outside auditor in the detection of fraud, and to analyze the extent to which corporate structure may allow fraudulent financial reporting to take place.

The Treadway Commission began its study in 1985 and over a two-year period undertook an exhaustive investigation of the root causes of financial fraud. Subjects of investigation and analysis included internal control systems, internal auditing, the significance of intra-corporate pressures for performance, management failures, and inadequacies of the accounting profession. Ultimately, the Commission undertook more than 20 separate research projects and briefing papers. In addition, the Commission investigated the views and perceptions of key financial regulatory agencies and groups, including the SEC, the FDIC, the Comptroller of the Currency, the American Institute of Certified Public Accountants (AICPA), the Auditing Standards Board, the Financial Executives Institute, and the Institute of Internal Auditors. Twice the Commission appeared before the House Committee on Energy and Commerce's Subcommittee on Oversight and Investigations as part of that subcommittee's inquiry into the adequacy of auditing, accounting, and financial reporting practices. Prior to its publication, 40,000 copies of an exposure draft of the Commission's report were publicly distributed for comment.

The resulting Report of the National Commission on Fraudulent Financial Reporting was published in October 1987. Among other things, it concluded the following: Foremost, "fraudulent financial reporting usually does not begin with an overt intentional act to distort the financial statements." Rather, the Treadway Commission found that fraudulent financial reporting frequently came about as "the culmination of a series of acts designed to respond to operational difficulties." What tended to happen, the Commission concluded, was that initially "the activities may not be fraudulent, but in time they become increasingly questionable" until, finally, someone steps over the line.

The Treadway Commission also found that, behind the individuals stepping over the line into financial fraud, was almost always undue pressure. It might be "unrealistic pressures, particularly for short-term results" or "financial pressure resulting from bonus plans that depend on short-term economic performance" or pressure from "the desire to obtain a higher price for a stock or debt offering or to meet the expectation of investors." At the core of fraudulent financial reporting, though, the Commission almost inevitably found pressure. The Commission stated:

The Commission's studies revealed that fraudulent financial reporting usually occurs as the result of certain environmental, institutional, or individual forces and opportunities. These forces and opportunities add pressures and incentives that encourage individuals and companies to engage in fraudulent financial reporting and are present to some degree in all companies. If the right, combustible mixture of forces and opportunities is present, fraudulent financial reporting may occur.

Any effort to combat fraud, therefore, had to start at the top. In particular, responsibility for reliable financial reporting had to reside "first and foremost at the corporate level." Thus, top management had to establish the proper "tone at the top"—an attitude that demanded truth and candor in financial reporting and that, just as important, saw to it that pressures for financial performance did not get out of hand. Such a tone at the top then had to penetrate every fiber of the enterprise so that it became part of the corporate culture. The Commission summarized: "The tone set by top management—the corporate environment or culture within which financial reporting occurs—is the most important factor contributing to the integrity of the financial reporting process."

The problem with the Treadway Commission's determination to place foremost responsibility for financial reporting on the tone set by top management was that, of all groups within an enterprise, it was probably top management that was most vulnerable to pressures from outside forces. Those forces might include investors, financial analysts, bankers, owners, or others—some of whom may not be expected to appreciate fully the importance of the tone at the top and who may rather maintain a greater interest in the bottom line. For top management, establishing the right amount of pressure to achieve results, while at the same time ensuring that at no level of the enterprise did the pressure get out of hand, would pose a formidable challenge.

It is for this reason that the Treadway Commission posited a key role in financial reporting beyond that of senior management. That key role was to be filled by the board of directors and, in particular, by its audit committee. Through "establishment of an informed, vigilant and effective audit committee to oversee the company's financial reporting process," a board of directors could thereby act as a backstop for senior management and undertake to ensure that a proper tone at the top and financial reporting system remained in place. The centrality of the audit committee's function to financial reporting was emphasized by the Commission's formulation of eight separate recommendations regarding audit committees that were directed to public companies:

- The board of directors of all public companies should be required by SEC rule to establish audit committees composed solely of independent directors.
- Audit committees should be informed, vigilant, and effective overseers of the financial reporting process and the company's internal controls.
- All public companies should develop a written charter setting forth the duties and responsibilities of the audit committee. The board of directors should approve the charter, review it periodically, and modify it as necessary.
- Audit committees should have adequate resources and authority to discharge their responsibilities.
- The audit committee should review management's evaluation of factors related to the independence of the company's public accountant. Both the audit committee and management should assist the public accountant in preserving his independence.
- Before the beginning of each year, the audit committee should review management's plans for engaging the company's independent public accountant to perform management advisory services during the coming year, considering both the types of services that may be rendered and the projected fees.
- Management should advise the audit committee when it seeks a second opinion on a significant accounting issue.
- Audit committees should oversee the quarterly reporting process.

To complement the efforts of the audit committee, the Treadway Commission also recommended an effective internal audit function that would report directly to the audit committee and thereby be positioned to act as the audit committee's eyes and ears. (See Exhibit 2–2.)

Consequences of the Treadway Commission Report

The reason the Treadway Commission report is central to any modern day assessment of those who stand to be blamed for financial misreporting is

Exhibit 2-2. Key Recommendations of the Treadway Commission for Public Companies

Recommendation 1: Top management must identify, understand, and assess the factors that may cause the company's financial statements to be fraudulently misstated.

Recommendation 2: Public companies should maintain internal controls that provide reasonable assurance that fraudulent financial reporting will be prevented or subject to early detection.

Recommendation 5: Public companies should maintain an effective internal audit function staffed with an adequate number of qualified personnel that is appropriate to the size and the nature of the company.

Recommendation 9: The board of directors of all public companies should be required by SEC rule to establish audit committees composed solely of independent directors.

Recommendation 10: Audit committees should be informed, vigilant, and effective overseers of the financial reporting process and the company's internal controls.

Recommendation 13: Both the audit committee and management should assist the public accountant in preserving his independence.

Recommendation 17: Management should advise the audit committee when it seeks a second opinion on a significant accounting issue.

Recommendation 19: Audit committees should oversee the quarterly reporting process.

that the report's publication basically marked a sea change in the allocation of financial reporting responsibility. Implicit in the report's findings and recommendations was the notion that reliance for the prevention of fraud on mechanisms outside the corporate structure—and, in particular, on the annual audit function—was not enough. Indeed, the Treadway Commission explicitly relegated the outside auditor to "a crucial, but secondary role" and cautioned that outside auditors could not be viewed as "guarantors of the accuracy or the reliability of financial statements." Rather, the genesis of financial fraud took place as a consequence of pressures and a tone within the company and, if financial fraud was to be prevented and detected at the outset, the mechanisms to do so must exist within the corporation itself. An effect of the Treadway Commission's findings and recommendations, therefore, was to shift responsibility for accurate financial reporting onto the shoulders of senior management, outside directors, internal audit, and—most important—audit committees.

Upon the report's publication in October 1987, the findings and recommendations of the Treadway Commission garnered almost extraordinary attention and support. Members of Congress instantaneously came to view its recommendations as authoritative. Legal writers discussed at length the Treadway report and advocated a level of diligence consistent with its recommendations. The national accounting firms separately took steps to apprise the directors and officers of their client companies as to precisely what was now expected of them according to the report's recommendations. Thus, the accounting firms published their own monographs, duly distributed to corporate officials, that highlighted the recommendations of the Treadway Commission and outlined their views as to what corporate officials, and audit committees in particular, should be doing. Management letters, typically issued at the conclusion of an audit engagement, explicitly or implicitly began to assume Treadway Commission recommendations as important criteria against which the corporate governance aspects of internal control systems were to be measured. The Treadway Commission's recommendations in effect became the touchstone for the evaluation of financial reporting systems.

Further Developments

The effect of the Treadway Commission's report did not, moreover, stop with the Commission's findings and recommendations themselves. The

Commission also affected a series of subsequent financial reporting initiatives and developments. Even beyond the four corners of the report, therefore, Commission findings and recommendations influenced the evolution of financial reporting. Among the effects was a further shift of responsibility for financial reporting to those within the reporting entity.

One of these further developments was a concerted effort by members of the accounting profession to make clear to the public that it was performing—in the words of the Treadway Commission—only a "secondary" role. Within the profession, this became colloquially known as the effort to close the expectation gap—the gap perceived to exist between what juries in accountant malpractice litigation seemed to assume to be the auditor's role and the auditor's role in fact. The impetus behind this initiative was a concern, rooted in the experience of individual CPA firms in audit malpractice litigation, that the public assumed a much greater level of responsibility on the part of the outside auditor than the outside auditor under professional standards was prepared to fulfill. That responsibility, the accounting profession sought to demonstrate, really belonged to management.

Here, too, one of the more significant results was a clearer allocation of responsibility for financial reporting between corporate officials and the outside auditor. One visible consequence was a revision of the standard form of auditor's report, which now stated explicitly on the face of the report what had earlier been buried in the underlying literature articulating GAAS: that the "financial statements are the responsibility of the Company's management," whereas the auditor's responsibility is only to "express an opinion on these financial statements based on our audit." Although the expectation gap initiative also involved some assumption by the auditor of increased responsibilities for the detection of fraud, it highlighted the primary responsibility as that of corporate management.

Still another development operated to affect the allocation of responsibility for financial reporting between corporate officials and auditors. That is the much-touted "litigation crisis" and the very real concern that, if the accounting profession remained at the forefront of liability for fraudulent financial reporting, every national accounting firm was going to be driven out of business. Headlines advertised not only extraordinary jury verdicts but extraordinary settlements as well. Ernst & Young's $400 million settlement with the federal government appeared in giant headlines on the front page of *The New York Times.*

The resulting appearance of professional vulnerability was furthered by business decisions made by the individual CPA firms: They started firing their clients. Accordingly, the financial press began to report impediments to expanding enterprise owing simply to the unavailability of financial statement audits. A March 1, 1993 article in *Business Week* is typical. In an article titled "Big Six Firms Are Firing Clients," *Business Week* reported:

> With growing regularity, major public accounting firms are turning their backs on many smaller banks, thrifts, and fledgling companies. Deloitte & Touche, for one, declined to audit about 60 companies trying to go public last year, more than half the 103 initial public offerings they actually evaluated.

Business Week described the reason as "no mystery." It was because "[i]n recent years, accounting firms have been forced to fork over hundreds of millions of dollars to settle lawsuits."

The prospect of accounting firms going out of business or firing clients turned the conventional wisdom—underlying the allocation of responsibility between management and the outside auditor—on its head. The conventional wisdom, typified by a 1983 decision by the New Jersey Supreme Court, had been that the placement of broad responsibility for financial reporting upon the outside auditor would operate, among other things, as a mechanism to enhance financial reporting and, at the same time, to diversify risk. The analysis was proved incorrect. The system was in trouble.

All of this culminated in broader scrutiny as to responsibility for financial reporting and a broader assessment of the extent to which corporate officials, rather than outside professionals, should be at the forefront of those held accountable for financial fraud. Courts began to take notice. In the thick of this reawakening emerged decisions such as the California Supreme Court's opinion in *Bily v. Arthur Young & Co.*, which scrutinized the role of an outside auditor and precisely what level of responsibility an auditor of financial statements was assuming. (See Exhibit 2–3.) Decisions placing broad responsibilities on auditors such as that in New Jersey came to be undermined or, in the case of the New Jersey decision itself, reversed by the legislature.

The Levitt Initiatives

The shift of primary responsibility for financial reporting to those within the corporation was thus well under way when a new catalyst surfaced: the dra-

Exhibit 2–3. Evolving Perceptions of Auditor Responsibility

"By certifying the public records that collectively depict a corporation's financial status, the independent auditor assumes a public responsibility transcending any employment relationship with the client. The independent public accountant performing this special function owes ultimate allegiance to the corporation's creditors and stockholders, as well as to the investing public. This 'public watchdog' function demands that the accountant maintain total independence from the client at all times and requires complete fidelity to the public trust."

United States v. Arthur Young & Co., 465 U.S. 805, 817–18 (1984).

"An auditor is a watchdog, not a bloodhound....As a matter of commercial reality, audits are performed in a client-controlled environment. The client typically prepares its own financial statements; it has direct control over and assumes primary responsibility for their contents....The client engages the auditor, pays for the audit, and communicates with audit personnel throughout the engagement. Because the auditor cannot in the time available become an expert in the client's business and record-keeping systems, the client necessarily furnishes the information base for the audit. Thus, regardless of the efforts of the auditor, the client retains effective primary control of the financial reporting process."

Bily v. Arthur Young & Co., 3 Cal. 4th 370, 399–400 (1992).

matic upsurge in reported instances of accounting irregularities in the latter half of the 1990s. In hindsight, the exposure of the accounting fraud at Leslie Fay—most notably in a series of high-profile stories in *The Wall Street Journal*—probably marked the beginning of the trend. Not long thereafter, newspaper readers were seemingly being greeted on a regular basis with headlines announcing the latest public company to fall victim to financial fraud. Perplexing to many, the underlying theme of each story was the same: massive accounting fraud perpetrated by some of the most senior officials in the company.

It was in April 1998 that the problem of accounting irregularities attained a level of prominence that made clear it was not going away any time soon. In that month Cendant Corporation—up to that point believed to be one of the spectacular success stories of the decade—announced that it, too, had fallen prey to financial fraud. For Cendant, the experience came about in a way that was particularly unfortunate: it had taken on the accounting problems through the acquisition of another company and the fraud, akin to an unstoppable virus, had infected its own financial reporting system. Within hours after public announcement of the fraud, investors watched in horror as the value of their stockholdings plunged by roughly $14 billion. A subsequent audit committee investigation (placed on the internet by Cendant itself) exhaustively documented a financial fraud the scope of which was almost breathtaking. Not insignificantly, the entire drama was played out in the pages of *The Wall Street Journal*, *The New York Times*, *Business Week*, *Newsweek*, *Fortune*, and almost every other notable business publication throughout the spring and summer of the year.

By the fall of 1998, then-SEC chairman Arthur Levitt had apparently decided that enough was enough. He tossed down the gauntlet in the form of a speech on September 28, 1998, which he entitled "The Numbers Game." Among other things, Levitt castigated public companies for a form of financial reporting that he referred to as "earnings management" which was, he said, in substance nothing more than "accounting hocus-pocus." Levitt admonished that he was "challenging corporate management and Wall Street to re-examine our current environment" and announced a new series of initiatives to that end. The solution, according to Levitt, was "nothing less than a cultural change." (See Exhibit 2-4.)

While Levitt's sense of urgency was unmistakable, the fundamental solutions he proposed were neither new nor particularly innovative. For his solutions, he turned, at root, to the fundamental precepts that had been published in the Treadway Commission's report 13 years before.

Accordingly, at the core of the Levitt initiatives was the concept of "qualified, committed, independent and tough-minded audit committees:"

Exhibit 2–4. Arthur Levitt's: "The Numbers Game"

Plans to improve the reliability and transparency of financial statements:

- Technical rule changes by regulators to improve the accounting framework

- Improved outside auditing in the financial reporting process

- A strengthened audit committee process

- Cultural changes on the part of corporate management and the financial community

---

And, finally, qualified, committed, independent and tough-minded audit committees represent the most reliable guardians of the public interest. Sadly, stories abound of audit committees whose members lack expertise in the basic principles of financial reporting as well as the mandate to ask probing questions. In fact, I've heard of one audit committee that convenes only twice a year before the regular board meeting for 15 minutes and whose duties are limited to a perfunctory presentation.

Compare that situation with the audit committee which meets 12 times a year before each board meeting; where every member has a financial background; where there are no personal ties to the chairman or the company; where they have their own advisers; where they ask tough questions of management and outside auditors; and where, ultimately, the investor interest is being served.

The SEC stands ready to take appropriate action if that interest is not protected. But, a private sector response that empowers audit committees and obviates the need for public sector dictates seems the wisest choice. I am pleased to announce that the financial community has agreed to accept this challenge.

The consequences of the Levitt initiatives are still unfolding, but an important one was the formation of the Blue Ribbon Committee on Improving the Effectiveness of Corporate Audit Committees. After hearings on the effectiveness of financial reporting systems and, in particular, corporate audit committees, the Blue Ribbon Committee in February 1999 issued a series of recommendations for new rules by the NASD, the NYSE, the American Stock Exchange, the SEC, and the AICPA, which, to a large extent, either duplicated or carried further the recommendations made by the Treadway Commission 13 years before. Again, we see an emphasis on the centrality of audit committees in the prevention of fraudulent financial reporting, accompanied by renewed emphasis on the role of internal audit.

In substance, the committee's recommendations, some of which were directed only to companies with a market capitalization of $200 million or more, were these:

- Audit committees should be comprised solely of independent directors.

- Members of an audit committee shall be considered independent only if they have no relationship to the corporation that may interfere with the exercise of their independence from management and the corporation.

- A non-independent director may be appointed to an audit committee only if the board, under exceptional and limited circumstances, determines that membership on the committee by the individual is required by the best interests of the corporation and its shareholders and the board discloses, in the next annual proxy statement subsequent to such determination, the nature of the relationship and the reasons for that determination.

- Audit committees should be comprised of a minimum of three directors, each of whom is financially literate (as described in a section of the report titled "Financial Literacy") or becomes financially literate within a reasonable period of time after his or her appointment to the audit committee. At least one member of the audit committee should have accounting or related financial management expertise.

- Audit committees should (i) adopt a formal written charter that is approved by the full board of directors and that specifies the scope of the committee's responsibilities and how it carries out those responsibilities, including structure, processes, and membership requirements, and (ii) review and reassess the adequacy of the audit committee charter on an annual basis.

- The SEC should promulgate rules that require audit committees to disclose in the company's annual proxy statement whether the audit committee has adopted a formal written charter and, if so, whether the audit committee satisfied its responsibilities during the prior year in compliance with its charter, which shall be disclosed at least triennially in the annual report to shareholders or proxy statement.

- The audit committee charter for every listed company should specify that the outside auditor is ultimately accountable to the board of directors and the audit committee, as representatives of shareholders, and that these shareholder representatives have the ultimate authority and responsibility to select, evaluate, and, where appropriate, replace the outside auditor (or to nominate the outside auditor to be proposed for shareholder approval in any proxy statement).

- The audit committee charter for every listed company should specify that the audit committee is responsible for ensuring its receipt from the outside auditor of a formal written statement delineating all relationships between the auditor and the company, consistent with Independence Standards Board Standard 1, and that the audit committee is also responsible for actively engaging in a dialogue with the auditor with respect to any disclosed relationships or services that may affect the objectivity and independence of the auditor and for taking, or recommending that the full board take, appropriate action to ensure the independence of the outside auditor.

- GAAS should require that a company's outside auditor discuss with the audit committee the auditor's judgments about the quality, not just the acceptability, of the company's accounting principles as applied in its financial reporting; the discussion should include such issues as the clarity of the company's financial disclosures and degree of aggressiveness or conservatism of the company's accounting principles and underlying estimates and other significant decisions made by management in preparing the financial disclosure and reviewed by the outside auditors. This requirement should be written in a way to encourage open, frank discussion and to avoid boilerplate.

- The SEC should require all reporting companies to include a letter from the audit committee in the company's annual report to shareholders and Form 10-K Annual Report disclosing whether or not, with respect to the prior fiscal year, (i) management has reviewed the audited financial statements with the audit committee, including a discussion of the quality of the accounting principles as applied and significant judgments affecting the company's financial statements; (ii) the outside auditors have discussed with the audit committee the outside auditor's judgments of the quality of those principles as applied and judgments referenced in item (i) under the circumstances; (iii) the members of the audit committee have discussed among themselves, without management or the outside auditors present, the information disclosed to the audit committee described in items (i) and (ii); and (iv) the audit committee, in reliance on the review and discussions conducted with management and the outside auditors pursuant to items (i) and (ii), believes that the company's financial statements are fairly presented in conformity with GAAP in all material respects. The SEC should adopt a "safe harbor" applicable to any such disclosure.

- The SEC should require that a reporting company's outside auditor conduct a SAS-71 (Interim Financial Review) review before the company files its Form 10-Q.

- SAS-71 should be amended to require that a reporting company's outside auditor discuss with the audit committee, or at least its chairman, and a representative of financial management, in person, or by telephone conference call, the matters described in AU Section 380 (Communications With Audit Committees) before filing Form 10-Q (and preferably before any public announcement of financial results), including significant adjustments, management judgments and accounting estimates, significant new accounting policies, and disagreements with management.

In the months following their publication, these Blue Ribbon Committee recommendations were the subject of vigorous debate. On the one hand, advocates of improved corporate governance maintained that the adoption of these recommendations was critical to improved financial reporting systems. Indeed, a report by the Committee of Sponsoring Organizations of the Treadway Commission caused some to suggest that, insofar as the report found that accounting irregularities tended to strike with frequency at smaller companies, the recommendations of the committee should be made applicable to companies with even less than the $200 million market capitalization proposed by the committee in certain instances as a cutoff. On the other hand, corporate defense lawyers understandably raised concerns about the corresponding increase in legal liability to boards of directors and, in particular, audit committees.

On December 15, 1999, the SEC approved a series of new rules as a consequence of the Blue Ribbon Committee recommendations. In substance, virtually all of the Blue Ribbon Committee's recommendations were adopted. Thus, the new rules:

- Required audit committees to include at least three members and generally be comprised solely of "independent" directors who are financially literate
- Defined *independence* more rigorously for audit committee members
- Required companies to adopt written charters for their audit committees
- Gave the audit committee the right to hire and terminate the auditor
- Required at least one member of the audit committee to have accounting or financial management expertise
- Required companies' interim financial statements to be reviewed by independent auditors before filing
- Required companies to provide in their proxy statements a report from the audit committee that discloses whether the audit committee reviewed and discussed certain matters with management and the auditors and whether the audit committee recommended to the board that the audited financial statements be included in the Form 10-K
- Required companies to disclose in their proxy statements whether the audit committee has a written charter and to file a copy of the charter every three years, and
- Required companies whose securities are listed on the NYSE or AMEX or are quoted on Nasdaq to disclose certain information about any audit committee member who is not "independent."

Approval of the new rules was followed eight months later with a report and recommendations by still another panel—the "Panel on Audit Effectiveness" of the accounting profession's Public Oversight Board. While primarily directed to enhancement of the effectiveness of the audit function, even this panel found itself emphasizing the pivotal role of the board's audit committee in enhancing both the company's financial reporting system and its outside and internal audit functions. Among other things, the panel emphasized the need for increased audit committee interaction with the internal and outside auditors and encouraged an outside auditor relationship which positioned the audit committee "as the external auditors' primary client." The panel also admonished audit committees to "increase the time and attention they devote to discussions of internal control with management and both the internal and external auditors" and to place particular emphasis on "management's and the auditors' views on (1) the control environment and (2) the controls (or lack thereof) over financial reporting." Here, too, one of the principal authorities cited by the panel was the Treadway Commission.

So Who Gets the Blame?

The principal consequence of all this is the resulting focus on those within the corporate entity as the principal safeguard against fraudulent financial reporting. This is not to say that management and boards of directors may no longer rely upon outside professionals for assistance. Nor is it to suggest that it will be incumbent upon executives and directors to aggressively second-guess the judgment of professionals or that outside professionals—be they auditors, lawyers, underwriters, or others—are to be exonerated from any responsibility for a failure of financial reporting systems. The point, rather, is that responsibility for financial reporting has evolved in such a way that ultimate responsibility for the integrity of the financial reporting system will be placed on those within the reporting entity. In other words, where fraudulent financial reporting should surface, among the candidates to share in the blame will be executives, directors, and—really in the hot seat—members of the audit committee.

What will they get blamed for? The answer depends on the particular circumstances at issue, but it is not difficult to pinpoint the fundamental aspects of a financial reporting system that investigators may conclude had broken down.

1. *Too much pressure.* Foremost, if the integrity of the financial reporting system has been compromised as a result of excessive pressure for performance, blame may find its way to those senior executives by whom that pressure was placed. True, investigators will

hopefully understand that all executives place upon operating personnel some level of pressure for performance and that, in the absence of some degree of pressure, optimal performance may not be attained. Nonetheless, senior executives may be criticized where the pressure reaches a level that compromises the truthfulness of the company's financial disclosures.

2. *An inadequately configured audit committee.* Where fraudulent financial reporting surfaces, both senior executives and outside directors may find themselves sharing in the blame in the absence of an adequately configured audit committee staffed with sufficiently independent, sophisticated, and diligent members. Particularly as a result of new independence and financial sophistication requirements by the NYSE and NASD (see Chapter 11), an audit committee whose membership consists, for example, of family members, professionals charging large fees to the enterprise, or individuals with little expertise in matters of financial reporting may be found not to measure up.

3. *An insufficiently diligent audit committee.* If an appropriately configured audit committee is in place, it may nonetheless find itself subject to criticism to the extent it has failed to deploy its talents by actively overseeing the company's system of financial reporting. This is not to suggest that an outside director, upon becoming a member of an audit committee, must immediately resign his day job and become a micro-manager, directing his energies to the inspection of general ledgers for suspicious-looking transactions. The audit committee members will be expected to remain at an oversight level. At the same time, though, the audit committee may be called upon to look into whether the basics of a sound financial reporting system are in place and, in particular, to seek the installation of mechanisms whereby the audit committee is provided with regular and reliable information as to just what is happening within the enterprise. Among other things, for example, the audit committee will want to inquire as to whether the financial reporting function is adequately supervised by a sufficiently sophisticated chief financial officer and whether the accounting department is adequately staffed and logistically capable of producing reliable reports.

4. *Lack of internal audit.* As financial reporting further evolves, executives and directors at larger companies may begin to suffer criticism in the absence of a viable internal audit function. An important function of internal audit would be to obtain direct information as to what is happening within the company and, in particular, the effect that the tone at the top or the environment is having on accuracy in financial reporting. At the moment, the role of internal audit in public companies has probably not developed to the point where the absence of a viable internal audit capability would subject audit committee members or outside directors to a substantial risk of criticism. On the other hand, things could be heading in that direction.

5. *Insufficient demands for information from the outside auditor.* Beyond effective use of internal audit, the audit committee may increasingly be faulted if it has failed to exploit fully the information available from the outside auditor. Audit committees are increasingly being encouraged to engage in an open and frank dialogue with the auditor while, at the same time, the accounting profession is encouraging auditors to respond in kind. Executives and directors may find themselves criticized where they do not seek to take advantage of the enhanced opportunity for information.

How serious is the exposure where there is a failure to install these basics? At the moment, financial reporting responsibilities are in a state of flux, owing to the uncertainty introduced into the established standard of care by the accelerating pace of change. Indeed, to put all this in context, today any number of well-meaning executives and directors, acting entirely in good faith, could probably be found to have in place financial reporting systems which, measured against the above criteria, are less than optimal. It goes without saying, moreover, that a failure of financial reporting systems by itself does not come anywhere close to demonstrating executive or director complicity in a fraud. Still, where the basics of a viable financial reporting system have not been established, senior executives, outside directors, and audit committee members may find themselves getting blamed from all sides. Increasingly, for example, even diligent audit committee members are being targeted as defendants in class action litigation and, at the same time, class action law firms are focusing on failures of internal control systems as an underlying predicate for securities claims. Regulators are looking askance at boards of directors and audit committees that fail to seek the installation of viable financial reporting systems. Corporate executives and directors may even find themselves liable to their outside auditor, which, under recent legal developments, may itself be entitled to sue corporate officials for fraud and negligence where the auditor has been deceived as to the existence of accounting irregularities in a company's underlying books and records.

The manner in which corporate officials' financial reporting responsibilities have expanded over the last 15 years, moreover, contributes to the existence of a lengthy paper trail pointing to corporate officials' financial reporting and corporate governance responsibilities. Recall, for example, the accounting firm monographs and newsletters mentioned earlier that assumed Treadway-style financial reporting systems as a basis for recommendations on internal control system improvements. Such information, calculated to increase awareness, may place a corporate executive, director, or audit committee member on the defensive to the extent that he has failed to act upon them. Consider as well the plethora of internal memoranda, correspondence, board packages, or even press reports on issues of potential inadequacies in, or improvements to, financial reporting systems. The net effect of such information is that, throughout corporate America, the bar is being raised. Those who fail to act in response may potentially find themselves defending their inactivity should fraudulent financial reporting surface on their watch.

Some—most notably skittish audit committee members and their lawyers—may complain that the new audit committee rules and the overall shift in oversight responsibility to audit committee members will serve to increase their exposure in litigation. To be sure, that is one way of looking at it. But it is not the only way. The fact of the matter is that, even before the new rules, audit committee members were being routinely named as defendants in class action litigation where accounting irregularities had surfaced. More than that, in the absence of a swift dismissal by the court, the termination of such litigation was almost always the same: a negotiated settlement which typically involved the payment of millions of dollars to compensate for shareholder losses. It is far from clear that the enhancement of audit committee oversight of financial reporting will, as a practical matter, change any of that. Indeed, in a broader sense, enhanced audit committee oversight may serve the members' own interests in avoiding litigation insofar as enhanced financial reporting systems operate to prevent accounting irregularities from occurring in the first place. In the end, that is the most effective mechanism for managing the litigation risk of all.

CHAPTER 3

THE IMMEDIATE AFTERMATH

Jack H. Nusbaum and John Oller

Once a potential accounting irregularity has been uncovered, the board of directors must immediately begin the process of investigating the matter and dealing with the crisis atmosphere that is likely to pervade the company in the immediate aftermath of the discovery. Indeed, crisis management is a phrase that aptly describes what happens in the first few days following the uncovering of a financial fraud. Although there is no standard time frame for when the aftermath begins once an accounting irregularity is discovered—it may be a day, a week, or three weeks after the discovery—there are typical events and issues that the company will need to consider in those first few days.

Chapter 3 addresses the period from the time a potential fraud is uncovered to the time the company concludes that the problem is real and sufficiently serious that it needs to be publicly disclosed and made the subject of an independent, full-scale investigation.

The Preliminary Investigation

Faced with a potential accounting irregularity, a company does not want to jump to conclusions. After all, when the problem first arises, the company typically has information that is, to say the least, imperfect. Hypothesize, for example, that a whistleblower has come forward in the manner described in Chapter 1. It may be that this individual misunderstood the facts, or lacks first-hand knowledge, or is withholding information. The whistleblower also may have overstated the problem—or understated it. Perhaps he is holding a grudge. The whistleblower may be wrong, and the company may be dealing with accidental accounting errors rather than irregularities or fraud.

In any event, the company will need to conduct a preliminary investigation to verify the problem and to determine how substantial it is. The preliminary investigation could be conducted by any number of people. Financial management could conduct it, unless the company believes financial management was involved in a fraud. Other options include the company's regular outside auditor, internal auditors, general counsel, or outside counsel. Or the preliminary investigation could be carried out by a combination of these people.

Early on in the preliminary investigation, the investigators will have to ask the company's chief financial officer and high ranking accounting and financial personnel what they know about the whistleblower's allegations. Perhaps after talking to these more senior financial personnel the investigators will conclude that a problem does not exist and it was a simple misunderstanding. Chances are, however, that it will not be as simple as that.

It is possible that some of the key financial people will confess when they are confronted with the facts. They may even go so far as to provide the investigators with a secret schedule that explains what happened. Even if their confessions are not so complete, they may acknowledge that they cut some corners, or bent some accounting rules, but still deny they did anything wrong. In either event, the company has now confirmed that there's at least substance, if not total truth, to the whistleblower's assertions and the problem is not going to go away.

The Initial Board Meeting

Let us now assume that the company reaches the point in its preliminary investigation where it has what it considers to be solid information that there's a serious potential or even likelihood that accounting irregularities occurred. That means that purchasers and sellers of the company's securities are likely to be trading on the basis of materially misleading financial statements. At this point, the company is going to want and need to disclose something as soon as feasible, if only to stop the daily increase in liability arising from each new trade based on false information in the market.

The next point in our aftermath timeline is the initial board of directors meeting, which needs to be convened very quickly—immediately, really—after the preliminary investigation has verified the existence of potential irregularities. The last thing the company's management wants is to have the board read about serious problems with the company for the first time in the newspaper.

Only someone who has been through a number of these initial board meetings can fully appreciate what it is like to be there, the types of problems the board typically faces, and the issues that typically arise. The following is intended to capture some of the flavor and substance of what typically transpires in these meetings.

Again, the environment in which the board finds itself can best be described as a crisis. People are in shock. The company has probably never faced anything like this before, and this is probably the first time any of the board members have gone through an exigency of this sort. In short, there is a lack of precedent to guide the board.

Not only do the board members have to go through an exercise they have no experience for, they also must do it with little information to guide them. Although the preliminary investigation may have clarified some things, there will be many more questions than answers at this point. The questions that will naturally occur include the following:

- How bad is the fraud?
- How far back does it go?
- Who did it? Who knew about it?
- Who should have known about it (even if they didn't know)?
- Which employees can the company keep?
- Who, if anyone, should the company fire?
- Who should the company hire to do a more thorough investigation?
- Is director and officer (D&O) insurance available?
- How long will an investigation take?

The board needs to act quickly in getting answers. Yet it is difficult for the board to get answers and make decisions, because the board is dealing with a situation where information is imperfect, suspicions are running high, people are nervous, and the entire environment is less conducive to the kind of open communication that's usually necessary for effective problem-solving. Indeed, the people with the real information may be actively trying to conceal it to protect themselves.

Following are some likely answers to some of the above questions:

1. *How bad is the fraud?*   The company can't know for sure, but it is probably worse than anyone thinks. That is, the company probably has a greater number of problematic transactions that affect more areas of the company (e.g., units, divisions, and subsidiaries) than first apparent. Unless the company is lucky enough to catch the fraud in the first stages, the fraud usually is not discovered until it has spread well beyond the area that the whistle-blower described.

2. *How far back does it go?*   The fraud probably goes back further than anyone thinks, again because fraud is usually detected after it has been occurring for a while. The nature of financial fraud is that it typically starts small. The perpetrator only wants to manipulate a single quarter's numbers in order to make that quarter's financial targets. However, it usually continues until more and more people are required to implement the fraud and more elaborate measures are required. Soon the fraud becomes so great that it can no longer be hidden.

3. *Who did it? Who knew about it?*   The CFO and other senior accounting personnel will be suspects in many cases. The great and often unanswered question is whether the CEO (or other senior non-financial personnel) knew about or condoned the fraudulent conduct, or at least should have known. These questions are difficult to answer because there won't always be a clear paper trail leading directly to the senior-most people.

   So while the board is in its initial meeting trying to resolve some problems, some board members may be wondering whether some of the people in the room are knowing participants in the fraud. The board may ultimately find that the chairman or CEO, the very person running the board meeting, is a participant.

4. *Who does the company keep/fire?*   In some cases there may be a temptation to want to terminate everyone who is suspected of having had anything to do with the fraud. The problem is that at this preliminary stage, before a full investigation has been com-

pleted, no one knows who was involved or the degree of their involvement. Some of the involved employees may have employment contracts, which may require some fairly stringent standard of cause in order to fire them or to terminate lucrative benefits to which they would otherwise be entitled. Here is a sample clause:

> Cause shall mean (i) conviction of any crime constituting a felony or involving moral turpitude, dishonesty, or theft; (ii) gross neglect or misconduct in the performance of employee's duties hereunder; (iii) willful failure or refusal to perform such duties; (iv) engaging in any conduct that is materially injurious to the company or the reputation of the company.

While engaging in financial fraud may well constitute "cause" as set forth in the sample clause, proving that an officer or employee actually is guilty of such behavior is not always easy, especially where the individual strenuously denies any allegation of wrongdoing.

On the other hand, the company may want to retain the employees who confessed (particularly lower-level employees or a whistleblower) to help the company conduct the investigation and assist in preparing restated financial statements.

5. *Is D&O insurance available?* The availability of D&O insurance often is a legitimate concern. For a variety of reasons, D&O insurance policies typically decline to provide coverage for deliberate fraud. Consider, for example, the following (fairly standard) clause:

> EXCLUSIONS
>
> The Insurer shall not be liable to make any payment for Loss in connection with a Claim made against an insured:
>
> (a) arising out of, based upon, or attributable to the gaining in fact of any profit or advantage to which an insured was not legally entitled;

* * *

(c) arising out of, based upon, or attributable to the committing in fact of any criminal or deliberate fraudulent act.

However, the extent to which such a clause would preclude coverage is not always clear. For example, not all directors and officers named as defendants in the inevitable litigations will necessarily be knowing participants, and the fraud of wrongdoing directors and officers is not usually imputed to innocent directors and officers under the policy. But there is one exception: D&O policies sometimes provide that execution of the insurance application by one of the perpetrators of the fraud may cause that person's knowledge to be imputed to other insured persons and to the company. As a result, coverage may be denied completely on the basis of a material misrepresentation in the application.

So one thing that needs to be checked is who signed the insurance application. And the board should be made aware of the insurance company's potential right to rescind the policy, and thereby deny any coverage, if the application was signed by one of the guilty parties.

Usually, the affected parties attempt to resolve insurance issues through negotiation rather than litigation, though exceptions do exist. It is not, however, uncommon for these issues to take a long time, sometimes years, to resolve. Will an insurance company deny coverage entirely if a perpetrator signed the application? Experience suggests that they rarely will, though they may have the right to do so. But it is a negotiating tool in their hands and a mortification for directors and officers.

6. *How long will an investigation take?* The board of directors will need to commence a more thorough investigation, and everyone will want the investigation done yesterday—for good reason. But there will be a tension between this time pressure and the need for thoroughness. Realistically, these investigations must be done and can be done in a manner of a few months, although for small, more contained problems it may be possible to shorten that time frame.

A Race Against Time

The last question—the length of the investigation—is in some ways one of the most important. Unbeknownst to the board in its initial meeting, the company—no matter how strong its financial position at the moment—may be on the verge of a cash crisis. The reason is that, if the company has any debt, it has potentially violated its lending agreement insofar as the financial statements earlier provided to the bank were false. For example, a lending agreement might provide:

> 12. REPRESENTATIONS AND WARRANTIES
>
> * * *
>
> 12.4 *Financial Statements and Projection.* (a) The Borrower has delivered to the Bank the audited balance sheet and related statements of income and cash flow for the Borrower and its consolidated Subsidiaries as of December 31, 1998, for the Fiscal Year then ended . . . . All such financial statements have been prepared in accordance with GAAP and present accurately and fairly the financial position of the Borrower and its consolidated Subsidiaries as of the dates thereof and their results of operations for the periods then ended.
>
> 13. EVENTS OF DEFAULT
>
> 13.1 *Events of Default.* It shall constitute an event of default if any one or more of the following events occurs for any reason whatsoever:
>
> * * *
>
> (c) Any representation or warranty made by the Borrower in this Agreement, any Financial Statement, or any certificate furnished by the Borrower or any Subsidiary at any time to the Bank shall prove to be untrue in any material respect as of the date on which made.

No matter how strong a company's relationship with its bank, a typical lending committee will often recoil in horror when accounting irregularities have surfaced, and a normal reaction is for the bank to clamp down on the availability of credit until an investigation is complete and new audited financial statements are available. Such a reaction is particularly unfortunate because the resulting cash crunch comes just at the moment when the company's credibility is on the line, it is the subject of significant distrust, and it suddenly has enormous and unexpected cash needs owing to the need to hire a team of professionals to dig out the fraud and restore the company's credibility. (See Exhibit 3–1.) Of course, the lack of audited financial statements makes raising cash from alternative sources equally difficult. Indeed, for these and other reasons, once an accounting irregularity has surfaced, it is a statistical likelihood that the corporate victim will be going into bankruptcy or some equivalent type of restructuring. To avoid that calamity, the company needs to complete an investigation and get new audited financial statements fast.

The need for an expedited investigation does not, however, stem only from a potential crisis in cash. The exchange on which the company's stock trades is not an entirely passive observer of all this, and another source of time pressure will result from its requirement for accurate information to allow the company's stock to continue trading. During the interim between the discovery of the problem and the completion of an investigation allowing the issuance of new audited financial statements,

Exhibit 3–1. Restoring Credibility

The company's board of directors will need to restore credibility with the following:

- The SEC
- Securities exchanges
- Auditors
- Lenders
- Suppliers
- Customers
- Shareholders
- Financial markets

the company will not be in compliance with the exchange's listing requirements. More than imposing a halt on trading, the exchange may require that the company's stock be delisted.

Still another source of time pressure will be the company's everyday interaction with suppliers, customers, and everyone else with whom it has to deal. At root, the problem is that nobody will believe anything the company says until an investigation is completed, the wrongdoers are identified, and corrective financial information has been blessed by the auditor through the auditor's issuance of a new audit report on corrected information.

Action Plan

Whether the board knows it or not, fast, efficient action is therefore a must. That requires crisp decisionmaking and clear allocation of tasks (see Exhibit 3–2). Otherwise, the board's "action plan" will simply consist of a lot of people milling around and nothing will get done. The board needs to find people to: contact the company's lenders, suppliers, important customers, and other key constituents; look at insurance questions and make sure the proper notices are sent to the carriers; address the issue of potential communication with the SEC and other regula-

---

Exhibit 3–2. Implementation Checklist

The company's board of directors will need to make sure the following items are completed to ensure a thorough investigation and to alleviate damages from the fraud:

- Prepare initial press release
- Form a special committee to investigate the fraud
- Retain forensic accountants
- Retain outside counsel
- Make personnel decisions
- Notify insurance carriers

---

tory agencies; deal with the securities exchange; coordinate the process of interviewing and hiring the professionals to do the investigation; and think about publicity and getting out a press release.

The Initial Press Release

That brings us to the initial press release. This communication is the one that tells the world the bad news that the company has uncovered a problem and that the financial statements can no longer be relied on.

A key aspect of the initial press release is that the board, no matter how much it would like to, does not completely control the timing of its issuance. That is significant because—all other things being equal—the board would prefer to hold off issuance of the press release until it has a better handle on the facts. Unfortunately, the information is rarely complete when the press release has to be put on the wire. Typically, the press release must be issued before the board would like.

There are several reasons. The first is simply the fact that failure to promptly issue a press release allows innocent shareholders to continue to trade based on fraudulent information. Every week, every day, every hour that goes by, shareholders are continuing to buy and sell the company's stock in reliance on numerical results that the board now knows are not correct. That does not mean that the board should be panicked into premature issuance of a press release which, in conveying incorrect or partial information, does more harm than good. Still, good conscience requires that the board issue a press release as soon as realistically feasible.

If good conscience doesn't do it, there's always the outside auditor. Under the standards of the accounting profession, an auditor is not allowed to sit by and watch financial markets trade based on false audited financial statements. Thus, as soon as the auditor gets involved—and early involvement of the auditor is almost inevitable—the auditor will almost immediately begin alerting the board to the need for a press release with corrective information.

Still another source of time pressure for the press release will be the potential for irregular trading in the company's stock. Once an accounting problem has surfaced, it is normally only a matter of time before rumors start to swirl. Making matters worse, accounting irregularities have an unfortunate propensity to surface soon before a previously scheduled date of a company's earnings announcement—the delay of which will only excite suspicions further. Throughout the entirety of the time that it's desperately assembling information for the press release, therefore, the board will be haunted by the specter that, at any given moment, significant disruptions will occur in trading of the stock. Should that happen, immediate action will be an imperative. The board may be called upon to issue a press release by the end of the day.

Throughout the time period preceding issuance of the initial press release, therefore, the board will be faced with a very real tension between the need for prompt disclosure and the need for accurate disclosure. Typically, the most tangible form of that tension will involve whether the company believes it is in a position in its initial press release to include corrected or "restated" financial information.

The reality is that the company in its initial press release will desperately want to alert financial markets as to what the restated financial results should be. Otherwise, financial markets may simply assume the worst. The countervailing concern is that whatever restated results the company provides may, upon a more thorough investigation, turn out to be wrong. The fraud may be bigger or it may go back further. Thus, the well-intentioned press release may end up being a disclosure document on which a brand new class of plaintiffs will seek to sue. Experience teaches that a company almost never gets pleasant surprises once it discovers fraud.

The following is a hypothetical press release that might be issued during the immediate aftermath of discovery of a potential accounting fraud:

> New York, NY, March 15, 2001—ABC Corporation (Nasdaq: ABC) has reached a determination as to the need to restate earlier reported financial results. A preliminary investigation has indicated that revenues were incorrectly recognized during the second and third quarters of 2000 and that earnings for each of those quarters will need to be restated. The preliminary investigation suggests that earnings may be restated from $.32 to $.25 per share for the second quarter and from $.41 to $.19 per share for the third quarter. The company has not yet determined

whether it will need to restate any results for fiscal years 1999 or 1998. At the present time, all such previously reported financial results should not be relied on.

Yesterday evening the independent directors of the board of directors terminated the employment of Chief Financial Officer John L. Jones. At the request of the board of directors, Chief Executive Officer Alan S. Smith has voluntarily taken a temporary paid leave of absence from the company.

The audit committee of the board of directors has hired Monroe, Tyler & Van Buren as special legal counsel to conduct an independent investigation of the matter and to explore the possibility of litigation against culpable parties. The law firm has hired the accounting firm of Pabst and Pabst LLP to conduct an independent investigation.

ABC Corporation is a leading manufacturer of ladies dresses and sportswear. With wholesale delivery capability to 124 nations, it provides a full line of ladies wear for the office, home, and social gatherings. It has twice won the coveted Stellar Award for women's fashions.

Incidentally, notice the absence of one word from the press release: "irregularity." At this early stage, it is not necessarily advisable for the company to include in its press release the assertion that the restatement is the result of an accounting "irregularity," given the poor quality of information and the fact that the company does not want to attribute the totality of a restatement to an "irregularity" unless it is absolutely, positively sure. The main point to be communicated is that financial markets should no longer be relying on the earlier financial results. Disclosure of the level of intent of the various participants can normally await a more thorough investigation.

Other Issues

Once the initial press release is issued, the board of directors must then turn to myriad additional issues. These include the following:

1. *Activate the audit committee.*   A committee of the board will need to oversee the upcoming investigation, and that responsibility will normally fall upon the shoulders of the audit committee as part of its duty to oversee the company's system of financial reporting.

The audit committee must therefore convene a meeting and make plans for the investigation to get under way. If for some reason the audit committee is not in a position to undertake that responsibility, then a special committee of the board will need to be created for that purpose.

2. *Retain forensic accountants.* The audit committee will potentially need to hire an independent accounting firm—one with experience providing financial-investigative or "forensic" services—to find the correct numbers. That is, the forensic accountants will have to uncover and piece together all the irregularities to facilitate the restatement of financial results.

   The forensic specialists, however, will not necessarily be the ones to audit and render an opinion on the restated financial statements. Companies often hire their regular outside auditors to issue the actual audit opinion. In fact, one of the most important decisions the company will need to make early on is whether to retain its regular outside auditor to opine on the restated financial statements or to bring in a new firm for this task. On the one hand, the incumbent auditor may be in the best position to complete the audit most quickly, which gets the company to its goal of restated financial statements most rapidly. In some cases, however, there may be a concern about the incumbent auditing firm's independence stemming from the possible allegation down the road that it should have uncovered the problem itself. These competing concerns must be balanced on a case-by-case basis.

3. *Retain outside counsel.* The audit committee will also need to select an independent outside counsel (i.e., not the company's regular outside counsel) to do the following:

   - Conduct and advise at the meetings
   - Direct the investigation
   - Conduct the interviews of company personnel and others who can shed light on the problem
   - Write an investigative report, assuming there is to be a written report
   - Deal with other counsel (for the company, for employees, for the SEC, for other regulatory agencies, etc.)

4. *Install new management.*   The company may need to hire new management (if old management has been suspended or fired), and it may have difficulty retaining valuable old management, because they may be demoralized and looking to leave a troubled situation. It is normal for the company's stock price to drop substantially following the initial press release, so any stock options management holds, which provide much of its compensation, may now be much less valuable or even worthless. At some point the company may want to consider appropriate incentives to induce critical personnel to stay with the company.

5. *Securities delisting.*   For companies whose shares are quoted on Nasdaq, revelation of accounting irregularities also raises the specter of Nasdaq delisting. Nasdaq has fairly stringent listing requirements, including that the company stay current in filing audited financial statements with the SEC. In the event the company's outside auditor were to withdraw its previous audit opinions, or withdraw from its current engagement, causing a delay in the filing of audited financials, Nasdaq could elect to delist the company's securities, thereby relegating them to the old pink sheets. Nasdaq may also delist in the extreme circumstance where the company's stock drops below a specified level in trading value. Of course, the company may apply for reinstatement if and when it resumes compliance with the Nasdaq requirements, but in the meantime it will have had its credibility and reputation in the marketplace badly damaged. A company whose shares are traded on the New York Stock Exchange may face analogous problems with that exchange.

6. *Secure documents.*   The board should promptly try to secure company documents and computer records from the perpetrators to keep them from being destroyed. In this increasingly technological age, it may not be enough just to lock suspected perpetrators out of their offices. The company may also have to retrieve the laptops the perpetrators carry home with them every night.

7. *Handle class-action lawsuits.*   Class action lawsuits are certain to roll in within a day or two after the initial press release. Although many corporate executives may have come to think of securities class actions as meritless annoyances, the types of class

actions the company faces in the wake of an accounting irregularity disclosure may not fall into this category. Keep in mind that the company's initial press release in all likelihood will have admitted at least one important element of a securities law claim.

8. *Indemnification.* The company's bylaws and charter need to be checked to see whether the company has an obligation to indemnify and provide defense costs, including for those who are suspected wrongdoers. Most bylaws these days generally provide for indemnification of the company's officers and directors to the maximum extent permitted by the corporation law of the company's state of incorporation.

    A typical state corporate law (Delaware, for example) provides that a corporation may indemnify:

    > . . . any persons, including directors and officers, who are, or are threatened to be made, parties to any threatened, pending or completed legal action, whether civil, criminal, administrative or investigative . . . by reason of the fact that such person is or was a director, officer, employee or agent of such corporation, or is or was serving at the request of such corporation as a director, officer, employee or agent of another corporation or enterprise [such as a corporate subsidiary]. The indemnity may include expenses (including attorneys' fees), judgments, fines and amounts paid in settlement . . . provided such director, officer, employee or agent acted in good faith and in a manner he reasonably believed to be in the corporation's best interests. . . .

Even if the company believes a particular officer or director did not act in good faith or in the best interests of the company, it is difficult to resist advancing defense costs to such person in the absence of an actual adjudication of wrongdoing. At least this is true where the bylaws provide that indemnification "shall" (rather than "may") be provided to the fullest extent permitted under state law, which is usually the case. Moreover, the practicalities of the situation may favor indemnification and advancement of defense costs insofar as a failure to do so may result in uncontrollable and highly public litigation by the departing executives back against the company which, in turn, could exacerbate already strained relationships between the company and pretty much everyone with whom it has to deal.

Thus, the company may find itself in the rather unpalatable position of having to pay the legal fees of separate counsel for persons whom the company believes were responsible for the fraud. Even though the company can (and often must) require an undertaking from the directors and officers to repay defense costs if they are ultimately found to have acted dishonestly or for improper personal gain, this will be small solace since, by the time the company is ready to collect, the line of creditors will be long, and assets to pay creditors probably long gone.

The Auditor's Upper Hand

As it sorts through these issues, one realization will loom larger and larger in the board's mind: to a significant extent, the company's fate now lies in the hands of its outside auditor. The reason is that, until the company can procure audited financial statements, it basically cannot function. Lenders, regulators, its securities exchange, suppliers, customers, employees—each of these will remain exceedingly skeptical of management until the company's integrity is reestablished and its credibility restored. The audit report in this context represents independent confirmation that the company has taken the first steps to getting its financial house in order, in providing reliable financial data, and restoring some level of institutional integrity.

For a board desperate to move beyond this mess, therefore, procurement of an audit report often becomes akin to the quest for the holy grail. It is the key to a return to normalcy. What may have seemed easy in the past, though, now becomes much more of a challenge. Auditors, too, are capable of emotional reactions to the discovery of fraud, especially when the fraud has developed in such a way that they can be counted among the victims. Just at the moment the company's need for an audit report is at the utmost, the auditor may be looking to the door. Auditor resignation in such a circumstance is far from unknown.

For that reason, the board's focus will soon shift to the auditor. In particular, it shifts to one of the biggest obstacles the board will face: getting new audited financial statements.

CHAPTER 4

GETTING NEW AUDITED FINANCIAL STATEMENTS

Harvey R. Kelly

What do the real numbers look like? What is the true financial condition of the company? How far back do the accounting problems go?

The instant potential accounting irregularities come to light, a company is sure to have to answer these and similar, endless questions. The questions emerge from everywhere. As the company's owners, its shareholders demand reliable financial information. Lenders, concerned about the company's financial stability and compliance with loan covenants, may threaten to cut off credit lines and demand loan repayments. Customers or vendors may seek to delay, renegotiate, or even cancel purchases or sales. Major transactions, such as mergers or pending financing transactions, may hang in the balance. And, of course, the Securities and Exchange Commission (SEC), stock exchanges, and other regulatory bodies will have a keen interest in exactly what has gone wrong. Frequently, regulators will halt trading in a company's stock pending receipt of adequate additional financial information.

Amidst all this uncertainty, one point becomes clear: the marketplace will demand to see corrected financial statements. Realizing the need for corrected or "re-audited" financial statements is the easy part—getting there is often more of a challenge. Chapter 4 explores issues that companies often confront in their attempts to get new audited financial statements right after the discovery of accounting irregularities.

Initial Involvement of the Outside Auditor

When potential accounting irregularities initially surface, the first task for the board of directors is to get the facts. However, the need to understand what has happened creates a very real dilemma for the board: Who is familiar enough with the company's accounting systems to quickly size up the problem, but at the same time is entirely free of suspicion? Directors rarely know enough facts in the early stages to allay fears that the CEO, the CFO, the controller, or other senior members of financial management may be directly involved. Indeed, experience shows that the very executives on whom the board typically relies for financial information often turn out to be somehow implicated in the fraud.

Unless such concerns are quickly demonstrated to be groundless, the immediate involvement of the outside auditor is therefore likely. The outside auditor has the expertise, experience, knowledge of generally accepted accounting principles (GAAP), and history with the company that make it the logical first choice to help the board of directors assess the situation. In fact, calling potential accounting irregularities to the immediate attention of the outside auditor typically has several important advantages to the company, such as:

- Making available the necessary expertise and resources to quickly determine whether accounting irregularities exist
- Limiting reliance on company personnel to evaluate the potential irregularities at a time when the identity of the perpetrator(s) may be unknown
- Enabling the auditor to fulfill its professional responsibility to evaluate the effect of suspected irregularities on previously issued audit reports

Consequently, one of the first things a board of directors typically does when faced with accounting irregularities is to bring in the incumbent outside auditor.

Effect on Previously Issued Audit Reports

Once called to the scene, the auditor may take as little as a few days to substantiate that the company does indeed have an accounting irregularity problem. When that fact has been determined, the auditor is immediately confronted with a serious issue: the possibility, if not likelihood, that the fraud goes back to the most recently filed Form 10-K, which includes not only the company's annual financial statements but the auditor's report on them. Thus, the discovery of irregularities may force the auditor to act to prevent further reliance on the previously issued audit reports, as required by American Institute of Certified Public Accountants (AICPA) professional standards when an auditor becomes aware of new information that relates to previously audited financial statements.

In situations involving material accounting irregularities that affect prior-years' financial statements, an auditor will almost inevitably conclude that reliance on previous audit reports must be discontinued. Under such circumstances, the auditor will advise the company to make appropriate disclosure to those who the company knows to be relying on, or who are likely to rely on, the financial statements and audit report.

One way the company can make that disclosure, if the effect of the accounting irregularity on the financial statements can be promptly determined, is to issue revised audited financial statements. However, the effect on the financial statements often cannot be determined without a prolonged investigation; thus, the prompt issuance of revised financial statements is frequently not an option. In such a circumstance, the auditor will ordinarily suggest that the company notify those who use the statements that the financial statements and accompanying audit report should no longer be relied upon. The auditor will also likely advise that the company tell the statement users that restated financial statements will be issued once the company completes an investigation. The auditor may also insist that the company notify the SEC, stock exchanges, and other appropriate regulatory agencies.

The board of directors must take the auditor's recommendation for such notification seriously. If the board fails to act on the auditor's suggestion, the auditor could notify:

- Regulatory agencies that the audit report should no longer be relied on

- Each person known to be relying on the financial statements that the audit report should no longer be relied on. (In the case of public companies, this can be accomplished by the auditor requesting that the SEC, the stock exchange, or other regulatory agency take whatever steps are deemed necessary to accomplish the required disclosure.)

The board might be tempted to avoid these disclosure obligations by excluding the auditor from the process; however, such an approach is ill-advised. Exclusion of the auditor may expose the company to even greater litigation and regulatory risk and almost certainly would destroy any working relationship between the auditor and the board. In any event, once accounting irregularities have surfaced, the involvement of the auditor is inevitable.

The Element of Mistrust

Unfortunately, the very mention of an accounting irregularity often leads to premature accusations and mistrust. Company executives, directors, and others almost without fail begin to accuse the auditor and ask questions such as:

- Where was the auditor?
- How could the auditor have missed this?
- Is it possible that the auditor was in on the fraud?
- Should we fire the auditor for not doing its job thoroughly?

At the same time, the auditor inevitably must face the following questions:

- Who at the company knew about the accounting problems?
- Which company personnel lied to us during the audit?
- Were documents deliberately withheld from us?
- Did the company forge documents?
- Who at the company can we trust?
- What other problems are out there?

Accusations at the outset are understandable but counterproductive. They create a certain level of tension, which, if allowed to fester, can be disastrous. Such an environment may cause the auditor to terminate the relationship and withdraw all previously issued audit reports, effectively leaving the company without audited financial statements. The company would then have to disclose publicly the auditor's resignation in SEC filings, which could elevate the concerns of regulators and shareholders. At a time when interested parties are already nervous about the company's financial condition, the abrupt departure of the company's auditor can be operationally unfortunate as well as a public relations disaster. Moreover, as described later, changing auditors will almost certainly delay the procurement of revised audited financial statements, which, the board of directors will quickly come to realize, is one of the most important tasks that it faces.

Usually, a more constructive approach for both the auditor and the company is to reserve judgment until the facts are known. Because the procurement of revised, credible financial statements is of paramount importance, the energies of management and the auditor should generally be directed to working with, not blaming, each other.

Benefits of Continuing the Audit Relationship

Once the auditor has reported back to the board of directors that corrected financial statements are necessary, the board then must decide who should assist in correcting them. In particular, the board must decide whether to stay with its incumbent auditor or to bring in a new auditor. (See Exhibit 4–1.)

The answer is not always obvious. Among the arguments for a new auditor will be the notion that "a new broom sweeps clean" and that the incumbent auditor may be a co-defendant in class action litigation. At the same time, the element of mistrust in the auditor-client relationship will be obvious to everyone, and some will inevitably view the retention of a new auditor as an opportunity to eliminate the resulting stress.

All of those views may be sound; however, they are largely trumped by one that is more important. Once an accounting irregularity has surfaced, of utmost concern to the board of directors will be the procurement of restated financial statements accompanied by a reliable audit report. As the days and weeks progress, the board will find that it is difficult for a public company to function without audited financial statements. The company's banking relationships will founder. Its lines of credit will dry up. The company will face significant inquiry from the SEC. It will be threatened with delisting by its stock exchange. Suppliers will begin having second thoughts and may demand cash on delivery. Customers will become skeptical as to the company's reliability. And, as time progresses, the doubts will only increase.

Exhibit 4–1. Selecting an Auditor

- Benefits of a new auditor
  - — Fresh look
  - — Clean break from the past
  - — Less tension in auditor relationship
- Benefits of continuing with the incumbent auditor
  - — Ability to audit restatements faster
  - — Access to information gathered in past audits
  - — Buy-in of past auditor to restatement requirements
  - — Ability to reaffirm opinions on unaffected years
  - — Avoids challenges of finding new auditor in a fraud environment
  - — Less burden on company personnel

The biggest issue in the audit relationship, therefore, is not the level of comfort with the incumbent auditor or whether a new broom will sweep clean. The biggest issue is getting re-audited financial statements as fast as humanly possible. In balancing the benefits and costs of continued use of the incumbent auditor, the following considerations will favor the incumbent auditor's continued retention:

1. *Speed.* The incumbent auditor can do it faster. In the absence of evidence to the contrary, the incumbent auditor will generally be able to rely on audit work it has already performed. Conversely, in order to be able to render an opinion on the financial statements as a whole, any new auditor would need to perform extensive audit procedures beyond areas affected by the accounting irregularities. Such additional efforts can be particularly time-consuming where the irregularities have affected multiple years.

2. *Information.* Often, the auditor's working papers will contain documents that shed light on the origin and parties responsible for the irregularities. For example, an auditor may have copies of altered documents (although such alterations may not have been

previously apparent to the auditor) or evidence of misrepresentations made to the auditor by company personnel. Termination of the auditor may hinder the investigation by delaying or even precluding audit workpaper access.

3. *Concurrence.* If a company opts to engage a different auditor, it increases the risk that the former auditor will later publicly contest the restatement. Such disputes can cast further doubt on the integrity of the company's financial statements at a time when the company can ill-afford such uncertainty.

4. *Prior-year audit reports.* When accounting irregularities are determined not to extend back to multiple years, a company may wish to continue to rely on prior-years' audit reports. For example, applicable rules and regulations generally require a company to keep on record a total of three successive years of audited financial statements. If the company terminates its incumbent auditor or otherwise isolates the auditor from the investigation findings, the auditor may withhold its consent to incorporate its audit reports from prior years. Conversely, an auditor that is sufficiently familiar with the investigation findings should be in a position to reaffirm previously rendered audit reports on years unaffected by the irregularities.

5. *New auditor reluctance.* At this particular moment in its corporate history, the company is not exactly a dream audit client. At least some members of management have probably committed fraud. Among the victims of the fraud is the incumbent auditor. It is not necessarily the case, therefore, that termination of the incumbent auditor will be followed by an onslaught of other auditors fighting to pick up the engagement. Depending on the circumstances, each of the other Big Five accounting firms (if your incumbent auditor is a Big Five firm, already you're down to four) may decide it is better to let this one pass. The enthusiasm of the other national or regional firms may not be any greater. Termination of the existing auditor—at least until another firm is lined up—can therefore leave the company in the completely untenable position of having no auditor at all. Again, a public company basically cannot function for very long without audited financial statements.

The Independent Forensic Accounting Team

All of these considerations do not mean that a company must rely exclusively on its incumbent auditor to conduct an investigation. After all, many will (fairly or unfairly) point to the fact that the incumbent auditor did miss the fraud once. Moreover, the "audit sampling" and "professional skepticism" approaches of a normal audit pursuant to generally accepted auditing standards (GAAS) are not necessarily optimal where deliberate misrepresentations have surfaced. Therefore, it frequently makes sense to bring in a separate accounting firm with special expertise in digging out fraud to complement the incumbent auditor's efforts. Thus will be introduced to the process the "forensic" accounting team.

The engagement of forensic accountants usually is controlled by the audit committee or some special committee of the board of directors charged with the responsibility of conducting the investigation. Although the scope of the forensic accountants' responsibilities can differ from investigation to investigation, their role normally will include the investigation of data that will assist the auditor in issuing a new audit report. Among other contributions, the forensic accountants are frequently called upon to facilitate the financial statement restatement by:

- Serving as technical accounting advisors to the audit committee and its lawyers
- Identifying and compiling documentary support that will be needed by both the company and its auditors to determine the proper financial statement presentation
- Acting as intermediaries between the company's management and auditor with respect to specified accounting issues
- Providing the company's auditor comfort that a credible, independent investigation into the irregularities is being performed
- Communicating relevant investigation findings to the auditor

The role of the forensic accounting team and its interaction with the outside auditor are discussed in greater detail in Chapter 6.

Responsibility for Restated Financial Statements

Notwithstanding the involvement of a battery of auditors and forensic accountants, the ultimate responsibility for preparing restated financial statements remains with company management. Management, with the assistance of its newly formed army of accounting investigators, must make its own determination as to whether accounting irregularities have occurred. If management concludes that irregularities resulted in financial statements that violated GAAP, the company must process accounting adjustments and issue revised financial statements that comply. Before the auditor issues an audit report on the restated financial statements, it will require appropriate members of the company's management to provide written representations that the financial statements are management's responsibility and have been fairly presented in accordance with GAAP. Management must, therefore, fully understand and document the corrections.

Although it may seem obvious that management should be knowledgeable about its own financial statements, the time-sensitive, pressure-filled environment of an investigation into accounting irregularities usually is unfamiliar territory to management personnel. In some cases, high-level financial managers, new to their positions as a consequence of personnel changes after irregularities have surfaced, may be dedicating most of their time to other newly obtained responsibilities. Often, irregularities are identified and quantified initially by the forensic accountants or an auditor rather than company personnel, who may find themselves largely or entirely left out of the picture. However, even in instances in which well-respected auditors and forensic accountants have identified, quantified, and documented restatement adjustments, management must ensure that the company maintains appropriate documentation of the nature and composition of such adjustments and takes responsibility for concluding that such adjustments are appropriate.

Restatement Requirements

A re-audit of previously issued financial statements can potentially uncover all kinds of issues—if only because time has passed since the original audit and things inevitably have not turned out exactly as previously estimated. Not every issue that surfaces, however, will require restatement of the financial statements. (See Exhibit 4–2.) Indeed, restatement to accommodate certain kinds of issues is forbidden by GAAP. Thus, one task facing management and its auditor will be to determine which issues require restatement and which do not.

Exhibit 4–2. Restatement Guidance

Accounting issues that require restatement:

- Misstatements arising out of errors
- Misstatements arising out of irregularities
- Misstatements arising out of illegal acts
- Misstatements arising out of bad faith estimates

Accounting issues that do not require restatement:

- Misstatements arising out of a revision of earlier good faith estimates
- Misstatements arising out of a change in accounting principle

---

As a general matter, the issues uncovered during a re-audit will fall into one of the following five categories:

1. *Errors.* Errors are unintentional misstatements or omissions of amounts or disclosures in financial statements. Errors may involve the following:
    - Mistakes in gathering or processing data from which financial statements are prepared
    - Unreasonable accounting estimates arising from oversight or misinterpretation of the facts
    - Mistakes in applying accounting principles relating to the amount, classification, manner of presentation, or disclosure in the financial statements
2. *Irregularities.* Irregularities (under the revised audit standards they are now called *fraud*) are intentional misstatements arising from fraudulent financial reporting practices, such as:
    - Manipulation, fabrication, or alteration of accounting records or supporting documents from which financial statements are prepared

- Misrepresentation in, or intentional omission from, the financial statements of events, transactions, or other significant information

- Intentional misapplication of accounting principles relating to the amounts, classification, manner of presentation, or disclosure in the financial statements

3. *Illegal acts.* Illegal acts involve violations of laws or governmental regulations.

4. *Inaccurate estimates.* Subsequent events may demonstrate that accounting estimates used in preparing the financial statements later proved to be inaccurate. Examples of accounting estimates that can be called into question include inventory valuation reserves, bad debt reserves, loss contract reserves, percentage-of-completion revenue recognition estimates, sales returns and allowance reserves, and warranty reserves.

5. *Changes in accounting policies.* Accounting policies represent the methods adopted by a company to account for transactions in accordance with GAAP. Sometimes two or more acceptable methods of accounting exist for certain types of transactions (the use of FIFO or LIFO to account for inventory being a good example).

The nature of the accounting issues determines whether previously issued financial statements require restatement. Misstatements arising out of newly discovered errors, irregularities, or illegal acts will require a restatement unless the amounts are not material or, in some instances, the financial statements are outdated.

On the other hand, the identification of inaccurate estimates underlying the financial statements does not necessarily call for restatement of prior-year financials. Virtually every company that prepares financial statements later discovers that its accounting estimates differed from how things actually turned out. For example, an entity's actual receivable write-off experience may be worse than a reserve for bad debts previously accrued due to unforeseen customer financial difficulties. Under GAAP, changes in estimates generally should not be accounted for by restating amounts reported in prior periods. Instead, the effects of changes in accounting estimates should be accounted for in the period the company changes its estimate and, in certain circumstances, in future periods.

The distinctions between these different types of accounting issues can be blurry. Distinguishing between an incorrect estimate that is the result of an error (which requires a restatement) and an incorrect estimate that is the result of reasonably unforeseen subsequent events (which does not) can be exceedingly subtle. The context in which the distinctions must be made, moreover, virtually guarantees that all such determinations will be heavily second-guessed. Thus, the restatement process frequently involves much discussion and debate among management, the auditor, and the lawyers.

Further complicating the process may be a natural desire on the part of management to seize the opportunity to change preexisting accounting policies even though those preexisting accounting policies already complied with GAAP. For example, to increase its credibility with the financial community, management may decide to adopt new accounting policies that, while still complying with GAAP, are more conservative than those previously used.

If a company elects to change from one proper accounting policy to another, the nature and justification for the change and its effect on income are to be disclosed in the financial statements in the period in which the company makes the change. Although GAAP provides for certain exceptions, companies generally are to report most changes in accounting principles by recognizing the cumulative effect on net income of the period of the change rather than as a restatement of prior-period results.

Restatements and Materiality

Assessment of the need for a restatement is complicated by another consideration. Financial statements must be restated only where the prior misstatement is one that is "material."

Assessments of materiality have always been a challenge, and the challenge has increased within the last several years. Historically, materiality assessments have typically involved the application of certain numerical thresholds. By convention, potential adjustments that were below 5% were less inclined to be viewed as material. Potential adjustments above 10% were more inclined to be viewed as material.

In August 1999, the staff of the SEC tried to jolt the financial community into a way of assessing materiality that focused not only on numerical thresholds, but also on the potential significance of the item to investors. The SEC's pronouncement was entitled "Staff Accounting Bulletin Number 99" or "SAB 99," and its gist was that "there are numerous circumstances in which misstatements below five percent could well be material." For SAB 99, assessment of materiality did not involve simply the application of numerical thresholds, but "qualitative factors" that "may cause misstatements of quantitatively small amounts to be material." Among such factors was "how the misstatement arose." According to SAB 99, deliberate misstatements were more likely to be viewed as material. SAB 99 provides: "It is unlikely that it is ever 'reasonable' for registrants to record misstatements or not to correct known misstatements—even immaterial ones—as part of an ongoing effort directed by or known to senior management for the purposes of 'managing' earnings."

Few can doubt that, in promulgating SAB 99, the staff of the SEC had its heart in the right place. It arguably made sense to prevent companies, prior to the issuance of their financial statements, from failing to correct for known misstatements of less than 5% solely in an attempt to sustain a company's stock price. Applied to the potential need to correct financial statements that have already been issued, however, the logic behind SAB 99's view of materiality becomes less compelling. Suppose, for example, that a company discovers that, in the previous year, it mistakenly reported earnings 1% higher than it should have because of an honest blunder in counting inventory. Insofar as the prior financial statements now include a "known misstatement," does that render the financial statements "materially" misleading? Does it make a difference if, rather than being accidental, the inventory misstatement was deliberate? Does it matter if the discrepancy happened two years, rather than one year, before?

At the moment, SAB 99's impact on such questions is unclear. Without actually saying so, SAB 99 by its terms appears primarily intended to address assessments of materiality in financial statements yet to be issued, rather than in financial statements that have already gone out the door. For now, suffice it to say that materiality assessments as to already-issued financial statements can be exceedingly challenging.

The Audit Process

Once the re-audit has commenced, management is often taken aback by the auditor's adoption of new procedures in conducting the actual audit testing (see Exhibit 4–3). The audit process, never a complete pleasure even under the best of circumstances, can become more exasperating once the auditor has been told that it was earlier the victim of lies. The auditor must then be more thorough and cautious during the re-audit, to the point where genuinely innocent employees may get frustrated as their integrity seems to be repeatedly called into question.

That frustration may be increased insofar as company personnel fail to appreciate exactly what the auditor is trying to accomplish during a re-audit. Common misconceptions among company personnel about the re-audit include:

- The auditor will confine itself to revisiting only those prior-year issues that the company has called to its attention
- The auditor can fully rely on work done and conclusions reached by the independent forensic accountants, so the auditor will not have to perform much additional work
- The auditor will only require the company to provide the same level of documentation as customarily requested in prior audits
- The company will only be dealing with the same personnel from the auditing firm that performed past audits of the company

In general, company employees should expect audits of restated financial statements, particularly those resulting from prior fraudulent financial reporting, to involve heightened auditor skepticism, more extensive evidence gathering, and expanded audit teams. All in all, it will generally be an entirely unpleasant experience for company personnel.

Evidence of a new approach in the audit, moreover, will be everywhere. The auditor might seek additional documentary evidence from outside the company. For example, if the fraud involved improper revenue recognition, the auditor may request expanded confirmations from the company's customers on issues such as contract terms, the existence

---

Exhibit 4–3. What to Expect from Auditors Auditing Fraud-Related Restatements

- New and expanded test procedures

- Increased demand for third-party corroboration

- Voluminous document requests

- More visible involvement of senior personnel and national office technical experts

---

of side letters, acceptance criteria, delivery and payment terms and timing, the extent of any continuing company obligations, and cancellation or return provisions.

Such an additional level of audit scrutiny can be burdensome and frustrating. The auditor may request documents that are voluminous, that have been sent to off-site storage, or, even worse, that cannot be found. The auditor may demand to see original documents when previously it accepted photocopies. The company may be asked to prevail upon its customers to research and confirm (or perhaps re-confirm) details about the customers' business with the company dating back several years. Management may believe it has provided the auditor sufficient explanation or documentation, yet the auditor will seek still more. Even innocent senior executives may get the feeling that its overzealous auditor no longer trusts anything anybody says.

Such a characterization usually is something of an exaggeration, but it does highlight an important dynamic that occurs in instances of financial fraud. Auditors, always obligated to conduct independent audits with an attitude of professional skepticism, must consider how the fraud previously escaped detection both by the company's internal control system and by the auditor. Once the auditor concludes that one or more members of management consciously committed fraud, the auditor may question the reliability of every representation or piece of evidence received from those individuals. The auditor may also question the reliability of every representation or piece of evidence prepared by subordinates of those determined to have perpetrated the fraud.

All of this is made more difficult for company personnel by the auditor's likely introduction of new audit team personnel to supplement (or replace) the previous engagement team, with which the company personnel may have been comfortable. The auditor may involve personnel not previously involved in the company's audit to ensure that the audit team possesses the knowledge, skill, ability, and experience commensurate with the risk. The addition of new accountants to the audit team, moreover, will not only take place among those individuals at the company's offices during the duration of the auditor's fieldwork: Beyond those in the field, the audit team will probably now include significant participation by the most senior technical representatives of the accounting firm's national office. In all likelihood, company personnel will notice constrained flexibility and discretion in those areas that require some level of judgment. Correspondingly, the process of decision making may be slowed. To some extent, company personnel may get the impression that the CPAs in the field are very much under the thumb of those at the auditing firm's national headquarters. In many instances, that impression will be correct.

The auditor's task can be further confounded by management confusion over how its incumbent auditor and its newly retained forensic accountants are supposed to interact. Thus, executives and employees sometimes mistakenly assume that the investigation performed by the forensic accountants from a different accounting firm will obviate the need for the auditor to perform much testing. After all, cannot the auditor accept the findings of these other professionals and still render an unqualified opinion? The answer is no. GAAS requires an auditor on its own to obtain sufficient competent evidential matter to afford a reasonable basis to express an opinion on the financial statements.

Representations to the Auditor

One issue that rarely creates a problem in a normal GAAS audit, but which can pose quite a significant problem after accounting irregularities have been discovered, is the auditor's need to obtain management representations.

The auditor's procurement of management representations is mandated by GAAS. Before the audit report is issued, the auditor is to obtain a representation letter setting forth, among other things, the representations of responsible executives that the financial statements are set forth in accordance with GAAP and that all pertinent information has been provided to the auditor. That representation letter is to be signed by executives whose knowledge of the financial reporting system is such that an adequate basis for the representations exist. Beyond the formal representations of the representation letter, any number of executives and accounting personnel will make separate representations during the course of the audit that sometimes will be noted by the auditor in its workpapers.

What can be routine in a normal audit, however, can become more of a problem once fraud has been discovered. Suddenly the normal procurement of management representations can be difficult, or even potentially impossible, insofar as executives from whom the representations would normally be obtained—such as senior financial executives or the CEO—may have been terminated or, even if not terminated, may no longer be viewed as completely reliable. In instances in which key management personnel have been terminated, moreover, the company may have filled newly vacated positions with individuals not previously associated with the organization.

New members of management may add credibility to the company, but they can also pose a challenge to the audit process. The auditor will demand from management written representations covering all previous years upon which the auditor must express an opinion. Executives new to the company may resist taking responsibility for the propriety of financial reports about which they, in truth, know little. Under GAAS, management's unwillingness to furnish written representations constitutes a limitation on the scope of the audit sufficient to preclude an unqualified opinion. It is also enough to cause the auditor to disclaim an opinion or to withdraw from the engagement.

Needless to say, an auditor disclaimer or resignation is the last thing management wants. Neither is likely to restore the confidence of shareholders, creditors, regulators, or others. The need for management representations can therefore delay the release of audited financial statements if not dealt with early in the audit process. At the outset, company management and its auditor should do their best to achieve a clear understanding of the personnel from whom the auditor will require written representations and exactly what those representations will consist of. Of course, even the best of planning in this area may be ruined if the investigation finds fault with individuals from whom the auditor planned to obtain representations.

Effect of Lawsuits on Auditor Independence

Amid all the uncertainty of the re-audit and investigative process, one matter is a virtual certainty—lawsuits will be filed. One question that often arises involves the effect of such lawsuits on the auditor's ability to continue in its capacity as the company's auditor.

Public accountants are governed by a code of professional ethics that requires them to be "independent" of the companies whose financial statements they audit. Beyond that, for an auditor to be able to render an informed, objective opinion on financial statements, the relationship between the auditor and the company being audited must be characterized by complete candor and full disclosure. There must also be an absence of bias on the part of the auditor so that the auditor can properly exercise professional judgment on the financial reporting decisions made by management.

Litigation concerning the propriety of a company's previous financial statements and the accompanying audit report can potentially interfere with the auditor's independence. For one thing, litigation that names both the company and the auditor as co-defendants can potentially turn the auditor and management into adversaries—and thereby chill the complete candor that, under GAAS, must characterize the audit relationship. Often, both the company and the auditor will come to the strategic recognition that lashing out against each other in litigation is foolish and counterproductive. Still, the potential for compromised independence poses a risk to issuance of a new audit report.

Whether independence is in fact deemed to be compromised involves a complex area of GAAS that is to be governed by the particular circumstances at issue. As a general rule, the following matters are considered to impair the auditor's independence and therefore would result in the auditor's resignation:

- The commencement of litigation by present company management against the auditor alleging deficiencies in audit work on the company's financial statements

- Under certain circumstances, the threat of litigation by present management of the company against the auditor alleging audit deficiencies if the auditor deems the filing of such a claim to be probable
- The commencement of litigation by the auditor against present management alleging management fraud or deceit

Conversely, litigation by shareholders or other third parties against the company and/or its auditor alleging violations of the securities laws or similar issues normally does *not*, in and of itself, necessarily affect the auditor's independence. Therefore, such lawsuits do not automatically result in the company's need to find a new auditor. Even such third-party litigation, however, can lead to an impairment of auditor independence under certain circumstances. Independence may be compromised if, for example, the company files a cross-claim against the auditor alleging that the auditor is responsible for financial statement deficiencies. A cross-claim filed by the auditor alleging fraud by present company management may also impair the auditor's independence.

On the other hand, the existence of cross-claims filed by the company, its management, or any of its directors merely to protect the right to legal redress in the event of a future adverse decision in the primary litigation (or, in lieu of cross-claims, agreements to extend the statutes of limitations) would not normally impair the auditor's independence, unless there was thereby created a significant risk that the cross-claim would result in a settlement or judgment in an amount material to the accounting firm or the company.

The issues are obviously complicated, and the complexities of the litigation environment preclude the formulation of hard-and-fast rules governing auditor independence in all actual, threatened, or possible circumstances. Accordingly, the best approach is probably to raise the issue of independence at the outset of the re-audit so that both the auditor and company management are completely familiar with the risks and can develop a common understanding of how those risks will be addressed.

The Bottom Line

The bottom line is that a public company that has experienced accounting irregularities needs to get restated financial statements fast. To be

sure, the company and its employees start out behind the eight ball—
the auditor, having already been the victim of a fraud once, will not want
it to happen again. Therefore, management must convince the auditor
that it has management's full support; that management has every interest in digging out all of the fraud; and that management will be completely candid and forthcoming in complying with all of the auditor's
requests for data, information, and corroboration. These tasks will not
be pleasant or easy, but for a public company, audited financial statements are a prerequisite for continued existence.

CHAPTER 5

DIGGING OUT THE FRAUD: THE LAWYERS

Stephen Greiner and John Oller

The auditors are only the first of a long list of constituents who may want to know what happened. Others include the Securities and Exchange Commission (SEC), the National Association of Securities Dealers (NASD), the New York Stock Exchange (NYSE), the company's creditors, its insurance company, and (though the incentives are a little different) shareholders and their class action lawyers. All of this means that the board of directors has to conduct a thorough investigation.

Purposes of the Investigation

In this chapter we discuss the investigative process. Generally, this refers to an in-depth investigation conducted by lawyers and forensic accountants retained by the company, its audit committee, its outside directors, or some other independent committee of the board of directors. Chapter 5 focuses on the investigative process from the lawyers' standpoint. Chapter 6 will focus on the role of the forensic accountants.

The principal purpose of the accounting irregularities investigation is to answer two fundamental questions: What happened? And who did it?

The first question involves the determination and quantification of the irregularities affecting the company's publicly filed financial statements. The investigation needs to identify, substantiate, and quantify all of the various irregularities (and distinguish them from any additional errors not involving fraud) before the company can achieve its primary goal of issuing restated audited financials.

This is not an easy task, for it will frequently be the case that what the company initially believed to be a relatively isolated, confined problem will turn out to be much more widespread, not only in terms of the number and seriousness of irregularities, but also in terms of the areas or business units affected, the time periods implicated, and the people involved. Thus, questions such as the need to investigate one area or another where no evidence of wrongdoing has yet surfaced or to question financial and accounting personnel at various subsidiaries or divisions that seem not to be involved will take on real importance.

This is especially true if a pattern of fraud emerges—if the same people seem to be involved in or directing the irregularities, or the same accounts tend to be affected. In such instances, it may become necessary to probe into those areas that fit the pattern even in the absence of any specific indication of wrongdoing. For example, if the company's controller is found to have engaged in fraud at corporate headquarters regarding the parent company's financials and that person has had regular dealings with assistant controllers at the company's various subsidiaries, it is reasonable to question whether any subsidiary's books might likewise have been tainted.

In most cases, the fraud will prove to be more widespread, more complex, will involve more people, and will implicate more fiscal periods than initially thought. This means that the investigation is likely to expand accordingly and will require more time, effort, and expense than initially hoped. As such, the investigative team must be prepared to go wherever the evidence leads it.

There are no guidelines that the investigators can use to determine when they should feel comfortable that all irregularities have been found; they will need to be alert to any red flags or patterns that suggest a need for further inquiry. Yet experience suggests that there is a high likelihood that the objective of answering "What happened?" will be achieved and that the investigation will allow the company to issue accurate restated financials. This is generally true even if the fraud is widespread and complex.

The second question—"Who did it?"—is really several questions: Who directed, who participated in, and who had knowledge of the accounting irregularities? The investigation may also seek to answer the more difficult question of who should have been aware of the accounting irregularities or perhaps some variant of that question.

These questions about culpability and responsibility will be of intense interest, as well they should be. They are really the questions on everyone's mind. And they will be questions that are the subject of intense speculation within and outside the company. The SEC, as well as other regulators, will be interested in questions of culpability and responsibility from an enforcement standpoint. The financial press will be writing and speculating about who knew what and when, and employees within the company—many of whom will be working side by side—will be wondering the same thing about their colleagues.

In the end, many of the principal architects and participants will almost certainly be identified. Perhaps all will be. But there may be some persons about whom suspicions run high whose involvement cannot be definitively determined, for reasons discussed below.

Who Conducts the Investigation?

In a typical case, and almost always in more complex investigations, outside counsel will be retained by the company (or more likely, by the audit committee or other special committee commissioned to oversee the investigation). The selection of outside counsel will often be made by or with substantial input from the company's general counsel and/or the chairperson of the audit or special committee. If outside counsel is retained by the company, the board will normally want to ensure the outside counsel's independence by passing a resolution that the outside counsel should report directly to, and be supervised directly by, the audit committee.

Optimally, outside counsel should be *independent* in the sense that it has no significant ties to the members of company management who conceivably may have been involved in the fraud. This will generally mean that a law firm other than the company's regular outside counsel will be hired to conduct the investigation. Outside counsel will also perform a number of noninvestigatory tasks, such as advising the audit or special committee at meetings; advising on press releases concerning the status of the investigation and other matters; and dealing with counsel for other constituencies, such as the company, individual employees, and the SEC.

Outside counsel, in turn, will generally retain what are known as *forensic accountants* to assist in the investigation. Forensic accountants are specially trained in ferreting out financial fraud from a complex set of accounting and financial records and their focus is more on the who, what, when, and how of what happened, rather than on auditing a set of financial statements. Forensic accountants tend to be more skilled in interviewing techniques, more cognizant of issues such as attorney-client privilege and other issues that may become relevant later in litigation, and more experienced in retrieving data from computer systems than are regular auditors. In general, forensic accountants from a firm other than the company's regular auditors will participate in the independent investigation. (The respective roles of the forensic accountants and the company's regular outside auditors, along with related issues, are discussed in greater detail in Chapter 6.)

One reason the forensic accountants are generally retained by the law firm (rather than directly by the company or special committee) is that this can enhance the argument that the work product of the accountants is privileged and can be kept confidential. Generally, the work product of attorneys, and agents working for attorneys, is entitled to be kept confidential, at least until it is voluntarily disclosed to others.

Both the lawyers and the forensic accountants conducting the investigation will need to work closely with people inside the company to gather the necessary facts and data. Indeed, from the outset of the investigation, swarms of lawyers and accountants may virtually take up residence at the company for weeks on end, securing various company and individual employee files and requiring assistance from clerical personnel such as secretaries and file clerks. Inevitably, this will cause some disruption to the company's day-to-day operations, which will require sensitivity on the part of the investigative team in going about its business.

Time Frame of the Investigation

The board of directors will frequently want to know, as early as possible, how long the investigation will take. In many instances, it will want the investigation done yesterday. As a result, there is an inevitable tension between the desire to resolve the matter quickly and the need to get it right the first time. One restatement is unpleasant enough. A second is not something that the company will want to experience.

For smaller, more confined problems that stay that way, it is quite possible to complete a detailed investigation in a matter of a few weeks or less. On the other hand, large, complex frauds may take several

---

Figure 5–1. Investigative Tasks

- Gather documents

- Retrieve e-mails and other computer data

- Interview witnesses

- Prepare a report

---

months to investigate fully. It would be highly unusual, however, for even the most complex investigation to drag on interminably, as the imperatives of the marketplace and the demands of the company generally will not allow for it. It is hard to overemphasize the pressure to complete the investigation as soon as humanly possible.

The government's investigation of the matter is quite another thing. Often, the government's investigations and inquiries will take years, so individuals who are potentially implicated in the fraud will not know where they stand until long after the internal investigation has been completed. In addition, private lawsuits by civil parties, such as shareholders, may take several years to be resolved. That means, again, that even after the internal investigation has been completed, the company will continue to be required to provide documents and files, and individual officers and employees (including former employees) may be required to provide testimony about their activities during the period in question. In many ways, the internal investigation is merely the beginning, rather than the end, of the process.

Tasks to Perform

Whatever the time frame involved, a great deal of work must be performed during the internal investigation (see Exhibit 5–1):

1. *Procure documents.* Foremost, relevant documents must be identified, secured, reviewed, and understood. Depending on the circumstances, such documents may include:

   - Individual correspondence files
   - Company central files

- Accounting records (e.g., general ledgers, journal entries, balance sheets, trial balances, memoranda, and other documents supplied to outside auditors)
- Budgets and projections (both company-wide and by division, subsidiary, or operating unit)
- Operating reports (e.g., monthly sales and revenue reports, expense reports, and profit and loss reports, again on a company-wide and unit basis)
- Personnel records (which may contain sensitive and confidential personal information)
- Telephone records
- Vendor files, including contracts and invoices
- Expense account forms and receipts
- Personal calendars, diaries, appointment books, and telephone messages
- Minutes of meetings of the board of directors and its committees, as well as agendas and presentation books
- Notes and memoranda from meetings and other interoffice memoranda
- Research analysts' reports

The task of obtaining such documents may entail preventing those who are suspected of being involved in the fraud from having access to their offices and may require removal of their files into secure locations.

2. *Retrieve database information.* Databases must be accessed and efforts made to retrieve information that has been deleted. As illustrated by the widely publicized Microsoft antitrust trial, e-mails are a potentially rich source of evidence in any case. E-mail communications tend to be more casual than formal interoffice memoranda and therefore either more or less reliable indicators of the truth, depending on one's point of view. Many corporate executives may not even realize that, depending on the company's software system, the e-mails, computer files, and other documents they thought had been deleted might actually be retrievable.

3. *Understand the accounting system.* A thorough understanding of the accounting systems and the functions of various accounting and financial personnel must be developed.

4. *Interview witnesses.* Witnesses must be interviewed—frequently more than once. The list of people to be interviewed would normally include at least the following:

   • Financial and accounting personnel at corporate headquarters and any relevant operating units

   • Senior level executives in management

   • The company's outside auditors

   • Internal auditors

   • Members of the board of directors and relevant committees (such as the audit committee during the relevant time period)

   • The company's legal counsel and compliance officers

   • Public relations or other personnel who communicated with the public and research analysts on financial matters

5. *Prepare a report.* Finally, a report generally must be prepared.

To accomplish the above tasks, a large team will be needed—probably larger than one might guess. To give some indication, as many as thirty or more forensic accountants and seven or eight lawyers may be needed in a large and complex investigation. The expense can be enormous.

Lack of Subpoena Power and the Interview Process

Unlike government investigators or private litigants in a civil lawsuit, the investigating team does not have subpoena power. The reason is that the internal investigation is essentially a private matter conducted voluntarily by the company and not as part of a lawsuit or regulatory action where the law provides for subpoenas.

The absence of subpoena power is significant and will shape the outcome of the investigation in many ways. It means, first, that the ability to interview witnesses is dependent on their voluntary cooperation, including their willingness to appear and to speak fully. It is particularly important to have the cooperation of at least some of the perpetrators, because these people can best point the investigators in the right direction so that they can ask the right questions and obtain the key documents.

Unfortunately, the atmosphere that will likely exist as the interviewing process begins could hardly be less conducive to obtaining cooperation. By this time:

- Employees will be largely aware of the problem
- Outside accountants and lawyers may have taken up residence at corporate headquarters and taken control of various files
- Rumors will be rampant
- Personnel in the accounting and financial areas will wonder whether they are suspected
- They will also wonder whether they did something wrong that they do not know about

Putting employees at ease in this setting and coaxing them to tell what they know are challenges. Nonetheless, experience suggests that most people will cooperate. Current officers and employees may be required to appear for interviews, because refusal may constitute grounds for termination. Many others will agree to be interviewed because they do not want to appear uncooperative or because they feel (rightly or wrongly) that they have done nothing wrong and have nothing to hide.

Still others may suspect (or even acknowledge) that they or their co-employees might have done something improper and they will want to appear to put their best spin on their own behavior (perhaps by explaining that they did not understand the complete picture or were directed by their superiors to engage in the acts in question).

Other people, however, may conclude that it is not in their best interest to appear unless they get advance briefings on the questioning and evidence or an opportunity to review documents before the interview. For example, they may ask for a specification of the allegations (if any) against them by other employees, a list of questions (or at least subject matters) that they will be asked, copies of any documents that will be shown to them at the interview, and copies of any significant documents on which their name appears (either as author, recipient, or cc). In other words, they or their lawyer will want to know what the investigators know before they decide whether to tell what they know. Although providing such information in advance may seem to facilitate and streamline the interview process (by ensuring that the witness is better prepared), it also has the potential to impair the kind of spontaneity that is conducive to learning the whole truth.

Some witnesses will ask to have their own counsel present during their interviews. The company may in fact be paying for such counsel where its bylaws require it, thereby creating a significant additional expense for the company.

The company generally has no legal obligation to honor an employee's request to have counsel present for the interview, and there is no particular reason for the company to encourage employees to retain counsel during the investigative stage. As a practical matter, though, witnesses will usually be permitted to have their lawyer present if they wish, even if no formal charges have been made against the employee. The presence of such counsel may actually facilitate the fact-finding process, although, again, there may be some tradeoff in terms of the witness's level of spontaneity.

It normally should be made clear to the person being interviewed that the attorneys conducting the interview do not represent him or her personally and, instead, that the attorneys represent the audit committee or other independent body. As a result, witnesses generally should be advised that their discussions and statements during the interview may not remain subject to an attorney-client privilege and that their statements may later be communicated to the company or outside parties such as the SEC. Even if a privilege applies, the company could elect to waive the privilege later and voluntarily provide to third parties the employee's interview statements. In some states, the lawyers conducting employee interviews may be ethically bound to advise the employee of these considerations, at least where it appears that the company's interests are adverse to the employee's.

In any investigation there may be some persons who see no reason to help and will decline to be interviewed altogether. Individuals such as former employees, including those discharged after the preliminary investigation and those who resign in the course of a more thorough investigation, may conclude that the risks of giving a statement for the record at an early stage are too great in light of the potential civil liti-

gation, regulatory, and criminal problems that they may face. For example, employees may be sued as part of a shareholder class action; the
SEC could bring an enforcement action against them (the result of
which could be a civil fine or other penalty); and, most daunting of all,
the U.S. Attorney's office or other prosecutorial body could bring a
criminal indictment. Thus, the familiar observation that "anything you
say can and will be used against you" is one that employees will be advised to take into consideration in deciding whether to be interviewed.

Questioning at the interviews will generally be done by the lawyers
or accountants or both. On occasion, a member of the audit committee
may ask to be present, and such a request may be honored because the
committee is the client of the lawyers conducting the investigation.

Another important consequence of the lack of subpoena power is that
witnesses cannot be questioned under oath and therefore the laws
against perjury do not apply. The interview setting will be less formal
than in a courtroom or even in a pre-trial deposition. Generally, a court
reporter or a stenographer will not be present to take down, verbatim,
what the witness says.

Most investigators will elect not to tape record the interview for fear
of intimidating the witness and chilling candor. Rather, the lawyers will
typically make handwritten notes of the interview (which will later be
typed), and it is always possible that a witness may subsequently deny
having said at the interview what the notes record (although such outright denials are rare). As a result, some witnesses may perceive that
they will not suffer the same adverse consequences from not telling the
truth as they might from testifying falsely under oath. Or they may be
less than completely forthcoming in their answers.

All of this can mean that the evidentiary record may not be as complete as one would like. But that does not mean that the fact-finding
process is not effective. In fact, it is. The documentary information will
provide much of what is needed, and many witnesses with relevant information will be willing to be interviewed and to tell what they know.
Indeed, for some the discomfort of having had information about the
fraud bottled up for months or years may lead to almost extraordinary
candor. The informal setting of the investigative interview and the fact
that information is not being taken under oath and transcribed will operate to encourage witnesses to talk more freely.

Unresolved Questions

It should not be surprising, though, that there may be certain persons whose knowledge and participation cannot be definitively determined. They may have been implicated in some way by persons who have been interviewed. Or their positions may have been such as to make it seem probable that they must have been involved. But they themselves may have appeared for interviews and denied any wrongdoing. And there may be no documents that clearly demonstrate their participation or knowledge.

What then? Are the investigators and the audit committee free to draw conclusions about such individuals from whatever available information exists? Should determinations be made as to issues of credibility based upon the known facts or even upon demeanor at their interviews? Can the investigators and audit committee act, in effect, as jurors and, if so, what standard of proof do they use? Should the investigators in these circumstances simply report the disputed facts, leaving to others with subpoena power (e.g., regulators, prosecutors, private litigants) the task of further inquiry and leaving to any ultimate fact-finders (e.g., the court, the jury) the determinations of guilt, innocence, or liability?

These are among the interesting and difficult questions that are likely to be faced as the conclusions of the investigation are formulated. Each investigative team and each audit committee will have to decide under the particular circumstances just how far they wish to go in drawing inferences or conclusions from the available information.

Even in the absence of clear proof of knowledge of accounting irregularities, the evidence will often be sufficient to allow the board of directors to determine whether various personnel should be terminated, even though it may leave issues of employment and severance benefits and the like to be sorted out later in negotiation or litigation. That is because the investigation is very likely to provide information about whether there was the wrong kind of "tone" within the organization—in effect, an acceptance or encouragement of what occurred. And this type of information may well be the basis on which the board decides that changes must be made. In fact, there may be instances where, even if it cannot be definitively determined who knew what, the company will feel compelled to clean house simply because the fraud is found to be so egregious and widespread. Care must be taken, however, not to publicly malign individuals whose culpability is not clear; otherwise, the company may face the prospect of suits for defamation. Under some states' laws, moreover, employees who can prove they were unjustly terminated, i.e., without cause, may be able to successfully sue for damages (although probably not for reinstatement).

In the end, the company can reasonably expect that the investigation will accomplish most of what it set out to accomplish: It will identify the accounting irregularities and many of the individuals involved and will allow directors to make appropriate judgments as to which officers and employees should be terminated.

The Report

Reports in accounting irregularities investigations run the gamut from oral presentations to lengthy written documents that review the evidence in great detail. The nature, length, and level of detail of the report will depend on the complexity of the case, the number of individuals interviewed, the time pressure to complete the report, the desires of the audit committee and outside auditor, and strategic considerations.

A number of factors should be considered in deciding whether to prepare a written report (see Exhibit 5–2). The company may want a written report to document the results of the investigation and to exonerate the innocent and identify the guilty. A written report may also help restore the company's credibility by demonstrating, quite tangibly, the efforts and lengths to which the company has gone to investigate wrongdoing and take corrective action. A written report that explains to the world what happened and who was involved in a clear and comprehensive manner may put to bed many rumors and prior speculation. Recent reports in these cases have been widely disseminated to the public, including on the Internet.

A written report also avoids the need for repeated oral presentations and the ambiguities and lack of precision inherent in that process. Without a written report, it is possible that the lawyers who conducted the investigation will have to make multiple oral presentations of their findings to various groups (e.g., management, the board, the audit commit-

---

Figure 5-2. Pros and Cons of a Written Report

Advantages of a written report:

- Assists in exoneration of the innocent

- Avoids lack of precision in oral presentations

- Avoids need for multiple oral presentations

- Regulators expect written report

- Thorough report enhances company's credibility

Disadvantages:

- Provides roadmap for plaintiffs

- Conclusions may be binding on the company and others

---

tee, insurers, outside auditors, regulators, the courts). The recipients of these oral presentations will undoubtedly recall the presentations somewhat differently and they may take notes which, if later scrutinized, could on their face seem inconsistent and be taken out of context. A single written report can largely avoid such problems.

Regulators, such as the SEC, may expect to receive a written report at the conclusion of the investigation. In those situations where the company may be seeking to convince the regulators not to take any further action (for example, because the investigation has concluded that no wrongdoing occurred), a written report may be a virtual necessity.

Regulators cannot require that a written report be prepared, but they will generally view a well-written, thorough report as a positive in the company's favor and a valuable tool in conducting whatever further investigation they make themselves. A comprehensive report will also provide a good road map to the regulators as to what areas are of importance, who the key players are and what they have said, and what documents are most critical (often the report will include an appendix or separate volume of important documents, including many or most of the documents referred to in the text of the report).

It is true that a written report will provide a clear trail for subsequent litigants, whether they be investors suing the company, officers or directors defending against such suits (or against suits by the company itself), or auditors involved in litigation. The conclusions in the report will generally not be binding in subsequent litigation on most of the individuals mentioned, but may very well include admissions that may be binding on the company. The report or its conclusions might also be binding on certain individuals, such as audit committee members or directors who endorse and act upon the report's conclusions.

To the extent the company views creation of a litigation road map to be undesirable, it will need to balance that concern against the considerations identified earlier that largely favor a written report. Another factor to bear in mind is that, even if the report is not written, subsequent litigants may be able to discover the essence of the report's findings and conclusions through other means (such as obtaining the investigative team's interview notes, memoranda or other work product, or the notes taken by recipients of oral presentations). That leads to the next topic, concerning the applicability of various privileges to the report and underlying work product.

Can the Report Remain Privileged?

Generally, if a written report is prepared by the investigative team and given to the audit committee which oversaw the investigation, that report will constitute an attorney-client communication. If the report receives no wider distribution it can effectively be kept confidential, if that is the committee's (and company's) desire.

However, for the reasons discussed earlier, the company may wish to distribute the report to the regulators, who undoubtedly will request a copy. If the company voluntarily provides the report to the government, the company may be deemed to have waived the attorney-client privilege. If the privilege is waived, then other outside parties (besides the selected recipients) may be able to obtain the report in the course of any subsequent litigation by serving a subpoena for its production.

The company might be able to secure an agreement by the government to keep the report confidential. Such an agreement may offer some protection against waiver of the privilege, but it is no guarantee.

Apart from the regulators, the company may wish to give the report to various other outside parties, such as its lenders, its D&O insurer, or the company's outside auditors (all of whom will be anxious to obtain a copy). Again, if the company elects to provide the report to any such parties, it may be deemed to have waived any privilege that otherwise might apply. To the extent the report is used for operational decisions or to determine those to be discharged or retained, that may also impede the applicability of the privilege.

While the decision to waive the privilege by providing the report to outsiders may seem difficult in the abstract, in practical reality it is not. Almost inevitably, the outside auditor will seek a report on the investigation's conclusions and, in some instances, may seek a copy of the written report itself. The board, therefore, is often faced with the dilemma of choosing between preservation of the privilege and the procurement of audited financial statements. Under most circumstances, that decision is not difficult. Without audited financial statements, the company dies.

As a result, it is prudent for the company and the investigative team to assume, from the outset, that the privilege may end up being waived and that the report will eventually become public.

Is the Investigators' Work Product Privileged?

Apart from the actual report, the company may desire to keep the interview notes, memoranda, and other work product of investigative counsel and the forensic accountants confidential. Such work product would likely be protected against disclosure by virtue of one or more legal privileges, but, again, there is a possibility that the privilege could be waived. For example, if the company provides the actual report to regulators or other parties, this could be deemed a waiver as to any documents (such as interview memoranda and notes) that constitute the backup for the report.

The government will often request the company to turn over not just the report but also the interview memoranda and other underlying documents themselves. If the company elects to do so, this could also constitute a waiver of any privilege as to those backup materials. Again, prudence dictates that, due to the uncertainty and the possibility of waiver, the company and investigative counsel should proceed from the outset on the assumption that all work product relating to the report and investigation will eventually become public.

CHAPTER 6

DIGGING OUT THE FRAUD: THE FORENSIC ACCOUNTANTS

Harvey R. Kelly

Although highly skilled, lawyers experienced in digging out the truth behind fraudulent financial reporting typically cannot do it alone. They need the technical expertise, the skills, and the familiarity with the intricacies of generally accepted accounting principles (GAAP) that public accounting firms possess. Frequently, however, not just any accountant will do. It is often of great advantage to retain those accounting professionals experienced in special investigations and, in particular, rooting out fraud. Such specialists are informally known as *forensic accountants*.

What Is a Forensic Accountant?

The term *forensic accountant* does not represent an officially recognized professional designation, such as certified public accountant (CPA), and *forensic accountant*, accordingly, can mean different things to different people. As a general matter, though, the term connotes a specialized type of financial professional whose expertise and experience is targeted to the excavation of the underlying facts in connection with financial misreporting. Where accounting irregularities have been detected, forensic accountants are frequently retained by the audit committee to assist the audit committee's law firm in digging out the fraud.

Why Hire a Forensic Accountant?

An audit committee investigation into accounting irregularities will not get too far, if it gets started at all, without the recognition that the audit

committee's outside law firm will need the technical assistance of experienced accountants. Certainly, the audit committee lawyers can do
much of the investigatory work—interviewing witnesses, reviewing
business files, interacting with the audit committee and others involved.
However, typically the investigation quickly plunges into depths of
analysis beyond the ken of the average attorney not schooled or deeply
experienced in accounting and financial reporting. In particular, areas of
the investigation requiring the expertise of specialized accounting professionals include the following:

- **Generally accepted accounting principles.** Most obvious, an investigation into accounting irregularities requires extensive knowledge and experience in working with GAAP. The ultimate question, of course, is whether the financial statements conformed to
  GAAP as represented in the company's financial statements and
  Securities and Exchange Commission (SEC) filings. Insofar as
  those manipulating the books will have frequently undertaken to
  misreport results by exploiting potential ambiguities in GAAP,
  hazy areas of financial reporting, and highly technical rules of accounting, intimate and extensive familiarity with those rules is
  critical.

- **Accounting conventions.** Beyond intimate familiarity with the
  technical rules, an accounting irregularity investigation requires
  knowledge of the conventions of accounting practice in the particular industry at issue or, more broadly, in the context of financial reporting overall. Frequently, the accounting irregularities will
  surface in areas in which GAAP do not necessarily provide crystal clear answers and the propriety of the accounting will turn on
  what is generally accepted. Therefore, the lawyers will need the
  help of those who have not only mastered the black-and-white pronouncements that constitute GAAP, but also the conventions as to
  how they are applied.

- **Bookkeeping and accounting systems.** In addition to expertise
  in GAAP and the conventions of financial reporting, the investigators will also need the availability of expertise in bookkeeping
  and accounting systems. The most important and revealing evidence is often tucked away in obscure and hard-to-find general

ledger entries, records of reserves, sales cut-off documents, bills of lading, account reconciliations, and other components of the company's bookkeeping process. Expertise in accounting systems allows the investigators to go right to the potential trouble spots.

- **Manpower.** Uncovering accounting irregularities can literally be like looking for a needle in a haystack. The perpetrators will have deliberately selected the most hard-to-find places in which to bury obscure and hard-to-detect entries. Without their cooperation (and with the specter of prison hanging over their heads, they frequently will not cooperate), uncovering the fraud can involve untold man-hours of combing books and records. Although law firms specializing in the area frequently have teams of attorneys ready to start working, it is not unusual for a massive financial fraud investigation to require more manpower than a law firm has readily available. For example, one large accounting irregularity problem involved the full-time efforts of approximately 80 professionals—a number that, by itself, is greater than the size of many law firms. For the national accounting firms, with their thousands of partners and tens of thousands of employees, literally no investigation is too big—even if they have to fly in CPAs from surrounding cities in order to staff the investigation.

- **Lower billing rates.** If an audit committee is still in doubt about retention of a team of forensic accountants, the next issue usually wins it over: billing rates. Although the top rates of the most senior public accountants can easily match or exceed those of senior partners in law firms, the billing rates of those at the most junior levels will frequently be lower for accountants than for lawyers. Not all aspects of the investigation are rocket science and for much of the investigation (e.g., checking the dates of years' worth of bills of lading), a junior-grade professional will be more than adequate. Though cost is not usually the foremost concern in fraud investigations, to the extent it can be considered, cost also militates in favor of the substantial involvement of forensic accountants to supplement the lawyers.

So far, all of the factors listed support the involvement of accountants to assist the lawyers. None of them, though, suggests the need for a forensic accountant rather than, say, use of the investigatory capabilities of the company's incumbent auditor. CPAs from the incumbent audit firm meet most of the requirements: they are familiar with GAAP, understand the conventions of financial reporting, understand the company's bookkeeping and accounting systems (probably better initially than would a newly introduced forensic team), can presumably make available the necessary manpower, and have billing rates that are competitive with the other firms. Why not, therefore, use the incumbent auditor not only to obtain new audited financial statements (see Chapter 4), but to dig out the fraud as well?

In truth, the answer is not always obvious. Sometimes, it may make sense to use the incumbent auditor to assist in the investigation, and audit committee investigations have been conducted with complete success on that basis. On the other hand, additional factors frequently support the need for a specialized forensic team from a different firm (see Exhibit 6–1). Among those factors are the following:

- **Awareness of the gravity of the situation.** Though it may seem strange, sometimes the discovery of accounting irregularities is sufficiently outside the experience of normal financial statement auditors that the CPAs on the incumbent engagement team may not immediately appreciate the seriousness of the situation. They may not, therefore, react with a dramatic and intense response. In one instance, for example, an audit engagement team partner responded to the potential discovery of accounting irregularities by

---

Exhibit 6–1. Key Benefits of Using Outside Forensic Accountants

Forensic accountants:

- Add objectivity and credibility
- Provide the investigation team with accounting expertise
- Supply much needed manpower in a time of crisis
- Enhance effectiveness and efficiency by adding individuals experienced in rooting out fraud

---

asking if the matter could wait several weeks to be addressed—apparently failing to appreciate that, all the while, investors would be trading on potentially fraudulent information.

Forensic accountants, in contrast, have been through the drill before. Because of their experience with accounting irregularities, they fully understand that, in all likelihood, the survival of the corporation is hanging in the balance. Frequently, they will be prepared to begin working within hours of having been retained, with a full army of experienced professionals who know precisely where to go and what to do during the critical first 72 hours. They will understand what they have to do and will act accordingly.

- **Objectivity.** It is entirely possible that the incumbent auditor will be able to field an investigative team every bit as energetic as another firm's forensic accountants. Even where that is the case, though, an additional factor, depending on the particular circumstances, may militate in favor of the retention of new forensic accountants from another firm: objectivity.

  Of course, CPAs are trained in objectivity and independence, and many excellent professionals will be able to rise above more parochial concerns to investigate with zeal, tenacity, and earnestness every path and trail—no matter to whom they may lead. In some cases, the special committee may be convinced that its incumbent auditor can field a group of forensic accountants that will be completely objective.

  Complete objectivity is one thing. The *appearance* of objectivity is another. Even under circumstances where the outside auditor is capable of being fully objective, some special committees may nonetheless determine that the appearance of objectivity favors the retention of a new forensic accountant.

  To whom will that appearance of objectivity be important? Pretty much anybody whose responsibilities include oversight of, or interaction with, the company, and who, therefore, has an interest in its credibility and integrity. Those who may be interested in an objective investigation include the Securities and Exchange Commission (SEC); the company's securities exchange; and the company's banks, suppliers, customers, venture capitalists, large investors, and shareholders. When accounting irregularities first surface, all of these parties will ask themselves whether the company can be expected to do the right thing. Retention of an outside forensic accountant with unquestioned objectivity may be a necessary step in satisfying everyone.

- **Experience with forensic investigations.** A final factor favoring the retention of forensic accountants is their experience in dealing with financial fraud. In truth, a normal outside auditor does not have to wrestle with fraud very often. It is not unusual for a CPA in an audit department to go through the entirety of his career without ever once having accounting irregularities surface on his watch.

  This lack of experience with fraud investigations can cause delays because, unlike those experienced in such investigations, the inexperienced accountant does not know that the fraud tends to take place in the same areas over and over again. Those experienced in the ways of forensic investigations can immediately zero in on the likely areas and quickly target questionable transactions and entries. An experienced forensic accountant will have been through it all before. When time is of the essence, such experience helps.

The Difference between a Forensic Investigation and an Audit

Implicit in the discussion so far is the notion that a forensic investigation, of the sort to be undertaken by the audit committee where accounting irregularities have surfaced, is somehow different than a normal generally accepted auditing standards (GAAS) audit. To those not steeped in the ways of the accounting profession, such a disparity may seem something of an anomaly. It is conventional wisdom that normal outside auditors have some responsibility for the detection of fraud. Can the fulfillment of that responsibility in a normal year-end audit pursuant to GAAS and the investigation of fraud pursuant to a forensic engagement be all that different?

The answer is yes. In essence, an audit pursuant to GAAS and a forensic investigation into fraud fulfill their objectives in two completely different ways. Although the goal of each is correctly stated financial statements, the avenues to those goals are noticeably different.

The main difference between a conventional audit and a forensic investigation involves the principal assumption that constitutes the engagement's predicate. In a normal GAAS audit, the predicate is that, absent evidence to the contrary, everyone is generally trying to tell the truth. That is not to say that an auditor is entitled to accept everything at face value. That is certainly not the case. However, a normal auditor under GAAS—again, absent evidence to the contrary—is entitled in the first instance to believe that documents have not been forged, that books and records have not been deliberately manipulated, and that management's representations to the auditor are true. Although the auditor does not assume the unquestioned honesty of management, neither does the auditor assume management to be dishonest. The technical term describing this predicate is *professional skepticism*. At its core, professional skepticism requires the auditor to be something of a skeptic but not to assume the falsity of everything everybody says.

That is not to say that the auditor consistently assumes that no fraud has taken place—though years ago testing for fraud was not even required. Today, the auditor is called upon by GAAS to make an informed and reasoned judgment about the risk of fraud and, in light of that judgment, to design audit tests that provide the auditor reasonable assurance that any such fraud would be detected in the audit if it were material to the company's financial statements. Even here, though, the predicate is not that the company is infected with defrauders.

In a forensic investigation, that predicate changes to the complete opposite. Once it has been established that the bookkeeping has been infected by defrauders, the issue for the forensic accountant is: How deep and widespread does it go?

Therefore, everyone is a suspect. Each member of the board of directors, each senior executive, those in middle-level management, right down to the truck driver transporting potentially fictitious goods—all must initially be subject to the forensic accountant's withering probe. True, most will not stay suspects for long. But at the outset, the forensic accountant takes nothing for granted.

As a practical matter, this means that all suspicious areas—and even those areas that are only potentially suspicious—will be investigated. Whereas, in the absence of evidence to the contrary, the outside auditor would ordinarily assume the genuineness of documents, forensic accountants exhaustively search for evidence that either validates key documents or establishes their falsity. Similarly, forensic accountants must be extraordinarily suspicious of the veracity and completeness of the statements of company personnel made during the investigation. Such statements may be unduly influenced by self-serving motives. For those within the company, credibility is something that now must be earned.

The principal features that distinguish a forensic investigation from a normal GAAS audit are these:

- **Purpose.** The principal purpose of a forensic investigation is to dig out the fraud. It is, in other words, to find out the who, what, when, where, and how of what happened. The purpose is not simply to audit the financial statements through sampling techniques, as is the case in a normal GAAS audit.

- **Documentary evidence.** A forensic investigation into accounting fraud will almost inevitably uncover forged documents. Thus, forensic accountants view all documents with what might politely be referred to as a "heightened degree of skepticism." Documents falling into suspect areas must be corroborated, supported, and verified. The documentation behind questionable transactions must be inspected, inquired into, and inspected again.

- **Other evidence gathering.** Forensic accountants employ additional evidence-gathering techniques beyond those used in an audit. Extensive interviews of company employees and third parties, often in the presence of lawyers, are typical. Searches of company computer files (including those thought to have been deleted by employees) are sought to provide further clues to the truth. Reviews of employee desk files are not uncommon.

- **Scope and materiality.** Forensic accountants typically are asked to investigate irregularities without regard to their materiality to the financial statements taken as a whole. Thus, small transactions, unlikely to be examined in a normal GAAS audit, may be scrutinized with care. On the other hand, a forensic investigation may leave entirely untouched areas that would be subject to significant testing in a normal GAAS audit. The level of scrutiny by a forensic accountant turns largely on the susceptibility of a particular area to manipulation and fraud.

- **Urgency.** Investigations into potential accounting irregularities almost always involve extreme urgency. As a result, the number of forensic accountants and other investigators that descends upon a company can easily exceed the size of the company's entire accounting department. Even if they are not bountiful in number, the investigation team will submit substantial information requests and expect to receive responses quickly. The forensic investigators, in other words, will operate on the assumption that expedited completion of the investigation is of paramount concern for everyone involved. On the other hand, a normal GAAS audit has to take place in a way that does not unduly interfere with the company's ongoing operations.

Immediate Objectives

If the audit committee decides to retain a team of forensic accountants, some of the newly hired accountants will often begin working within hours of being engaged. The first objective will be to learn everything possible about the fraud based on available sources. Who, what, when, where, how—all of these will be the subject of immediate questioning by the forensic accountants, even while the complete forensic team is in the process of being assembled (see Exhibit 6–2). The forensic accountants, of course, will be under no delusions. It is almost inevitable that, whatever information they obtain at the outset, the fraud will turn

---

Exhibit 6–2. Typical Approach of Forensic Accountants

- Focus on the who, what, when, where, and how of what happened
- Consider all suspects
- Be on the alert for forged documents
- Conduct extensive searches of company documents and computer files for evidence of fraud
- Formally and informally interview key company employees

---

out to be deeper and more widespread than initially described. Still, the accountants have to start somewhere, and the available pool of information is obviously the right place.

Part of the initial inquiry into the fraud will involve examining the telltale documents that have surfaced to date. Frequently, the initial detection of accounting irregularities will be accompanied by suspicious documents, such as forged bills of lading, mysterious schedules of reserves, or, possibly, memoranda providing a window into the fraud. Members of the forensic team will be dispatched to explore clues that the initial set of documents will, in all likelihood, present.

All the while, the forensic accountants will be gaining an understanding of the business. Metaphorically speaking, the forensic accountants' role requires that they plunge into the deep end without more than a quick understanding of a company's operations, accounting system, or perhaps even the complete nature of its business. Thus, initial inquiry into the specific areas of fraud will be accompanied by an assessment of broader aspects of the business—who runs it, what it does, how it is set up.

With some level of initial orientation complete, an immediate objective becomes assisting the lawyers in the preservation of evidence from the likely malefactors. Today, with core financial records almost entirely computerized and frequently accessible from home, this can be more difficult than one would think. If it has not been done already, the supervisor of management information systems will be requested to preserve all computerized information and to shut down access by those who are suspected of participation in the fraud. To preclude physical destruction of paper, locks on doors may be changed and security personnel instructed to physically impede the reentry of suspected participants. In one instance of accounting irregularities, the local police force was summoned to physically stand guard at company headquarters with a directive to bar any attempted access by the newly discharged CEO and CFO.

Needless to say, all of this can be extraordinarily disruptive to the company's normal operations—many of which, in all likelihood, will suddenly grind to a halt. An additional objective of the forensic accountants, therefore, will be to determine those aspects of the accounting system and the documentary evidence that require isolation and to free up operating personnel to get back to work in those areas that are theoretically unaffected. Even if it completely uncovers the fraud, a forensic investigation is not a success story if it destroys the company in the process.

Framing the Issues

With the completion of an initial orientation and preservation of key evidence, it is time for the forensic accountants and the lawyers to sit down together and determine the issues to be explored. By this point, both the forensic accountants and the lawyers will have a fair handle on the principal areas of fraud and a sense as to what additional areas may be involved. Based on that knowledge, they will together agree upon a strategy for turning over every stone so that the totality of the deceptions may be uncovered and corrective statements made.

To the uninitiated, this may seem somewhere between a daunting task and an impossible one. A normal public company keeps thousands or millions of documents. Do the team members assume every one is false? If not, how do they distinguish between those that need to be checked and those that do not? And what about employees, officers, and directors? Is everyone from the chairman of the board down to the messengers in the mailroom to be the subject of interviews?

Obviously, no investigation could proceed in such a way. Still, one financial restatement is horrific; a second is unacceptable. The extent of the fraud, therefore, is no excuse for lack of thoroughness in uncovering the deceptions wherever they may be. Framing the issues, therefore, largely entails important judgments as to those areas to be explored.

It is at this point that the experience of the forensic accountant again proves its worth. Experience will have shown that financial fraud tends to involve the same areas over and over again. Therefore, each new investigation does not necessarily involve completely starting from scratch. Given an initial orientation into the nature of the fraud, experienced forensic accountants will start out with a pretty good idea of where to look.

And where is that? In essence, it is in those areas of the company's financial statements that involve flexibility or the use of judgment in the application of GAAP. These are the areas where fraud typically begins largely because the corresponding lack of clarity and black-and-white rules render the fraud (at least at its origin) difficult to detect. As the

Exhibit 6–3. Common Accounting Fraud Areas

Revenue recognition

- Premature recognition of sales
- Phantom sales
- Improperly valued transactions

Reserves

- Bad-faith estimates
- One-time charges

Inventory

- Overvaluation
- Nonexistent inventory

Expenses

- Delayed expense recognition
- Improper capitalization of expenses

Other

- Related party transactions
- Acquisition accounting

fraud proceeds, the need for more extreme manipulations causes it to branch out into other areas. Even then, though, areas involving judgment and lack of clarity are preferred by the perpetrators.

Thus, one typically does *not* find fraud in areas where the rules are clear and the account balances objectively verifiable. An example is cash. When it comes to cash, the rules under GAAP are straightforward and the balances are easy to check—they can simply be confirmed with the bank. Similarly, physical assets, such as plant, property, and equipment, are not exactly easy to manipulate. It would be difficult to explain, for example, the reason that the recorded value of a company warehouse suddenly tripled when, under GAAP, the proper value to be set forth is the warehouse's depreciated cost.

Still, that leaves plenty of areas of the company's financial reporting that are susceptible to manipulation (see Exhibit 6–3). Some of the more common areas are discussed below.

Revenue Recognition

These days, revenue recognition is one of the first places to look. There are two reasons. First, today financial misreporting seems to be driven by the perceived need to meet analyst quarterly expectations, which itself leads to the recognition of revenue as a prime candidate for manipulation. Second, management often resorts to creative sales techniques involving complex revenue recognition rules as a way to come up with at least a few extra pennies of earnings. One study of alleged accounting irregularity cases found that, over a two-year period, issues involving revenue recognition were implicated 40% of the time.

What are the devices by which revenue recognition may be manipulated? The most obvious is the one discussed hypothetically in Chapter 1: accelerating shipments. Frequently, financial fraud starts with shipment acceleration, which, as the treadmill effect goes into full gear, evolves into keeping the quarter open for a day or two and then longer and thereafter recognizing revenue on post-quarter orders or, after that, orders that have not been received at all. The evolution of the fraud, accordingly, tends to follow a natural progression. It starts out in an ostensibly innocuous way and evolves into a manipulation of records that is blatantly indefensible.

Quarter-end shipment manipulations, though, are only one of the more obvious ways that revenue recognition is susceptible to fraud. Another frequent area involves *bill-and-hold transactions*—transactions in which revenue can be recognized even though the product has not been shipped. Revenue recognition on bill-and-hold transactions involves compliance with a laundry list of criteria. Where accounting irregularities have surfaced, it is not unusual to find revenue recognized even when the specific criteria have not been met.

Similarly, consignment sales have historically been fertile ground for fraud. A consignment sale, of course, involves the placement of a product in another location, such as a retailer, with an obligation to take back the product in the event it is not sold. Whereas GAAP delays the recognition of revenue until the product is sold by the consignee, manipulators of financial records have on occasion seized upon shipping documents as a basis to recognize revenue before the actual sale has taken place.

Special discounting constitutes still another area where manipulations historically have been found. Special discounting frequently comes about based on a need for a spike in revenue as quarter-end is rapidly approaching. In order to obtain the necessary orders, the sales force may be instructed to offer special terms that then are not candidly reported to the company's accounting department. The result is a recognition of revenue, part of which (if, for example, the special terms involve a discount in price) or all of which (if, for example, the terms involve a particular right to return) should not have been taken into account.

Another area in which fraud is frequently found involves so-called barter transactions, that is, transactions in which the medium of exchange is not cash but a product or service of theoretically equivalent value. Barter transactions can be notoriously difficult to value insofar as their economic effect must be translated into cash when, in fact, no cash has changed hands. The resulting ambiguity is rife with opportunity for exploitation.

Reserves

Beyond revenue recognition, another area with the potential for manipulation involves the use of reserves. Although the term *reserves* is used broadly, in this instance we are talking about pools based on an estimate that either reduces the value of an asset (e.g., an allowance or reserve for bad debts) or establishes a liability for costs expected to be incurred in the future (e.g., damages relating to a lawsuit).

The reason reserves may be candidates for manipulation is straightforward. Reserves by their nature almost always involve some element of prediction. The precise number, therefore, can never be known. Under GAAP, the appropriate reserve level is determined according to the best estimate of management based upon its reasoned and informed judgment.

With regard to some reserves, the opportunities for manipulation are fairly constrained. If, for example, a company has consistently experienced a 90% collection rate on its receivables over the last 20 years, it is hard to argue that suddenly the reserve should be reduced from 10% to 2% absent any demonstrable changes in circumstances that would dramatically improve collections. Frequently, though, the appropriate reserve is not clear. That is particularly the case in new or evolving industries where the track record of performance is either nonexistent or short.

In recent years, reserves in the form of restructuring charges taken at the time of a merger or corporate reorganization have become a controversial topic (and a particular hot-button with the SEC). Restructuring charges are supposed to cover one-time costs, such as the costs of consolidating two companies, relocating or eliminating redundant operations, or paying severance to terminated employees. The charge is generally recorded and labeled as a special or unusual charge in the company's financial statements.

The danger inherent in such reserves arises from the potential desire by management to overstate the restructuring charge (i.e., create an excess reserve) so that the excess can be used to bolster income in future periods. Many believe that Wall Street analysts tend to ignore or discount the effect of restructuring charges as one-time or extraordinary, so the company's managers may reason that they are better off taking a hit to income up front and later reversing the excess reserve into income (thereby improving profits).

Inventory

For those defrauders interested in tradition, inventory manipulation is the vehicle of choice. One of the most famous frauds of the century—McKesson-Robbins during the 1930s—involved inventory fraud. It was specifically because of the inventory fraud at McKesson-Robbins that GAAS were rewritten to require auditor observation of a client's inventories and inventory measurement processes.

Today, inventory remains rich with opportunity for cooking the books. One reason is the need to record inventory at the lower of cost or market. Although cost is objectively verifiable, market value may not be as readily demonstrable. GAAP necessitate judgments as to the point at which recorded inventory levels should be reduced or, perhaps, written off completely.

Another problem with inventory involves the clumsiness inherent in physical inspection and verification. Although GAAS generally require an auditor to undertake some level of physical observation of inventory, even here the auditor relies on techniques of statistical sampling and random tests. In the event of fraud, such tasks are never foolproof. Fraud perpetrators have been known to go to such extremes as filling boxes with bricks, sealing the boxes, and labelling and counting the boxes as though they contained valuable inventory. Other methods used to circumvent the physical inspection and verification process include manipulating inventory counts at locations not visited by the auditor and falsifying records regarding inventory reported to be in transit at the time the auditor visited the site.

Expenses

Although manipulation of expenses is not a vehicle of first choice, a defrauder may turn to it to help cover his tracks. The manipulation of expenses is more difficult than, say, the manipulation of reserves, because expense amounts are normally objectively verifiable and, under GAAP, there is little room for discretion. Nonetheless, expense recognition can be delayed, thereby artificially enhancing the calculation of profitability.

One aspect of the recording of expenses, moreover, is more susceptible to fraud than the others. That involves the distinction between expenditures that are to be expensed and expenditures that are to be capitalized. Insofar as the distinction under GAAP can involve judgments regarding the nature of the cost or its future benefit to the organization, the opportunity for manipulation is enhanced.

Each of these areas will be a potential candidate for investigation as the lawyers and forensic accountants determine their approach to the audit committee investigation. As to each area where inquiry is warranted, the discussion will involve the location of relevant documents, those in a position to participate in the fraud, and the possible extent of misreported amounts.

At no point, though, will either the lawyers or the forensic accountants allow themselves to be deluded into thinking that this initial framing of issues will be the last one that takes place. Rather, each will fully appreciate the extent to which fraud tends to start out small in one area and then, as it grows, spread into other areas. Insofar as minor account manipulations are harder to detect than large ones, in the early stages the fraud will likely have resulted in modest manipulation to multiple accounts. Only when the opportunity for modest revision in many accounts has been exhausted will the perpetrators allow the fraud to grow to noticeable levels in any particular one of them.

Any initial framing of the issues, therefore, is going to be temporary.

The parameters of the investigation will always be changing as the weeks and months proceed.

Conducting the Investigation

Once the issues have been framed, the investigative team sets forth on its quest to find the truth. Ultimately, many avenues will be explored. At this stage, though, the quest begins with a fundamental undertaking: to develop a detailed understanding of the company's accounting system, with particular focus on the computerized general ledger.

Today, virtually all public companies maintain a computerized general ledger system. This general ledger represents the primary accounting tool of the company. Each and every transaction is recorded in the ledger. Each entry into the general ledger will include background information that, for the experienced forensic accountant, is abundant with potential clues.

Among the wealth of information potentially stored in the company's general ledger, for example, may be the following:

- The journal entries that the company recorded to implement the fraud
- The dates upon which the company recorded fraudulent transactions
- The sources for the amounts recorded (e.g., an automated sub-accounting system, such as purchasing or treasury, versus a manually prepared journal entry)
- The company employee responsible for entering the journal entries into the accounting system
- Any adjusting journal entries that may have been recorded

The general ledger journal entries, therefore, give an investigator a key starting place into the who, what, when, where, and how of the manipulated entries. Dates, amounts, key-punching employees, and related data may immediately become available. That is not to suggest that the general ledger will provide all of the answers. But it is an excellent place to start.

Examination of other aspects of the general ledger system—and the company's accounting system as a whole—will yield other clues. For example, inspection of quarter-end or year-end journal entries may reveal patterns of reserve manipulation, revenue enhancement, or other peculiar activity taking place as each financial reporting period draws to its close. Unusual manual entries—potentially the result of senior executive directives—may surface. Anything that appears out of the ordinary, in the context of the normal flow of the company's operations, may be a candidate for investigation.

The investigation obviously does not stop with clues gleaned from the general ledger or other aspects of the accounting system. Much more is involved. For example, frequently a useful step is to assess the extent to which a company has accounted for certain transactions in accordance with their underlying terms. Thus, the forensic accountants will often scrutinize the terms of contracts and other documents underlying important or suspicious transactions. Such scrutiny may include a search for undisclosed terms, such as those that may be included in side letters or pursuant to oral agreements. The forensic team may coax information from knowledgeable company personnel outside the accounting function, such as those in sales, about the possible existence of special terms or other considerations not reported to the accounting department. It is not unusual for the forensic accountants to contact those outside the company to corroborate important records as they become available.

Although the avenues of investigation may be somewhat straightforward at the outset, before long they will look like a road map of Paris. Inevitably, therefore, no matter how well-framed the issues at the outset, the investigation will largely depend upon the experience and gut instincts of the forensic investigative team. Although manipulative patterns are almost certain to exist, inevitable as well are unique tricks and manipulations owing to the creativity of the perpetrators and their particular needs of the moment. In the end, the adequacy of the investigation will come down to the zeal, tenacity, and ingenuity of the forensic team.

Interacting with the Lawyers and the Attorney-Client Privilege

As the investigation progresses, one mechanical issue involves the division of labor between the lawyers and the forensic accountants. What is to be done by whom? Related to that is the extent to which attorneys must participate in every discussion in order to maximize applicability of the attorney-client privilege.

As to the division of labor between lawyers and forensic accountants, there are no clear rules of delineation and the best approach depends upon the particular circumstances at issue. Important interviews of senior financial executives may be conducted jointly—with both a lawyer and an accountant in attendance. At the other end of the spectrum, interviews of lower-level accounting department personnel may involve only the accountants. Interviews of others may involve only the lawyers.

One aspect of the interview process that will become apparent fairly quickly is the practical impossibility of lawyer participation in every interview—at least in an investigation of any meaningful scope. Many or most interviews conducted by the forensic accountants will not be structured in any formal sense; rather, they will take place in momentary intervals throughout the day as documents surface, need to be explained, and then lead to new documents and explanations in turn. Concerns regarding efficiency, staffing, cost, and simply the availability of manpower will largely preclude the possibility of attorney participation in all such conversations. One thing the lawyers will need to check, therefore, will be the extent to which conversations between the forensic accountants and company personnel will be privileged even absent the involvement of a lawyer. If the company's lawyer has directed it, as the lawyer's client, to communicate with an accountant engaged by the lawyer, who is then to interpret the accounting aspects so that the lawyer may give better legal advice, then communications by the client reasonably related to that purpose ought to be privileged. The forensic accountants will typically inquire as to the structure of the investigation in order to maximize the applicability of the privilege.

One characteristic that both the attorneys and the forensic accountants will need to have in common is a capacity to put people at ease and to solicit candid information—a task that is particularly difficult in the context of an investigation into fraud. In all likelihood, certain employees will have already been discharged. Company operations will be in something of a state of turmoil. Entirely new faces will be combing through filing cabinets, asking difficult questions, setting up ad hoc offices in every inch of available space. And employees will be keenly sensitive to the fact that preservation of their employment may depend on the substantive answers given in interviews.

Soliciting information under such circumstances is difficult at best. The forensic accountants, like the lawyers involved, therefore will need to possess the interpersonal skills and diplomacy that cultivate an atmosphere in which employees are willing to talk.

Coordination with the Outside Auditor

Coordination with the lawyers spearheading the investigation, though, may turn out to be easy compared to the challenge of coordination with another group of professionals investigating the fraud at the same time. That group of professionals is the engagement team of the company's incumbent outside auditor.

The problem is this: The company needs its incumbent auditor. As discussed in Chapter 4, the company needs audited financial statements fast, and the quickest route to the procurement of audited financial statements is a re-audit by the incumbent auditor. Already having been lied to once, the incumbent auditor will not be in a particularly good mood. At best, the relationship between the company and its auditor will be strained.

Add to this already-strained relationship another accounting firm whose mission it is to second-guess, among other things, the reasons the fraud took place and was not discovered. One of the last things the incumbent auditor wants to hear is that now a new accounting firm (by the way, a competitor) will be combing through the books and records and finding out just who missed what. The forensic accountants undertaking that investigation, moreover, will probably have a fairly good sense of GAAS and will be almost unable to avoid second-guessing the diligence with which they were applied.

A natural consequence would be for the incumbent auditor and the forensic accountant simply to avoid each other. That, though, is a luxury that neither can afford. Ironically, each needs the other. The forensic accountant needs the incumbent auditor because the incumbent auditor has possession of knowledge and workpapers that can get the forensic investigation off to a more rapid start. Information about period-end adjusting journal entries, conversations with management regarding suspicious transactions, even important aspects of the audit chronology—all of these will be just sitting in the incumbent auditor's workpapers waiting for the forensic accountant's review.

But the need for information is not simply a one-way street. The incumbent auditor also needs information from the forensic accountant. In particular, as extra protection regarding the integrity of its re-audit, the incumbent auditor needs to know the results of the forensic accountant's investigation. Was the CEO in on the fraud? The CFO? Which individuals within the accounting department were involved in the fraud? These are all key questions that, to the extent not determined during the audit, will need to be answered before the auditor is prepared to issue a new audit report. For the incumbent auditor, simply turning away from the forensic accountant and offering no cooperation is not a realistic option.

An uneasy truce will therefore be established. The incumbent auditor will normally allow the forensic accountant access to its workpapers to assist in the speed and efficiency of the forensic investigation, and the audit committee will agree that formulation of a conclusion as to the adequacy of the incumbent auditor's work is not a purpose of the audit committee investigation. That is not to say that no aspect of the investigation will turn up evidence that might ultimately be used against the auditor. The mere fact that the auditor did not catch the fraud probably makes the discovery of some such evidence inevitable. But the audit committee will agree that, with regard to the incumbent auditor, it will not try to make things worse than they already are.

As the forensic investigation and the re-audit of the financial statements simultaneously draw to their conclusions, one issue that can be potentially troublesome is the manner in which the audit committee's conclusions are to be presented for outside auditor consideration. For understandable reasons, the auditor may prefer to receive a written report outlining the scope of the investigation, the details of the fraud, those found to have been participants, and the quantification of numerical consequences. The company, however, for equally understandable reasons involving the class actions, may not want such a written report to be drafted. If such a report is drafted, moreover, the company may not want to provide the report to its outside auditor, which could then potentially compromise applicability of the attorney-client privilege.

No written rules determine the manner in which the results of any investigation are to be transmitted to the outside auditor or, for that matter, that the results should be transmitted at all. The mechanism by which information is to be transmitted, therefore, depends upon the particular needs of the company and the auditor under the unique circumstances at issue.

Knowing When to Stop

With incomplete witness interviews, lost or destroyed records, and seemingly endless accounting records and transactions, how do the forensic accountants know when to end the investigation?

No fraud investigation concludes with absolute assurance that all irregularities have been identified or all wrongdoers caught. Nonetheless, the investigation should be sufficient to assist the directors and company management in forming their determination as to:

1. Whether previously issued financial statements require restatement

2. Which company personnel bear responsibility for the irregularities

3. What steps can be taken to minimize the risk that accounting irregularities will recur in the future

There will be no guarantee that every improper transaction has been completely uncovered. On the other hand, there *should* be a strong level of conviction that the investigation has been as thorough and complete as the circumstances will permit.

CHAPTER 7

CLASS ACTION LAWSUITS

Michael R. Young

After the first several weeks of an accounting irregularity crisis, it may be that the board of directors will have occasion to be almost amazed at the speed and efficiency with which it has addressed many aspects of the problem. If all has been properly handled, the board will have undertaken an investigation, alerted the public through a press release, terminated the employment of those whose complicity was clear, and handled innumerable problems involving creditors, employees, suppliers, and others. Looking back, individual board members may be genuinely astonished at the alacrity with which difficult issues have been handled.

There is at least one aspect of the problem, however, where speed and efficiency of resolution most notably will not be the case. That is the aspect dealing with the inevitable class action litigations. For the board, the litigation will likely proceed with exasperating inefficiency, delay, and expense. It is to this process of dealing with class action lawsuits that we now turn.

What Is a Class Action?

Broadly stated, a *class action* is a type of lawsuit in which a single representative individual is permitted to sue on behalf of an entire group of similarly situated individuals known as a *class*. In the wake of an accounting irregularity, a class action theoretically comes about when an aggrieved shareholder contacts a lawyer and explains that he has been harmed. The law then generally permits that single shareholder to sue on behalf of all similar shareholders.

Although the conceptual justification for class action litigation begins with the predicate of an aggrieved shareholder reaching out to a lawyer to seek redress, the reality is somewhat different. Shareholder class action litigation tends to be prosecuted by just a small number of highly specialized law firms and, over the years, these firms have developed practices and relationships that enable them to take the lead in commencing shareholder litigation almost on their own. A practical consequence is that, within 24 hours after issuance of a press release revealing the occurrence of accounting irregularities, the class action lawyers will normally have their lawsuits already prepared.

The Commencement of Class Action Litigation

The catalyst for commencement of the litigation will be the initial press release (see Exhibit 7–1), which will tell the class action lawyers pretty much everything they feel they need to know to prepare their first complaint. Among other things, the lawyers will glean from the press release that accounting irregularities have surfaced, that earlier Securities and Exchange Commission (SEC) filings are false, which line items on the financial statements are affected, and the board of directors' preliminary information as to how far back the accounting irregularities go. With that information in hand, the class action lawyers will quickly extract from their word processor an earlier complaint filed in a similar case and quickly insert the specifics regarding the particular company at hand. In their haste to be the first to file a lawsuit, the process of revi-

Exhibit 7–1. Typical Stages of a Securities Class Action

- Initial press release
- Series of complaints
- Consolidated complaint
- Motion to dismiss
- Document productions
- Depositions
- Settlement (if necessary)
- Trial (almost never)

sion is not always completely thorough. In one famous instance, class action lawyers described Philip Morris as being part of the toy industry.

From the perspective of the board of directors, the consequence will be that, within a day or two after the issuance of the company's initial press release, the directors will begin receiving a number of seemingly duplicative lawsuits in which the only significant difference seems to be the name of the representative shareholder seeking to represent the interests of the class. In truth, a shareholder gains no meaningful strategic advantage over the defendants in rushing to be named the class representative. In the end, only one class of similarly situated shareholders will be certified and only one complaint ordinarily will survive. Rather than trying to get a strategic advantage over the defendants, the interest of a plaintiff in rushing to be named the class representative is to get an advantage over the other plaintiff shareholders—or, more precisely, their lawyers. For a class action plaintiff's lawyer, having one's client named the class representative opens the door to the lion's share of the legal fees.

The Likely Defendants

Although the class action complaints may not be precisely identical, in all likelihood they will focus upon the same general group of individuals and companies as defendants. The candidates of those likely to be named in the class action complaints are as follows:

- **The company.** The corporate entity will almost inevitably be named a defendant. Also named may be a parent company or holding company. The plaintiffs will argue that the corporate entity or entities are responsible for the wrongdoing of their individual officers and directors.

- **Any officers who have resigned, been terminated, or placed on leave.** It may be that the initial press release will have identified particular officers who have resigned, been terminated by the board, or placed on paid or unpaid leave. The plaintiffs' lawyers will infer from any such corporate action the officers' complicity in wrongdoing. Such officers, therefore, will almost inevitably be named as defendants in the complaint.

- **The CEO and the CFO.** Prime candidates to be included as defendants in the class action lawsuits include the chief executive officer and the chief financial officer. The plaintiffs will infer from their positions some level of complicity. To the extent that they have signed what have now turned out to be incorrect SEC filings, such as a Form 10-K or Forms 10-Q, the likelihood of them being named as defendants increases.

- **Particular officers.** Beyond the CEO and CFO, other officers may be named as defendants depending upon the nature of the fraud (as described in the press release) and a particular officer's proximity to it. For example, if the fraud involved improper revenue recognition on consignment sales, the plaintiffs may seek to include as a defendant the officer or officers with responsibility in that area. Similarly, if the fraud involved improprieties at some remote location, those responsible for operations or the financial reporting function of that location may be named.

- **Members of the audit committee.** Increasingly, class action complaints are including as defendants members of the audit committee. The reason apparently stems from the trends discussed in Chapter 2, whereby responsibility for the prevention and early detection of fraudulent financial reporting has shifted to those within the corporate enterprise and, in particular, the individual audit committee members. From the existence and growth of undetected accounting irregularities, the class action plaintiffs will infer that the audit committee has not done its job.

- **Outside directors.** At the moment, the extent to which outside directors tend to be included as defendants in class action complaints is in a state of flux. Historically, all outside directors would be named as defendants almost as a matter of course. Congress's passage of federal securities law tort reform in the mid-1990s, however, operates as an important impediment to the inclusion of the entire board—at least in the absence of evidence suggesting an individual director's knowledge or complicity. The trend seems to be in the direction of class action lawsuits that do not include as defendents the entire board.

- **Underwriters.** An emerging trend in class action litigation is the inclusion as defendants of underwriters where the company has had occasion to publicly issue stock within the last three years. For the corporate issuer, this is particularly unfortunate insofar as typical underwriting documents will provide for corporate indemnification of the underwriter in the absence of the underwriter's own wrongdoing. The desirability from the plaintiffs' perspective of inclusion of the underwriter is not entirely clear, though it may result from a hope that, indemnification or not, the mere inclusion of the underwriter as a defendant will act as an incentive for the underwriter to pay some amount in settlement to get out.

- **Selling shareholders.** An issuance of public stock within the prior three years may also open the door to the inclusion as defendants of any shareholders who participated as sellers in the offering. Plaintiffs may seek to show their complicity in the accounting irregularities based upon inferences drawn from their natural desire to see the stock price sustained or increased during the period prior to their sale.

- **The outside auditor.** Several years ago, inclusion of the outside auditor in an accounting irregularities case occurred almost without exception. Today, the inclusion of the outside auditor as a defendant—at least in the first complaint—has become something of a rarity. As with the inclusion of outside directors, the reason stems primarily from the federal securities law tort reform legislation in the mid-1990s, which erected barriers to naming the outside auditor, at least without particularized facts showing auditor complicity. It would not be unusual, therefore, for the initial wave of class action complaints to completely omit the auditor from among the numerous defendants.

  However, that is not to say that the auditor will be left out forever. An important objective of the plaintiffs will inevitably be assembling detailed evidence sufficient to make claims against the auditor stick. At that point, the auditor will in all likelihood join the ranks of defendants in the case.

Sorting Out Parties and Counsel

Although the intensity of the initial barrage of lawsuits may create an appearance that the class action litigation will proceed with ferocity, that appearance will quickly change as the case gets bogged down almost from the outset. There will ordinarily be several reasons but foremost will be the need for the plaintiffs and their law firms to sort themselves out. Typically, any number of plaintiffs and law firms will have filed complaints, but theoretically only one plaintiff under the law is to become the lead plaintiff and only one law firm is to become lead counsel. The filing of class action complaints, therefore, will be followed by a series of discussions and negotiations among various plaintiffs' law firms as to which will emerge as the leader of the others. Given the potential fees at stake for the lead plaintiff's law firm, this is arguably one of the two most important negotiations that will take place.

For the defendants, the resulting hiatus will provide a welcome respite. The main reason stems from the fact that the initial class action complaints will arrive within days of the initial press release, a time during which the defendants will already be preoccupied with operational and financial crises and emergencies that seemingly must be handled on a daily basis. More than that, the defendants will have some sorting out to do among themselves. Among other things, they will want to sort out their own representation.

A complicating factor in arranging for the defendants' representation will be that, unfortunately, not every defendant will have precisely the same interests as every other. At one extreme, for example, will be those defendants by whom the accounting irregularities were perpetrated. At the other extreme will be those defendants who are falsely accused and who, in truth, are entirely blameless. Those two groups—and others that fall somewhere in the middle—may not share precisely the same interests on every issue that will arise in the case. Accordingly, the need for different lawyers to represent different groups of defendants will soon become apparent. At the same time, any outside professionals who have been named as defendants will in all likelihood seek their own representation.

The initial weeks of class action litigation, therefore, will be largely occupied with the plaintiffs, the defendants, and their new lawyers trying to sort themselves out.

The Consolidated Complaint

At one point, both sides will have successfully coordinated among themselves to the point where they are ready for the battle to begin, and it will be incumbent upon the plaintiffs to fire the first salvo. The projectile will be in the form of a *consolidated complaint*—that is, a single complaint that consolidates all of the material allegations, legal claims, and parties of the others. In essence, the consolidated complaint will reflect a distillation of the information and charges hastily thrown together into the earlier separate complaints. In drafting the consolidated complaint, the plaintiffs may decide to add claims, delete claims, add defendants, delete defendants, expand the time frame at issue, shorten the time frame at issue, or otherwise adjust the contours of the plaintiffs' contentions. Although the particulars of any consolidated complaint will depend upon the circumstances at issue, certain claims will be included almost inevitably. They are the following:

- **Section 10(b).** The one claim that is sure to be a fixture of any accounting irregularities lawsuit is a claim pursuant to a provision of the Securities Exchange Act of 1934, known as Section 10(b), and a corresponding SEC rule, known as Rule 10b-5. Directed against fraud in the secondary market of publicly traded securities, Section 10(b) makes it unlawful for any person directly or indirectly "to use or employ, in connection with the purchase or sale of any security," any "manipulative or deceptive device or contrivance" in violation of SEC regulations. In substance, Section 10(b) makes it unlawful to deliberately say anything of consequence that is false or misleading in connection with the purchase or sale of a security. Among the data subject to the prohibitions of Section 10(b) are significant inaccuracies in a company's financial statements that are filed as part of its Form 10-K or Form 10-Q.

    Although Section 10(b) is broad in its scope, a critical prerequisite of a claim limits its applicability. Section 10(b) imposes liability only upon those who acted with *scienter*—that is, with "intent to deceive, manipulate, or defraud." In other words, Section 10(b) does not impose liability on those who accidentally make false or misleading statements, even where the person who made the statements was negligent.

    Exactly what is needed to plead and prove "intent to deceive, manipulate, or defraud" is an issue that plaintiffs' and defendants' lawyers have been arguing about for more than 25 years—ever since the United States Supreme Court declined to reach the issue in the famous footnote 12 of its 1976 decision in *Ernst & Ernst v. Hochfelder*. The key point is that Section 10(b) does not impose liability for mere accidents or negligence.

- **Section 20.** A claim pursuant to Section 20 is frequently a companion to a claim pursuant to Section 10(b). Section 20, also a provision of the Securities Exchange Act of 1934, operates to impose liability on those who control another person who makes a significant false or misleading statement in SEC filings "unless the controlling person acted in good faith and did not directly or indirectly induce the act or acts constituting the violation or cause of action." Thus, for example, a consolidated complaint might allege that a large shareholder of a company at which accounting irregularities were discovered should be equally liable with the company. An inside director or high-ranking officer may also be alleged to control the corporation. The actual facts and circumstances that constitute control under Section 20 are frequently an issue of significant dispute.

- **Section 12(a)(2).** Unlike Sections 10(b) and 20 of the 1934 Act, Section 12(a)(2) of the Securities Act of 1933 (often still referred to as "Section 12(2)" based on the original statutory provision) does not apply to false or misleading statements in connection with secondary market purchases or sales of securities. The role of Section 12(2), rather, is much more limited: It applies only to false or misleading statements that are made in a prospectus, which has been interpreted to mean that only shareholders who bought in a public offering may sue under this statute. Although Section 12(2)'s scope is more limited, proving a violation of Section 12(2) is easier for a plaintiff than proving a violation of Section 10(b), because a Section 12(2) claim does not require proof that the false statement was deliberate. Under Section 12(2), therefore, when the statutory elements are met, even a person who accidentally says something that is false can be held liable.

  Courts have held that in the typical firm-commitment underwriting of a public offering (where the shares are sold by the company to the underwriter and then to the public), only the underwriter (and others who directly solicited the plaintiff's purchase) can be liable under Section 12(2). Defendants can avoid liability, however, by showing that they conducted a reasonable "due diligence" investigation of the information in the prospectus.

- **Section 11.** In some respects, Section 11 of the Securities Act of 1933 (applicable to registration statements) is the most draconian of them all. It potentially imposes liability on every person who signs a company's false or misleading registration statement, every person who is a director of such a company, every accountant who prepared or issued a report on a part of the registration statement, and every underwriter of the security at issue. In substance, Section 11 operates to make each of these potentially liable where the registration statement contains false or misleading information, although everyone except the company has a defense to the extent they conducted a reasonable investigation and had "reasonable ground to believe" that the registration statement was true, which they have the burden of proving. (The law also recognizes that it is easier for non-experts to justify the reasonableness of their beliefs as to those parts of the registration statement prepared by an expert, such as an auditor of the financial statements.) Under Section 11, the company can be held liable whether it had reasonable ground to believe in the truthfulness of the statements or not.

- **Section 15.** Analogous to Section 20, Section 15 of the 1933 Act operates to impose liability on "every person who . . . controls any person liable under Section 11, or 12."

While each of these provisions is relegated to a particular context of the securities markets, their collective thrust is the same: It is unlawful to make significant false or misleading statements. Where a significantly false and misleading statement has been made, liability may potentially be imposed upon the company; those who control the company; and the company's officers, directors, underwriters, and accountants.

Liability Implications of the Initial Press Release

These provisions obviously pose a particular problem where a company has issued a press release announcing the discovery of accounting irregularities. The press release by itself could operate to establish some of the key elements of a securities law claim against the company and individuals directly associated with it, the most notable of which being the fact that a significant false statement has occurred. One reaction to the company's press release would be that, once it is issued, there would seem to be very little left to argue about.

In fact, however, the imposition of liability under the securities laws, even after issuance of a press release conceding that accounting irregularities have taken place, can give rise to exceedingly vigorous litigation. There are several reasons, including the fact (as discussed more fully below) that the amount of damages allegedly suffered by the plaintiffs' class will be hotly disputed. Another reason that litigation may be intense, even after a company's "confession" of false financial statements, involves the fact that the various individual defendants directly associated with the company, in all likelihood, will fall into one of the three categories outlined in Chapter 1. One category is those who will be perceived as plainly guilty. A second category is those who, when the facts become available, will be perceived as plainly innocent. The third category is those who could go either way.

Some of the most significant battles in the class litigation will revolve around those who should fall into the third category. The reason is that often this third category is where the money is. As to those individuals in the first category—those who are plainly guilty—they frequently will not have personal assets worth pursuing. Nor will they typically be eligible for coverage under the company's director and officer (D&O) insurance policy, insofar as D&O policies generally exclude coverage for deliberate acts of fraud. For the plaintiffs, therefore, those individuals who are plainly guilty will ordinarily be of little financial interest.

Of even less interest will normally be those falling into the second category—those who are plainly not guilty. Though the legal system may be somewhat inefficient, it nonetheless ultimately serves to impede the prosecution of claims against those who did nothing wrong. For this reason, this category of defendants, too, will be of little financial interest to the plaintiffs.

That naturally leaves the third category—those individuals who may or may not bear some blame. True, their financial assets may be no more substantial than the plainly guilty. However, the D&O insurance policy will treat them somewhat differently. The absence of unequivocal evidence establishing their guilt at the outset will in all likelihood cause the D&O insurer to begin financing their defense. At the same time, the D&O insurer's mind-set will shift to acceptance of the proposition that these individuals are not deliberate defrauders but, instead, those who are at worst guilty of reckless fraud—something for which the D&O insurer will pay. The battle over the liability of those falling within this third category of defendants, therefore, is in substance a battle over the proceeds of the D&O policy. Depending upon the amount of the policy, that battle can become quite intense.

Of those directly associated with the company, that leaves one defendant: the company itself. A key to assessing the company's vulnerability will obviously involve those facts to which the company has already admitted in its initial press release. As mentioned earlier, almost inevitably the company will have admitted a misstatement of fact insofar as it is precisely such a misstatement that has triggered the need for a press release in the first place. Moreover, to the extent the company has announced the discovery of accounting irregularities, it will have revealed that at least someone within the corporate enterprise has misstated financial results deliberately.

It does not necessarily follow, however, that the company will be the principal target of the class action plaintiffs. Keep in mind that many of the class action plaintiffs will still be shareholders and, to the extent that they use the judicial system to extract a cash payment from the company, they are in a sense simply taking money from one pocket and placing it in another—through a judicial vehicle involving enormous transaction costs, insofar as a significant percentage of each dollar thereby extracted goes to the class action lawyers. On the other hand, to the extent that the class includes those who are no longer shareholders, their reluctance to seek a cash payment from the company will be significantly less pronounced. Another complicating factor, moreover, results from the fact that, where accounting irregularities have surfaced, the company's cash position may be somewhat tenuous. As discussed in Chapter 3, for example, the company may be in violation of debt covenants. To the extent that cash is not available, the interest of the class action plaintiffs in the company as a defendant correspondingly decreases.

In any event, with the consolidated complaint having been prepared and filed, the ball, so to speak, is now in the defendants' court. It is incumbent upon the defendants to respond. The preferred vehicle is through a *motion to dismiss.*

The Motion to Dismiss

A motion to dismiss is a document filed with the court and served on the plaintiffs' lawyers that assumes as its predicate (as it must) that the allegations of the consolidated complaint are true. Nonetheless (the motion goes on to contend), the plaintiffs may not prevail because the law provides no remedy based on the pleaded and assumed facts. Thus (the motion will conclude), the lawsuit should be judicially terminated without further ado.

The precise defenses to be raised in such a motion depend upon the unique facts and circumstances of any particular case. Almost inevitably, though, one defense in particular will be included in such a motion. Where Section 10(b) claims have been alleged—as they almost always will have been—the defendants will call into question whether, as to each separate defendant, the consolidated complaint has adequately alleged a sufficient awareness of the facts to render that particular defendant culpable. In the technical jargon of the procedural rules, the defense will be presented that the consolidated complaint does not adequately allege scienter.

The need to adequately allege scienter stems from the fundamental principle that Section 10(b) imposes liability only upon those possessed of an "intent to deceive, manipulate, or defraud." Federal procedural requirements—designed with the goal of protecting innocent citizens from baseless allegations—require a plaintiff seeking to allege a Section 10(b) claim to set forth with specificity the precise circumstances making clear that such an "intent to deceive, manipulate, or defraud" did in fact exist. Thus, the complaint must allege, for example, participation in a conspiratorial meeting, receipt of a telltale memorandum, or other circumstances laying a factual predicate for the allegation that an "intent to deceive, manipulate, or defraud" was possessed by each defendant.

Whether a consolidated complaint does, or does not, adequately plead scienter is something that, in a typical accounting irregularities case, plaintiff and defense lawyers may end up arguing about for months. Among the issues of contention will be such things as the legal requirements of a satisfactory complaint (the courts disagree with each other), the types of factual allegations that will satisfy those legal requirements (as a practical matter, the court has a great deal of discretion), and the extent to which a plaintiff failing to include adequate allegations should be given the opportunity to amend its consolidated complaint in order to make another try. By the time the adequacy of the complaint's allegations is ultimately resolved, more than a year may have gone by.

This passage of time, though, is not necessarily to the disadvantage of the defendants. The reason is that, under the tort reform legislation of the mid-1990s, during the pendency of the motion to dismiss, the plaintiffs' pre-trial investigation (formally known as *discovery*) may not proceed. The filing of a motion to dismiss, therefore, largely puts the class action litigation on hold and gives the defendant officers and directors time to deal with other pressing business problems.

The Prospects of an Early Settlement

Throughout the initial stages of the litigation, one thought that will never be far from either the plaintiffs' or the defendants' minds is the possibility of an early resolution of the case through a negotiated settlement. Logically, an early resolution would seem to make eminent sense. If a material accounting irregularity has surfaced, then both sides should theoretically recognize the strong likelihood that a number of shareholders have been harmed. The principal remaining obstacle would seem to be the calculation of resulting damages under the law and the negotiation of an appropriate settlement amount. Neither would seem like an insurmountable obstacle.

Moreover, strategic considerations would seem to heavily favor an early negotiated resolution. For the plaintiffs, an early settlement can maximize recovery by tapping into the reservoir of D&O insurance when it is at its fullest point (i.e., before it is depleted by the expenditure of defense costs) and, for that matter, can result in a recovery for shareholders before the incurrence of substantial legal fees. For the defendants, an early settlement brings a prompt end to the unpleasantness and helps individuals of questionable complicity keep their reputations intact. A particular advantage of an early settlement for the company stems from the removal of the horrific distraction of time-consuming litigation at a time when the company has more important operational and financial issues on which to focus.

Nonetheless, although some preliminary discussions of settlement may take place, an early resolution of the litigation is by no means assured and, in fact, is relatively rare. The normal reasons are not particularly profound. Usually the plaintiffs want more money than the defendants (or, more precisely, the defendants' insurance companies) are willing to pay. That is not to say that early settlements never happen, but they are the exception rather than the rule.

The Process of Discovery

In the absence of a settlement, the court will be given the time it needs to resolve the motion to dismiss. Although, with resolution of the motion, some or even most defendants may find themselves dismissed from the case, it is entirely possible that some defendants will remain. For those remaining defendants, the next step is to begin the pretrial investigation known as *discovery*.

The process of discovery has two main components. One is that the parties will request each other's documents as well as the documents of non-participants in the litigation who may have interesting information. The other component involves taking sworn testimony through *depositions*. Discovery involves other investigative techniques as well, such as written questions known as *interrogatories*, but the production of documents and the taking of depositions are the two main vehicles for gathering information.

Unfortunately for the defendants, in a class action, discovery tends to be a one-way street. That is to say, it is largely a process in which the plaintiffs investigate the defendants. The reason is straightforward: The plaintiff shareholders tend to have much less information of importance to the case. One securities defense lawyer has analogized the role of a defendant in a class action to that of a punching bag. You take punch after punch but get to give very little in return.

The Production of Documents

The first step to the discovery process will be a *document request*. This consists of a list of documents to be made available to the plaintiffs.

The list will normally seek documents such as board packages, board minutes, internal financial reports (e.g., snapshot reports, flash reports), monthly financial statements, and less generalized documents pertinent to the particular irregularities at issue. Under the rules, the defendants get 30 days to respond, though this is almost always extended to add at least another month.

It is usually during the process of collecting documents that the defendants are given the first opportunity to experience remorse that the case did not settle during the pendency of the motion to dismiss. The reason is that something unfortunate almost always turns up. This is not to fault the diligence of the directors at the time of the operative events. It is merely a consequence of the fact that, with the benefit of hindsight, seemingly wholesome financial reports or operating documents may contain clues that arguably should have put directors on notice that something was afoot.

What's an example? Assume a board of directors has spent the past year reviewing monthly and quarterly financial statements at a time when, unbeknownst to the board, the company was improperly seeking to accelerate revenues at quarter-end by prematurely shipping merchandise to customers who did not want it. As time passed, things looked fine to the board of directors and, in fact, the board was pleased to see earnings maintain a fairly steady pace of disciplined growth. With the accounting irregularities having been exposed, however, the seemingly innocuous financial statements now suggest a different story. A comparison of monthly revenues reveals that, for the first month of each quarter, revenues were almost non-existent; in the second month, revenues started to trend upward; and, in the third month, they accelerated dramatically. Absent some peculiarity in the buying practices of customers, careful scrutiny of the revenue pattern at the time might have given rise to questions as to the reason for the pattern.

Still, such documents must be turned over to the plaintiffs who will then scrutinize them for exactly this kind of information. That is not to suggest that the defendants' lawyers will turn over all requested documents without a fuss. Compliance with some requests for documents may be so burdensome, disruptive, or seemingly redundant that the defendants will formally refuse, thereby giving rise to another dispute to be resolved by the court. The process of requesting, producing, and arguing about documents may be expected to take another few months.

The plaintiffs' request for one document in particular may be expected to give rise to especially vigorous litigation. That is the plaintiffs' attempt to obtain the investigative report of the special committee or audit committee (which was discussed in Chapters 4 and 5) if a written report has been prepared. For the plaintiffs, procurement of the report would be invaluable. Insofar as it reflected candid interviews conducted by the committee's own counsel, it would provide to the plaintiffs' lawyers the best information to date as to exactly what happened, how it happened, which financial statement items were influenced, the reasons behind the accounting irregularities, and the varying degrees of guilt of each of the potential participants. Extraction of such information through the discovery process—in which witnesses will inevitably be more guarded and less candid—could literally take years. In the committee report, the information may be neatly packaged and available for the price of a photocopy.

Resolution of the plaintiffs' ability to get such a report will, in all likelihood, ultimately involve the court. The extent to which the plaintiffs should be entitled to such a report has been the subject of extensive judicial rulings and a plethora of published decisions. Alas, the decisions give support both to plaintiffs who would seek production of the report and defendants who would oppose it. Resolution of this issue, too, can be expected to take months.

Addition of the Outside Auditor

It is typically during the document-production phase of discovery that efforts will begin in earnest to add as a defendant the outside auditor. The principal reason will be that the auditor is no doubt heavily insured and therefore provides an exceedingly deep pocket from which to fund a substantial verdict. Moreover, if the accounting irregularities have gone on for more than one year, as they almost inevitably will have, the auditor would have issued an audit report that, insofar as it offered assurance as to the financial statements' conformity to generally accepted accounting principles (GAAP), was arguably incorrect. As the plaintiffs delve into the defendants' documents, therefore, a key objective will be uncovering telltale memoranda, financial reports, or other documents implicating the auditor in the accounting irregularities.

For the company, the prospect of inclusion of its outside auditor as a defendant in the case presents dilemmas that are both significant and strategically difficult to sort out. At best, the company's reactions will be mixed. On one level, the addition of a deep pocket to the group of defendants may be perceived to offer the prospect of a reduction in the damages that will be sought from the original members of the defendant group. To that extent, addition of the auditor as a defendant would seem to work to the company's advantage. Countervailing business considerations, though, may strongly militate in the other direction for reasons discussed in Chapter 4. Keep in mind that, while the litigation is proceeding, one of the company's most important goals will be to procure restated audited financial statements, and the most efficient way to get restated audited financial statements is to stick with the existing auditor. If the auditor is named a defendant, for reasons discussed above, that potentially jeopardizes the auditor's independence. Therefore, the addition of the auditor as a defendant carries with it the risk of enormous business problems.

As one examines the issue more deeply, moreover, the strategic complications only get worse. Inevitably, some of the more removed outside directors will feel betrayed by the auditor insofar as the auditor failed to discover and expose the fraud. For them, the thought of claims against the auditor might seem to make sense. Those closer to the center of wrongdoing, in contrast, may have a sense that, in truth, it was the company and its personnel who actively conspired to defraud the auditor. If anyone has a claim against anyone else, they might surmise, it is the auditor who has a claim against them. On close inspection, even the benefit of an additional "deep pocket" as defendant may not operate to the company's advantage. Recent statistical evidence suggests that, where the auditor is included as a defendant, the portion of the overall now-increased settlement amount paid by the company increases significantly.

Mercifully, whether the auditor ultimately gets named as a defendant is not a decision the defendants will get to make. It will be up to the plaintiffs and, after that, to the judge on the auditor's inevitable motion to dismiss. If the auditor is to remain a defendant in the case, experience teaches that the minimization of hostilities among defendants will, in all likelihood, work to all of the defendants' advantage as the litigation proceeds.

The Taking of Depositions

As the process of document discovery draws close to its conclusion, the parties will turn to the second phase of the pretrial discovery process: the taking of depositions.

Any number of senior executives or outside directors have been through the process of a pretrial deposition. Basically, it is the process by which one sits in a conference room while the plaintiffs' lawyer asks questions and a court reporter transcribes both the questions and the witness's answers. Throughout the deposition, lawyers will interpose objections to particular questions being asked. One recent development is to videotape the entire process.

The deposition process usually offers a second opportunity for the defendants to regret that the case has not settled, insofar as the process itself frequently brings to the surface information that, in hindsight, might have indicated to innocent executives or outside directors the possibility of financial reporting improprieties. More than that, the process itself is fraught with peril stemming from the fact that potentially incriminating documents from previous years can be extracted from the files and the witness quizzed about their content as if he or she saw them only yesterday. The opportunities for failed recollection, inadvertently inconsistent testimony, or simply honest mistakes exist at every turn. Although corporate defendants will normally be exceedingly well prepared for the process, the process by its nature inherently presents substantial risk.

Dynamics Favoring Settlement

As the case proceeds further through discovery, for everyone the prospects of a negotiated resolution will begin to look more attractive. "Everyone," by the way, may include not only the defendants and their insurance companies but also, in all likelihood, both the defendants' lawyers (whose legal experience may stop short of actually having to appear in front of a jury) and the lawyers for the plaintiffs (who at trial would actually be at risk of losing the contingency fee they at this point view as their birthright). As the case proceeds, therefore, the dynamics between the opposing parties will gradually shift in the direction of a pretrial resolution.

The biggest catalyst for a pretrial resolution, though, may not come from the lawyers for the plaintiffs or the defendants but from the trial judge itself. Generally speaking, a federal judge of normal temperament will view a multi-month jury trial about GAAP as about as much fun as a root canal. More than that, such a trial would upset the court's calendar, distract the judge from other urgent judicial business, and overwhelm the judge's staff with paperwork. The judge will view a failure of the case to settle as something akin to a personal failure.

At a propitious moment in the discovery process, therefore, the judge will likely convene what is known as a *settlement conference*. The ostensible purpose of the conference will be for the judge to use his authority to try to move the parties to a mutually acceptable damage amount. Attending the settlement conference will be attorneys for the plaintiffs, attorneys for the defendants, attorneys for the insurance carriers, and representatives of the clients with settlement authority themselves. In fact, only one group will not be in attendance: the actual plaintiff-shareholders. They are left out of the process completely.

The settlement conference itself proceeds in a fairly predictable way. Once the assembled attorneys and clients have settled down (they will frequently fill almost to capacity the judge's courtroom), the judge will normally begin by asking to speak privately with the plaintiffs' lawyers. In that meeting, he will dutifully listen to the plaintiffs' carefully rehearsed presentation, write down their damages estimate, and then tell them what a terrible case they have. Next, the judge will ask to speak privately with the defendants' lawyers. He will then listen to *their* carefully rehearsed presentation, write down *their* damages estimate, and then tell them what a terrible case *they* have. He will then reconvene a meeting of everyone in his courtroom and announce that the prospects of settlement are dim because the parties appear to be very far apart.

Indeed, they will be. Before the settlement conference, each side will have hired a *damages expert*, essentially an economist schooled in calculating damages to be as high (for the plaintiffs) or as low (for the defendants) as the confines of the numerical evidence will allow. At this stage in the litigation, it is not unheard of for the estimates of the plaintiffs' expert and the defendants' expert to be literally hundreds of millions of dollars apart. At an initial settlement conference, therefore, there will typically exist a wide chasm between the plaintiffs and the defendants to be closed.

Securities Law Damages

The underlying explanation for the disparity in damage estimates lies in the fact that the estimation of damages for securities law violations—and, for this purpose, we will discuss principally Section 10(b)—is not entirely a precise exercise in mathematics. Under the securities laws, the amount of damages is measured by the difference between the price a shareholder paid and what the price *would* have been if the truth had been known at the time of purchase. The first of the two numbers—what the shareholder actually paid—is easy. It is the second of the two—what the price would have been had the truth been known—that opens the door to advocacy.

Estimating damages thus becomes largely an exercise in speculation aided by all of the stock valuation methods and tools of the most sophisticated teams of economists that money can buy. Topics for debate include the extent to which the stock price was influenced by market factors (rather than fraud), the performance of the industry, the performance of comparable companies, and the non-fraud performance of the stock itself.

For a single share of stock purchased on a single day, this would be complicated enough. In a typical accounting irregularities case, however, at issue normally will be millions of shares of stock purchased and sold over a period of years at wildly different prices through industry ups and downs. Trading patterns among plaintiff shareholders, moreover, will have varied dramatically. Included as part of the class of shareholders may be momentum investors (who arguably pay little or no attention to value), day-traders (who may have traded hundreds of times a day), mutual funds (whose trading patterns would have varied depending upon their stated objectives and goals), and institutional investors (who may not have traded at all). Throw into the mix warrants, options, and short-sellers, and there is much to argue about.

Everyone has complete confidence, of course, that a jury would easily figure it out. For the judge, he is looking forward to his next slip-and-fall case.

Ultimately a Settlement

For all of these reasons, no matter how determined the parties, it is an unusual class action that settles in the first settlement conference. In fact, the judge may have to convene several more spanning a period of several months. Slowly, however, and with painstaking deliberateness, the parties will start to move toward each other. Recalcitrant directors will be prevailed upon to show flexibility. Participating deep pockets (i.e., the accounting firm, underwriters, investment banks) will think hard about the toll the inevitable bad press is taking on their reputations. The plaintiffs' lawyers will increasingly focus on the potential loss of their contingency fee. Thus, the numbers of each will start to move toward each other.

So at some point the parties will probably come to an agreement. A form of settlement agreement will be extracted from one of the law firms' computers (probably in a form that these very lawyers have used many times before), marked up to reflect the precise terms of the resolution, and signed. The most difficult part will be over.

Successful execution of a settlement agreement, though, will not completely end the matter because, to this point, one group will have remained completely unaccounted for. That group is the plaintiff-shareholders themselves. The normal process of resolution will leave them out completely and, although the law presumes their interests have been protected by their counsel, the danger always exists that their lawyers' concern with the anticipated contingency fee may appear to cloud their judgment as to what's best for the shareholders themselves. The law thus imposes an additional procedural device to protect the shareholders. That device is the requirement of court approval, after notice to the shareholders, of any settlement terms.

The next step once the settlement agreement has been signed, therefore, is to give notice to all shareholders so that each can individually decide whether to participate in the settlement or not. Among other things, the names and addresses of the class member plaintiffs need to be ascertained, the class notice must be sent to each, a hearing on the settlement terms must be held, class members will be called upon to submit proofs of claim setting forth the particulars of their stock purchases and sales, and these proofs of claim must then be scrutinized to isolate those for which a recovery is genuinely warranted.

This process, too, can add several months. Once the settlement terms have been agreed upon, though, these procedural requirements are left largely to the plaintiffs' attorneys and their retained administrators to work out. For the defendants, it will be time for them to lick their wounds and vow never to let it happen again.

CHAPTER 8

DEALING WITH THE D&O INSURER

Ty R. Sagalow and Michael R. Young

The commencement of class action litigation will bring to the fore a document whose principal function to that point will have been to sit quietly in a filing cabinet. That document is the director and officer (D&O) insurance policy. Among other things, the defendant officers and directors, and perhaps the company itself, will call upon the D&O policy to pay lawyers, to finance damages experts and, they hope, to finance all or a portion of any settlement. When an accounting irregularity first surfaces, the newly named defendants will no doubt be comforted by their understanding that D&O insurance generally provides coverage for conventional securities class actions and that, assuming compliance with the notice provisions and other prerequisites of the policy, reputable D&O carriers are fairly straightforward in abiding by the policy requirements.

Unfortunately, a situation involving accounting irregularities does not necessarily give rise to a conventional securities class action of the sort that D&O policies are specifically designed to address. The reason is that, in a conventional class action, the defendants will normally have available the defense that they told, or at least tried to tell, the truth. In an accounting irregularities class action, in contrast, that defense largely will not be available. At least one person within the organization, and frequently more than one, will have deliberately lied. The company, moreover, will have already admitted that it got the numbers wrong.

In a situation where accounting irregularities have surfaced, therefore, the insurance posture changes somewhat. And the defendant officers, directors, and company will likely find themselves facing, among other things, a policy exclusion that explicitly disclaims coverage for deliberate fraud. When accounting irregularities have surfaced, accordingly, officers, directors, and the company itself soon find themselves encountering significant issues as to coverage under the policy.

Chapter 8 explores D&O insurance issues. First, it provides an overview of the typical D&O policy and focuses on important policy provisions relevant to securities class action litigation. Then it zeroes in on those provisions that can be troublesome where accounting irregularities have surfaced.

The Structure of a Typical Policy

The typical D&O policy is an elaborate system of parts, each with a separate function. At root, the traditional policy is typically built around two central promises that reflect the dual purposes of this type of insurance. In older policy forms, the separate promises were treated as separate policies. Most modern policies, however, treat the two promises as two insuring clauses in one policy form. One promise, typically called Coverage A or the *individual side* coverage, promises to pay or reimburse officers and directors for losses they have suffered as a result of wrongful acts for which they are not indemnified by the company. The second promise, frequently called Coverage B or *company reimbursement* coverage, promises to reimburse the corporation for amounts that it has had to pay as indemnification of officers and directors for losses they have suffered as a result of wrongful acts within the meaning of the policy. Today, many policies also contain a third promise, entity coverage, that provides direct coverage for certain claims against the corporation itself.

The front page of a typical D&O policy is a *declarations page*, which functions as something of a specification sheet for the policy. The declarations usually state the following:

- **The policy period.** Since the mid-1980s, the policy term has most often been a year, but beginning in 1996, two- or three-year terms became increasingly available.

- **The name of the parent or named corporation.** The typical policy will cover the directors and officers of the named corporation and its subsidiaries, as defined.

- **The limit of liability of the insurer.** That is, the maximum combined amount that the insurer is liable to pay with respect to all claims, in the aggregate, made during the policy period or any extended reported period.

- **The retention or deductible amounts.** The amounts by which the company and the individual insured are agreeing to self-insure each of their losses.

- **Coinsurance.** The amounts, expressed as a percentage, of every loss by which the company and the individual insured are agreeing to self-insure.

- **The premium and any surcharges or installment terms.** This is simply the price of the insurance.

For purposes of analysis, it may be helpful to think of the body of the policy as consisting of several principal parts, regardless of whether the policy writer presents them separately in the text. The insuring clauses, as discussed above, form the initial principal part of the policy. These are the promises that form the heart of the bargain between the insureds and the carrier. The second part is the defining terms, which must be carefully reviewed, as they materially affect the extent of coverage offered by the policy. The third part is an exclusion section, which describes broadly those areas of liability that are not covered under the policy. The next part sets forth general terms and conditions of the policy, which establish important procedures, presumptions, and conditions to coverage, including provisions relating to notice of claims to the insurer, the insured's and insurer's rights with respect to the defense of a claim and subrogation of losses, circumstances in which the policy may be canceled, the right of the insured to elect an extended reporting period or discovery period, and, sometimes, an agreed mechanism for alternative dispute resolution. A particularly important provision in this part of the policy is one that describes the circumstances in which the insurer will advance costs to the insured. The final part is the endorsements—a series of side agreements between the insureds and the carrier reflecting points of negotiation and adjustments to the premium. This customized section of the policy has enormous practical impact, as it can either diminish or enhance the value of the policy to the company and the insured officials.

Analysis of a D&O Policy

Because of the complexity of the policies and the huge effect the exceptions and conditions imposed in them have on coverage, the best way to understand D&O insurance may be to go through the policy as would an insurer when faced with a claim.

Three preliminary tests must be satisfied before a claim can be considered for coverage under the policy:

1. A *claim* must have been made against the insureds during the policy period.

2. The claim must be for a *wrongful act* committed by the insureds.

3. The insureds must have experienced a *loss*.

These tests arise, logically enough, under the policy's *insuring clause*. If these preliminary tests are satisfied, then a review of the policy's exclusions and other conditions must be made in order to make a final determination of coverage. (See Exhibit 8–1.) All of these are examined in the following section.

A Claim Must Have Been Made During the Policy Period

D&O policies, like professional malpractice and other similar liability policies, are *claims-made* policies. That is, they provide coverage only for *claims* that have been made first against an insured during the policy period.

Exhibit 8–1. D&O Insurance Issues

- Existence of a *claim* made during the policy period
- The claim must be against an *insured*
- The claim must be for a *wrongful* act
- The insured must have incurred a *loss*
- The claim must not be *excluded*
- The insurer must be timely notified

Some policy holders may confuse the claim on which a claims-made policy is predicated with the claim that must be made by an insured when it gives the insurer notice of an insured loss. The claim referred to in the term *claims-made* does not refer to the notice by the insured to the insurer, but to a demand by a third party against the insured seeking to hold the insured responsible for the consequences of some alleged wrongful act.

The first inquiry, therefore, focuses on what constitutes a claim. Surprisingly, in the past it was not uncommon for a D&O insurance policy not to contain a definition for claim. In the absence of a defining term in the contract, as the years progressed the meaning of claim became subject to conflicting judicial interpretations. Because of the potential ambiguity and expense associated with judicial interpretations of undefined terms, policy holders increasingly grew to demand that important terms be defined. Accordingly, almost all modern D&O policies contain a definition of the term claim.

Under some policies, especially those written years ago for higher-risk coverage, the term claim is fairly restrictive. Given prior judicial determinations, a basic definition of claim for most risks would generally contain four types of coverage:

- Civil proceedings, such as lawsuits

- Criminal proceedings (post-indictment)

- Administrative proceedings (post notice of charges)

- Monetary or nonmonetary damages or relief for all of the above

A typical definition of *claim* that fulfills all these requirements would be the following:

1. A written demand for monetary or nonmonetary relief, or

2. A civil, criminal, or administrative proceeding for monetary or nonmonetary relief that is commenced by:

   a. service of a complaint or similar pleading, or

   b. return of an indictment (in the case of a criminal proceeding), or

   c. receipt or filing of a notice of charges.

Recently, the definition of claim has been the beneficiary of several additional, and significant, enhancements. These enhancements were brought on by civil, criminal, administrative, or regulatory investigations, and by grand jury proceedings. D&O policies are claims-made policies and cover only claims that are first made during the policy period.

Closely related to the claims-made concept is the establishment of a retroactive date. A *retroactive date* or *prior acts date* is a starting point for coverage under the policy—the first date in which covered wrongful acts may occur. For both the insureds and the insurer, the placement of the retroactive date can be of great significance to the amount of risk covered under the policy. For example, a retroactive date that is concurrent with the inception date of the D&O policy would limit coverage severely. In such a case, both the wrongful acts as well as the claim arising out of those wrongful acts would have to occur during the policy period in order for a claim to be covered. This concept is so central to many D&O policies that some policies actually have a reference to the retroactive date in the insuring clauses. On the other hand, sometimes policies can be negotiated with no retroactive date. In such instances, wrongful acts occurring at any time in the past or during the policy period would be covered.

The Claim Must Be Made Against an Insured

The definition of *insured* plays an important role in a coverage determination. Until recently, the term *insured* usually meant those directors and officers whose acts were protected. However, recent policies have greatly expanded the definition to include the company for certain designated claims, in particular securities claims. Modern D&O policies, therefore, will include as insureds officers, directors, and the company itself.

As a general matter, the term *director* describes those individuals who are elected by the shareholders of the corporation. Similarly, the term *officer* describes corporate officers appointed by the board of directors.

In the past, directors and officers had to be listed individually to be insured, and persons who thereafter became directors and officers during the policy period had to be submitted to the insurance company for approval. However, today almost all policies provide blanket coverage for all directors and officers and automatically include all directors and officers elected or appointed after the inception date.

But it should not ever be assumed that individuals hired by management and given generic titles, such as vice president, are automatically covered. Most insurers have the ability to add by endorsement divisional officers or other types of managers or supervisors as insureds to the policy upon request of the parent corporation. In addition, policies may contain endorsements automatically adding all employees as insureds in the cases of employment practices coverage or securities claims coverage. However, the terms of the policy should be checked to verify any information or assumptions.

The Claim Must Be for a Wrongful Act

Assuming that one has a *claim* against an *insured* made during the policy period, the next question is whether the claim alleges a *wrongful act*. The definition of wrongful act will vary somewhat from policy to policy. A typical definition would read as follows:

> Wrongful Act means any breach of duty, neglect, error, misstatement, misleading statement, omission or act by the directors and officers of the company in their respective capacities as such, or any matter claimed against them solely by reason of their status as directors and officers of the company.

Definitions of wrongful act generally require, as a predicate for coverage, that the directors or officers be acting in "their respective capacities as such." A number of issues arise out of this *capacity requirement.* The most common example of a claim that could run afoul of this requirement is a claim made against a director or officer because of his service at the request of the insured corporation on the board of another corporation that is not a subsidiary. Although the director in question might view his service on the other corporation's board as a mere extension of his capacity as a director or officer of the insured corporation, no insurer is likely to agree with him. Claims arising out of such outside directorships are normally excluded from the policy unless such coverage is specifically provided. This restriction in coverage may take the form of an *outside directorship exclusion* or may be inferred from or made explicit in the definition of wrongful act. However, outside directorship coverage is commonly available by endorsement.

An interesting question arises with respect to the capacity requirement when the director or officer is also rendering professional services to the corporation. Carriers take markedly different views as to whether, for example, an officer-attorney rendering legal services to the corporation was acting in a covered capacity if he is sued as a result of those professional services. Other allegations that may fall outside the insured capacity are those that involve conduct by directors and officers that concern acts that are self-interested, such as ventures involving corporate officials but not corporations, or other acts that are not within directors' and officers' official sphere of responsibility. The position of virtually every insurer will be that at least some, and possibly all, such acts would not be covered by the policy even if such coverage were not already barred by public policy or standard policy exclusions, which they generally are. Outside directors who provide legal, consulting, or other services to the corporation not directly related to their service as directors also may find that those activities are not covered.

The Insured Must Have Incurred a Loss

D&O policies require that, in order to qualify for coverage, the insured must have incurred a loss. A *loss* with respect to an individual insured is generally defined as any amount for which the insured is legally liable and that arises out of a claim made against him for wrongful acts. With respect to the corporate reimbursement side of the policy, a loss may encompass any amount for which the corporation indemnifies its directors and officers for covered wrongful acts by such directors and officers. Further, in the event that the policy provides entity coverage, the corporation may also recover for losses it incurs arising out of securities claims made against the corporation itself.

A typical definition of *loss* includes all "damages, judgments, settlements and defense costs" incurred in the defense and investigation of a claim. Losses covered by the policy thus do not include losses incurred by the corporation unless entity coverage is bargained for separately.

It almost goes without saying that the directors or officers must have suffered real legal liability for there to be a loss under the policy terms. In the past, some defendants have attempted to settle a claim without the consent of the insurer, with the proviso that the plaintiff could not look to them for payment, but must proceed directly against the D&O insurance policy. Carriers have resisted such attempts to create what they perceive to be an inchoate or artificial loss and courts have upheld the insurers' position.

It is usual for a D&O policy's definition of loss to be limited by specific exceptions. One illustrative exception, mentioned earlier, prevents payments made pursuant to settlements without legal recourse to the insured. Other typical exceptions include punitive and exemplary damages, fines and penalties, taxes, and "matters uninsurable under the law pursuant to which the policy is construed." The historic logic behind these limitations is that fines, penalties, and punitive damages are really designed to be punishment to wrongdoers, not compensation to wronged plaintiffs, and they are, or should be, uninsurable as a matter of public policy.

Another issue affecting the scope of covered losses is the treatment of interrelated or causally connected wrongful acts. D&O policies typically provide that all claims arising out of *interrelated wrongful acts* are deemed to arise out of the first such claim. Arguably, this provision has benefits for both the insurer and the insured. For the insurer, it ensures that all risks associated with claims arising out of the same or related wrongful acts will be captured within one policy period and thus will be subject to one liability limit. The danger to the insurer of omitting such a requirement is that insurers that fail to include such language may be found liable under separate policy limits for multiple related claims filed over a several-year period. On the other hand, such a provision may also contain benefits for the insured. First, it may permit the insured to move coverage to another carrier, reserving the argument that any future claims arising out of the interrelated wrongful acts of a previously submitted claim will be covered by the former policy. In addition, most policy forms also indicate that all claims that are interrelated for the purpose of imposing a single limit also obtain the benefit of applying a single retention.

The Claim Must Not Be Excluded

If a *claim* occurs during the policy period against an *insured* and alleges a *wrongful act* creating a *loss* for the insured or for the corporate policy holder that indemnifies him, the next avenue of inquiry is whether the claim has been excluded either by the *exclusion section* of the policy or by the *endorsement section*.

In a typical D&O policy, exclusions generally fall under three categories. They are those relating to:

- Specific conduct of an insured
- Coverage provided under other policies
- Issues of public policy or areas of difficult exposure

Most exclusions are found in the basic policy form, but many are often added by endorsement. There are also various fairly standard exclusions that (for historical reasons) are always added by endorsement. Because exclusions block coverage under the policy, it is the insurer that bears the burden, in the event of any coverage dispute, of demonstrating that the exclusion applies and that the language of the exclusion is clearly stated. Typical exclusions are as follows.

Conduct Exclusions

Conduct exclusions preclude coverage of acts that the carriers deem to be uninsurable or inappropriate for coverage. Typical conduct exclusions concern claims based on:

- Illegal remuneration
- Short-swing profits
- Criminal or deliberately fraudulent acts, or the gaining of any personal profit or advantage to which the insured is not legally entitled

As discussed in detail later, the third of these exclusions—for criminal or deliberately fraudulent acts—can play an important role in determining D&O coverage where accounting irregularities have surfaced. For the moment, the important point is to recognize not only the exclusion but the fact that a policy may provide that the exclusion is triggered not merely by allegations, but by a final adjudication or other finding of fact. The reason is that virtually all class action complaints allege deliberate fraudulent acts. If the exclusion were triggered by a mere allegation, the exclusion would swallow the policy.

Exclusions Due to Other Policies

A number of exclusions in the D&O policy are meant to protect the policy from being used to cover claims that are, or should be, covered under another type of policy. Such exclusions include:

- Claims to which an earlier D&O policy was applicable
- Claims arising out of litigation pending as of or completed before the continuity date (the *pending and prior litigation exclusion*)
- Claims based on wrongful acts of a director or officer of a subsidiary corporation occurring either before it became a subsidiary or after it was spun off
- Claims based on or attributable to any failure or omission to effect or maintain insurance
- Claims that are insured against by any other policy or policies, except presumably for D&O policies written specifically to provide excess coverage in addition to the coverage provided by the primary policy

Although these exclusions are rather straightforward in intent, there are nevertheless issues of interpretation of which a corporation should be wary. For example, exclusions preceded by the word *for* are typically interpreted narrowly to exclude only those items specifically stated. For the insureds, such a narrowing of the exclusions is a benefit. In contrast, older policy forms may begin with broader introductory phrases, such as "based upon, arising out of, or attributable to," which is catch-all introductory language that broadens the scope of the exclusions.

One exclusion that is subject to significantly varying interpretations is the seemingly innocent exclusion for *pending and prior litigation*. In its most acceptable form, the exclusion precludes coverage for "claims arising from any pending or prior litigation as of the continuity date, as well as all future claims or litigation based upon the pending or prior litigation or derived from the same or essentially the same facts that gave rise to the pending or prior litigation." Other broader, and therefore less preferable, versions of the exclusion might also exclude any "demand, suit or other proceeding . . . decree or judgment entered against any" director, officer, or the insured corporation.

The Insured v. Insured Exclusion

The purpose of the *insured v. insured exclusion*, now standard in almost all D&O policies, is easy to understand. The underwriting philosophy behind a D&O policy is to provide coverage for claims brought by third parties against an insured corporation's management. There are two reasons classically given for the insured v. insured exclusion. First, providing coverage for a claim brought by an insured against another insured, or brought by the company against an insured, would support potentially collusive arrangements between insiders. Second, even in the absence of collusion, the insured v. insured exclusion is needed to prevent coverage for boardroom infighting.

Although the reasons for the exclusion are understandable, some of the original phraseology used in older policies was overly broad and gave rise to considerable confusion. For example, an early broad form of this insured v. insured exclusion read as follows:

> The Insurer shall not be liable to make any payment for Loss in connection with any claim or claims made against the Insureds . . . which are brought by, or on behalf of, any other Insureds including but not limited to shareholders' derivative suits and/ or representative class action suits, brought by one or more past, present or future Directors and/or Officers including their estates, beneficiaries, heirs, legal representatives, assigns and/or the Company against one or more past, present or future Directors or Officers.

Because the broad language of such early forms of exclusion might be deemed to exclude even judgments paid in shareholder derivative actions (coverage of which is one of the principal advantages of insurance over indemnification), policies subsequently came to be modified to clarify the exclusion. Newer forms of the exclusion create significant exceptions for shareholder claims that can be shown not to have been made in collusion with an insured or the company and for wrongful discharge complaints against management by former officers. For example, a modern insured v. insured exclusion might read:

> The Insurer shall not be liable to make any payment for Loss in connection with any claim or claims made against the Directors or Officers . . . which are brought by any Insured or the Company; or which are brought by any security holder of the

Company, whether directly or derivatively, unless such claim(s) is instigated and continued totally independent of, and totally without the solicitation of, or assistance of, or active partici- pation of, or intervention of, any Insured or the Company; provided, however, this exclusion shall not apply to wrong- ful termination of employment claims brought by a former em- ployee other than a former employee who is or was a Direc- tor of the Company.

This form of the exclusion is intended to screen out the possibility of suits by the company, or by individuals acting as proxies for the board or the company, while at the same time permitting most non-collusive share- holder class or derivative actions to be covered.

Endorsements

Most of the exclusions listed above are so generally applied that they have become part of the preprinted policy form. Sometimes, however, exclusions that are more fitted to the particular circumstances and risks of an individual company are added by endorsement. *Endorsements*, un- like exclusions, may be either restrictive or expansive, and thus may best be viewed as the result of bargaining and customization of the ba- sic policy form.

A sample of some of the restrictive endorsements that might be found in a typical policy include:

- Deletions from coverage of specific directors or officers against whom actions or investigations or known claims are pending when the policy is written
- *Reorganization of business* exclusions, which provide for termi- nation of coverage in the event of a takeover or insolvency

Endorsements, of course, are also frequently used to expand cover- age under the policy. Examples of such expansive endorsements include those:

- Amending the term *insured* to include divisional officers, employ- ees, or other non-officers
- Expanding the definition of the insured company to include foun- dations, trusts, partnerships, or other noncorporate affiliates

- Obligating the insurer to advance defense costs, if such advancement is not already provided in the boilerplate of the policy

- Expanding or clarifying the worldwide applicability of the policy

- Providing multi-year discovery or run-off periods or making the policy applicable to a particular acquisition that the company is contemplating

- That are state amendatory endorsements required by state law, which typically expand coverage by providing longer advance notification of cancellation, the ability to elect discovery periods, and sometimes other benefits to policy holders mandated by state law

The Insurer Must Be Timely Notified

Assuming that a *claim* has been made against an *insured* during the policy period alleging a *wrongful act* creating a *loss* and that the claim is not excluded by any of the *exclusions*, the policy will require that the claim be submitted on a timely basis to the insurer. As mentioned earlier, the D&O policy is a *claims-made* contract. A necessary part of the claims-made concept is that both the insured and the insurer know with reasonable certainty at the time the policy is created or renewed whether coverage under the expiring policy has been triggered by a claim. Notification requirements are taken extremely seriously in the claims-made context, and the failure to give timely notice may jeopardize coverage. D&O policies usually require that insureds notify the insurer "as soon as practicable" of any claims made against them during the policy period (or discovery period, if elected). Higher-quality policies might add a small window after the end of the policy to facilitate the submission of claims made against the insured late in the policy period. A typical provision of that type might read as follows:

> The Company or the Insureds shall, as a condition precedent to the obligations of the Insurer under this policy, give written notice to the Insurer of a Claim made against an Insured as soon as practicable and either:
>
> (1) any time during the Policy Period or during the Discovery Period (if applicable); or

(2) within 30 days after the end of the Policy Period or the Discovery Period (if applicable), as long as such Claim(s) is reported no later than 30 days after the date such Claim was first made against an Insured.

Some more restrictive policies may require notice to be given within a certain period—such as 30 days—after the claim is first made.

In addition to the notice-of-claim provisions, most D&O policies also permit insureds to notify the insurer of circumstances that may give rise to a claim in the future. If such notice is given before the policy expires, the insurer will treat any subsequent claims arising out of those circumstances as claims first made within the policy period. A typical provision would read like this:

> If during the Policy Period or Extended Reporting Period (if exercised) an Insured becomes aware of any circumstances which could give rise to a Claim and gives written notice of such circumstance(s) to the Company, then any Claims subsequently arising from such circumstances shall be considered to have been made during the Policy Period or the Extended Reporting Period in which the circumstances were first reported to the Company.
>
> The Insureds shall, as a condition precedent to exercising their rights under this coverage section, give to the Company such information and cooperation as it may reasonably require, including but not limited to a description of the Claim or circumstances, the nature of the alleged Wrongful Act, the nature of the alleged or potential damages, the names of actual or potential claimants, and the manner in which the Insured first became aware of the Claim or circumstances.

The advantage to the insured of submitting such a notice of circumstances is that it preserves the insured's rights under the existing policy. If a claim arises out of such circumstances after the expiration of the policy period, the policy will treat the claim as if it were made during the policy period and therefore covered. Of course, such a claim likely would be excluded from coverage under a subsequent policy due to that subsequent policy's *prior-notice* exclusion. As a practical matter, therefore, giving notice of circumstances is something that should be approached with caution.

The Loss Must Be in Excess of the Retention Amount and Not Within Any Applicable Coinsurance Percentage

Having properly submitted to the insurer a claim that falls within the scope of the insuring clause and that meets the essential definitions of the policy and is not excluded by the exclusion section, the policy holder finally gets to ask the key question: How much of the loss will be paid by the policy?

This avenue of inquiry relates, in major part, to the retention and co-insurance sections of the policy. Typically, the insurer is liable to pay only that loss that is in excess of the applicable retention or deductible amount and, in the event of coinsurance, in excess of the applicable coinsurance percentage. Both retentions and coinsurance percentages are forms of self-insurance; their effect is generally to lower the amount of premium that the insurer otherwise would require, in exchange for some or all of the insureds' assumption of a portion of the risk.

The D&O Policy and Accounting Irregularities

That's basically how a standard D&O policy works. Where accounting irregularities enter the picture, though, particularly difficult issues of interpretation emerge. The reason, as mentioned at the outset, is that a typical D&O policy is primarily intended to address a conventional securities class action—that is, a class action in which the defendant officers, directors, and company do not admit they've deliberately said anything wrong. Where accounting irregularities have surfaced, that is by definition not the case. If the company has issued a press release admitting to irregularities, it has already gone a long way to conceding the existence of fraud. Even absent the admission of irregularities, the mere acknowledgment of need for an earnings restatement concedes that earlier numbers were incorrect.

Where accounting irregularities have surfaced, therefore, a series of difficult issues needs to be faced. These might be divided into the following five categories:

- The *deliberate fraudulent act exclusion*
- *Imputation* from one insured to another
- The need for a *factual adjudication*

- The problem of "loose cannons on the deck"
- The *application process*

The Deliberate Fraudulent Act Exclusion

The starting point in assessing coverage in the wake of accounting irregularities is ordinarily the *deliberate fraudulent act exclusion.* To reiterate briefly, this exclusion typically provides:

> The Insurer shall not be liable to make any payment for Loss
> in connection with any Claim made against an Insured:
>
> * * *
>
> (c) Arising out of, based upon or attributable to the commit-
> ting in fact of any criminal or deliberate fraudulent act;...

Interpreted in accordance with its plain meaning (which the insurer
will be wont to do), this means that the D&O policy expressly excludes
coverage for deliberate fraudulent acts. That is, the policy excludes coverage for claims arising out of fraudulent acts that the perpetrator inten-
tionally undertook. If the exclusion does not contain the restrictive ad-
jective *deliberate* (and many policies do not), the breadth of the exclusion may be even broader, potentially excluding *all* fraudulent acts. The
policy will also exclude coverage for criminal acts, which accounting
irregularities may very well involve. If the coverage analysis were to end
there, it would seem a fairly straightforward proposition that coverage
would be denied.

Fortunately for the officers, the directors, and the company, the analysis does not end there—at least if the policy only excludes coverage for
deliberate fraudulent acts. The reason stems from the fact that, although
some within the organization may have deliberately misstated financial
results, it is not necessarily true that everyone named as a defendant will
have knowingly participated—or perhaps participated at all. In particular, among those who were not participants in the irregularity, but who
still may nonetheless be named as defendants in the class actions, will
frequently be additional officers and directors of the company. Will the
insurer deny coverage as to them? Here, the policy provisions may suggest a different outcome. Although an enlightened D&O policy excludes
coverage for deliberate fraud, it *provides* coverage for fraud that arises
out of recklessness.

One interpretation of the policy, therefore, would have the defendants falling into one of two groups. One group would include those who were deliberate participants in the fraud. The other would include those who were not deliberate participants in the fraud and who, at worst, were only reckless. One possible outcome, therefore, is that the insurance carrier will deny coverage to the former but provide it to the latter.

Imputation from One Insured to Another

If only life were that simple. First, it is not always entirely clear who acted with a deliberately fraudulent intent—particularly when one is focusing upon potential participation in the fraud by a corporation. Second, in determining who possessed the requisite intent and who did not, another important provision comes into play. That is a provision providing for *imputation* from one insured to another—be the insured a natural person or an entity.

As a general matter, imputation works like this. If one person knows of the fraud, but another does not, then (in the absence of imputation) the insurance consequences should follow the separate knowledge of each. The innocent defendant gets coverage; the knowing defendant does not. However, this result can be unfair to the insurance company which, after all, has accepted a risk in good faith reliance on an understanding that it was not being misled. The doctrine of imputation, therefore, will in some instances impute the knowledge of a deliberate wrongdoer into the state of mind of another. For example, under many circumstances, a senior executive's knowledge of wrongdoing might be imputed to the company, thereby making the company, as a matter of law, a deliberate wrongdoer as well. Similarly, knowledge of one officer or director may potentially be imputed to another. This approach, while perhaps understandable from the perspective of the insurance carrier, may nonetheless have harsh consequences for those insureds who are truly innocent. The issue thus arises as to the extent of imputation for purpose of determining insurance applicability.

Here, too, different insurance carriers approach the issue differently, but many insurance policies will contain an imputation provision to address precisely this dilemma. For example, on the issue of imputation from an officer or a director to his company, a policy might provide as follows:

> For the purposes of determining the applicability of the forego-
> ing exclusions . . . only facts pertaining to and knowledge pos-
> sessed by any past, present or future chairman of the board, presi-
> dent, chief executive officer, chief operating officer or chief fi-
> nancial officer of the Company shall be imputed to the Company.

Similarly, on the issue of imputation from one officer or director to
another, the policy might read like this:

> The Wrongful Act of any Director or Officer shall not be imputed
> to any other Director or Officer for the purpose of determin-
> ing the applicability of the [deliberate fraudulent act exclu-
> sion].

Or the policy might contain a provision that reads:

> For the purpose of determining the applicability of [certain]
> exclusions, the facts pertaining to and the knowledge possessed
> by any Insured shall not be imputed to any Natural Person In-
> sure. . . .

On the issue of imputation, the provisions among various insurance
carriers are far from standardized. As a general proposition, though, the
extent of imputation from one defendant to another will be determined
according to the policy's terms. In the absence of an imputation provision
(these days a rarity), the extent of imputation from one defendant to another will be determined in accordance with the applicable state law.

The Need for a Factual Determination

The coverage analysis, though, is still not over. Yet another provision
now comes into play. It is the provision, found in many policies, that
limits an exclusion of coverage based on deliberate fraudulent acts to
instances where there has been a *final adjudication* or other finding of
fact. A typical provision may, for example, exclude coverage for deliberate fraudulent acts "if a judgment or final adjudication adverse to the
Insured(s) or an alternative dispute resolution proceeding establishes that
such criminal or deliberate fraudulent act occurred." Or a provision
might indicate that the exclusion is premised upon a factual finding.
Where such a provision exists, the insurance carrier may not, therefore,

simply premise an exclusion of coverage based upon (for example) a press release admitting the existence of accounting irregularities. Rather, the insurance carrier must first obtain a determination to that effect.

The ease or difficulty with which an insurer might obtain such a determination will largely be driven by the facts. Indeed, factual disputes can exist even where the company has conceded that accounting irregularities have taken place. For example, although the company may be more than willing to blame a particular executive as a perpetrator of the fraud, that executive may not be disposed to agree. He may, rather, point the finger at someone else, say it was all an innocent mistake, or deny the existence of irregularities completely. It is not the case, therefore, that a determination of fact will necessarily be swift or that the outcome is sure. Rather, the parties may be in store for years of document productions, depositions, and perhaps even a trial before the underlying facts can be known and determined.

Making the process still more complicated is the fact that precisely what constitutes a final adjudication (on those policies that use that particular phrase) may not itself be entirely clear. The defendants can be expected to argue that the policy thereby requires a judgment in the class action litigation. Such an interpretation can operate to the singular advantage of the defendants insofar as virtually no class action litigation goes through trial to a final judgment. On the other hand, such a position may have the undesirable consequence of motivating the insurer to withhold consent to a settlement based upon an expectation that a finding of fraud at trial would trigger the exclusion. The insurance carrier may also argue that a final adjudication involves any judicial determination of deliberate wrongdoing. Accordingly, the insurance carrier may assert that a judicial declaration in, say, a separate declaratory judgment action brought by the carrier would suffice under the policy. As in most contract disputes, the actual meaning may largely turn on the understanding of the parties at the time the policy was signed. A definitive resolution of such issues may require a separate judicial determination— and therefore still more litigation.

The Problem of "Loose Cannons on the Deck"

Let's take a moment to recap. Accounting irregularities by definition involve deliberate false statements and therefore potentially trigger the deliberate fraudulent act exclusion of a normal D&O policy. Each defendant will fall into one of two categories: those who were knowing participants and those who were not. Due to the rule of imputation, though, the knowledge of those who were knowing participants may be imputed to some or all of those who were not. But first a factual determination is required.

The further one gets into the analysis, therefore, the messier it becomes. Now it will get even worse. Because strategic and practical concerns may cause the insurer to think twice about a denial of coverage even to those individuals as to whom it has a legal right to do so. The explanation lies in what might be referred to as the problem of "loose cannons on the deck."

The problem comes about as follows. At first blush, it might seem to make all the sense in the world for the carrier to deny coverage where it has the legal right. Given the fractured interests of the defendants in typical accounting irregularity litigation, each defendant or similarly situated group of defendants will frequently need their own law firms as well as their own entourage of experts, forensic accountants, and others. All of these can be exceedingly expensive. It would seem entirely logical, therefore, for the insurance carrier to seize upon the policy's exclusions and limit coverage to the full extent possible.

Except for one thing. That is whether it really makes sense for the insurance carrier to limit coverage. The reason it may *not* make sense is that an outright denial of coverage to the deliberate wrongdoers may mean they will lack the financial resources to retain counsel at all. A foreseeable consequence, therefore, may be that the wrongdoers will end up completely unrepresented by counsel in the class actions. That may operate to no one's interest. Certainly it is bad for the deliberate wrongdoers. But more to the point, it can be exceedingly unfortunate for the other defendants—not to mention the carrier insuring them—insofar as those without lawyers may behave like loose cannons on the deck, careening back and forth through the swells and troughs of the litigation and wreaking havoc in the process. It is not without precedent, therefore, for some insurance carriers to recognize the legal right to deny coverage to some, but to go ahead and provide coverage for them nonetheless. The deliberate wrongdoers become the beneficiaries of their own lack of resources and their ability, through the inadequacy of their own representation, to compromise the defense of others.

The Application Process

We're getting to the end, but still not there yet. One final hurdle needs to be overcome. That is the injection of uncertainty into the insurance coverage arising out of representations and information given to the insurance carrier as a result of the insurance application process itself.

Here is the context. As part of the application process, an insurance carrier will normally seek submission of an application form to be accompanied by financial information on the company. The application will seek background information on the company and will normally be signed by a senior executive, such as the CFO. It may include a representation that the individual executing the application, as well as others in the company, are not aware of any circumstances that would give rise to a claim. The financial information sought by the carrier, in turn, will typically include the company's most recent Form 10-K and, perhaps, more recent quarterly information.

The problem is that, where accounting irregularities have surfaced, the information given to the insurance carrier may in fact be false. The insurance application may be false, for example, insofar as it disclaims knowledge by any officer of circumstances that would give rise to a claim. Correspondingly, the financial information may be false insofar as, to the extent the fraud goes back into prior reporting periods (as it probably does), the financial information is infected by—and, for that matter, may be the same as—the false financial information that is giving rise to the class action litigation. Making matters worse, it is possible, if not likely, that among those signing (or deemed to be signing) the insurance application on the part of the company will have been the CFO, who will frequently himself be implicated in the underlying fraud.

On top of all of the other coverage issues, therefore, is heaped the problem that the insurance carrier itself may be a victim of the fraud. To the extent it can prove the misrepresentations were material and that the policy was issued in justifiable reliance upon them, the carrier may potentially have still another basis to deny coverage and, now, to rescind the policy.

That is not to suggest that an attempt to deny coverage or rescind the policy will necessarily follow. Among the issues the carrier would want to consider would be, as mentioned above, materiality and justifiable reliance, and the carrier may have the uphill burden of proving those prerequisites. Here, too, the issue of imputation may arise. If the carrier acts too aggressively, moreover, there is the potential for a fairly severe downside. Beyond the possibility of harm to the insurer's reputation, the newly uninsured officers, directors, and company may themselves commence bad-faith litigation against the carrier premised upon the contention that the denial of coverage was made in bad faith. Historically, in front of a jury, insurance carriers have not always seemed to stand an even chance. On the other hand, neither the insurance industry nor the public welfare will necessarily be well served by a system of insurance that allows defrauders to obtain insurance coverage based on deliberately fraudulent applications.

So issues arising out of the insurance application process create yet another level of problems for the defendant officers, directors, and company. As if they didn't have enough problems already.

So How Does All This End Up?

When all is said and done, how does the coverage issue end up? Unfortunately, there is no easy answer. The answer, rather, turns on the specific terms of the insurance policy and, frequently just as important, the attitude, size, and reputability of the insurance carrier.

At one end of the spectrum, some carriers will recognize the perils of an outright denial of coverage, be openly disdainful of litigation as a mechanism to resolve insurance coverage disputes, and therefore be a willing participant with the class action defendants in an attempt to mutually define the precise contours of the policy. Among the considerations taken into account may be the carrier's own reputation and its desire to be perceived in the market as a supporter, rather than an adversary, of those it has elected to insure. This is particularly so given the likely innocence of many of those officers and directors named as class action defendants. More than that, an experienced and quality carrier will recognize the value of working as a partner to the insureds in devising a litigation strategy that is assisted by its own deep reservoir of experience in analogous situations—experience that the insureds themselves will typically lack.

But not all insurance carriers approach the issue in that way. At the other end of the spectrum, at least one of the smaller carriers has responded to the detection of accounting irregularities with a complete denial of coverage and the commencement of separate litigation by the carrier against the officers, directors, and company. The ostensible purpose of such litigation is a judicial declaration that the carrier may walk away from the policy completely.

For the officers, the directors, and the company, an outright denial of coverage by the insurance carrier can be catastrophic. The reason has little to do with the need to fund a class action settlement, and everything to do with the more immediate problem of up-front cash. Frequently, as the class action litigation proceeds through the early stages, the cash position of the company will be getting more and more dire. In all likelihood, the company will be in default on lending agreements; lenders may be seeking to withdraw from the relationship; and lines of credit may have suddenly dried up. At the same time, the company will likely be undergoing significant drains on its cash resources—stemming from the need to obtain a re-audit of its financial statements, the need to hire a new law firm to commence a special investigation, and particular needs of operations to sustain the enterprise in a time of crisis.

Of the utmost importance to those named as defendants in the class actions, therefore, will be the immediate availability of up-front cash with which to finance their defense. Making the need all the more pronounced will be the reluctance of outside professionals to become involved absent assurance that their fees can be paid. Putting aside the insurance carrier's ultimate position as to coverage, therefore, the critical issue at the outset is the carrier's willingness to begin financing the defense. Absent up-front cash, the defendants may end up tottering on the brink of litigation default.

The Best Approach

All in all, D&O insurance thus becomes another potential headache for the board of directors and senior executives when accounting irregularities have surfaced. The issues can be difficult, the frustrations many, and the availability of coverage—at least during the early stages—not completely certain. Ideally, both the insureds and the insurance carrier will share a common appreciation for the desirability of an agreed-upon approach to the potential coverage issues. A preferred approach, for example, may be one that permits the parties to settle the underlying class action litigation and then, if necessary, resolve any disputes between themselves through some alternative dispute resolution mechanism, such as arbitration. In the future, it may be that sophisticated carriers will find blended-risk solutions to the insurance problem.

The overriding objective on the part of both the insurer and the insureds, though, is the minimization of disputes between themselves. In that way, they may effectively cooperate to obtain an optimum result for the company and the other insureds in the underlying litigation.

CHAPTER 9

DEALING WITH THE REGULATORS

Joseph T. Baio

Just as class action lawsuits are a predictable consequence of the discovery and disclosure of accounting irregularities, so too are the investigations and formal proceedings that are typically brought by the Securities and Exchange Commission (SEC) and the regulatory arms of the stock exchanges. Unlike class action lawsuits, however, these regulatory matters can proceed relatively quickly, and they must be considered and dealt with by the company's management from the outset of the crisis.

The SEC and the stock exchanges enforce a variety of rules designed to protect investors who buy and sell the stock of public companies. A company that has been providing false financial statements to investors inevitably has violated a collection of these rules, and the consequences of those violations can be severe. The SEC has the power to investigate and punish companies and their responsible agents for misleading the public. The stock exchanges can delist the securities of companies that do not adhere to their quantitative and qualitative requirements. In dealing with these potential repercussions, company managers hope to minimize the penalties that the company will suffer for its past sins, to regain credibility in the eyes of the regulators, and to create an environment where the company can successfully move forward. Although all these goals cannot always be met and each crisis will pose its own unique problems, this chapter identifies some techniques for dealing with the regulatory problems that follow the disclosure of accounting irregularities.

The SEC: The Power to Investigate, Correct, and Punish

The SEC, created by an act of Congress in 1934, is the government agency with principal responsibility for the administration and enforcement of the federal securities laws. The SEC is composed of five members who are appointed by the President, with the advice and consent of the Senate, for five-year terms. The SEC directs a number of divisions, each of which has a large staff of lawyers, accountants, engineers, investigators, examiners, and others.

Describing itself as an "independent, non-partisan, quasi-judicial regulatory agency," the SEC is designed to provide some measure of protection for investors by policing securities markets to keep them fair and honest. The SEC does not assess and relay the value or quality of any particular security; actually, it can be a crime to represent that the SEC has done so. Instead, the SEC works to ensure that companies that sell their stock to a large group of investors—these companies are called *issuers*—publicly disclose the information necessary for investors to make informed choices and to help provide honest markets in which those securities are traded. The SEC's regulatory activities therefore fall into two broad categories: corporate disclosure and market fairness. In its role as enforcer of corporate disclosure rules, the SEC works to identify, investigate, and prevent financial fraud and to punish those who engage in it (see Exhibit 9–1).

Disclosure Requirements

The first piece of legislation that provides an oversight and enforcement mechanism for the federal securities laws was actually passed shortly before the SEC came into being. The Securities Act of 1933 made it illegal (subject to some exceptions) to offer a security for sale to the public unless that security was registered. An issuer registers a security by

Exhibit 9–1. SEC Objectives

- A thorough investigation
- Corrected financial statements
- Improved financial reporting systems
- Punished wrongdoers

filing a registration statement with the SEC. The registration statement contains two parts. One part is the prospectus, which must be provided to every purchaser of the security. The second part, which contains additional information and supporting documents, is available to the public but need not be transmitted to every purchaser.

The 1933 Act identifies some of the information to be included in the registration statement, but it also gives the SEC some discretion to add required material and permit certain omissions. The SEC has exercised this authority to develop a number of different forms suitable for different categories of issuers. Generally, an issuer must provide a description of its business and holdings, a description of the security it is offering with an explanation of the relationship between the new offering and pre-existing securities, information about company management, and financial statements audited by independent public accountants. The registration statement must be signed by the issuer's principal officers and at least a majority of the board of directors.

Some months after passing the 1933 Act, Congress passed the Securities Exchange Act of 1934 which, in addition to establishing the SEC, extended corporate disclosure requirements. Unlike the 1933 Act requirements, which are imposed at the time a registration statement is filed, the 1934 Act disclosure obligations are ongoing. As long as securities of a company subject to the 1934 Act are being traded, the company must file annual and other periodic reports to update continuously the information submitted in the original filing. These requirements extend to most issuers with more than 500 shareholders and $1 million in assets, regardless of whether their securities were listed and traded on a national exchange.

Three basic reports are filed with the SEC under Section 13 of the 1934 Act and they are designed to assure that the public gets accurate and timely information about a company. These are (1) Form 10-K, an annual report; (2) Form 10-Q, a quarterly report; and (3) Form 8-K, a report filed whenever certain specified events occur. Both Forms 10-K and 10-Q include a company's financial statements, and the financial statements in Form 10-K must be audited. The Form 10-K must be signed by the issuer, by the company's principal officers, and by a majority of its board of directors. Thus, corporate disclosure under both the 1933 and the 1934 Acts involves representations by many responsible individuals, all of whom are at some risk if the company's financial statements prove to be false.

Additional Provisions

The 1934 Act doesn't just establish disclosure requirements. As amended over the years, it contains a number of different provisions that hold individuals accountable for violations of the disclosure rules. For example, Section 10(b) of the 1934 Act makes it unlawful for any person directly or indirectly "to use or employ, in connection with the purchase or sale of any security, . . . any manipulative or deceptive device or contrivance" in violation of SEC rules and regulations. This statute can serve not only as the basis for a private, class action lawsuit, as discussed in Chapter 7, but also for an action brought directly by the SEC against the company, as well as those who control it, direct it, operate it, underwrite its financings, and keep its accounts. The same applies to the other anti-fraud sections of the 1934 Act discussed in Chapter 7.

The rationale behind these laws is clear. Companies act through human beings. The SEC cannot effectively enforce corporate disclosure requirements if it cannot regulate those people who act on a company's behalf. The SEC's regulatory reach must extend to *all* of the principal actors, so that one group cannot attempt to shelter itself behind another. By linking anti-fraud provisions to disclosure requirements, the 1934 Act puts the SEC in the business of regulating not only the company itself but also its controlling shareholders, directors, officers, underwriters, accountants, and lawyers.

Financial Fraud Investigations

The SEC has express legislative authority to combat accounting irregularities. More recently, it has become clear that the SEC also has the will to attack the problem. In a series of speeches beginning in the fall of 1998, the SEC's then-Chairman, Arthur Levitt, challenged the financial community to stop "accounting hocus-pocus." The SEC views transparency and comparability as the "touchstone" to this country's financial reporting system. The SEC believes that accounting tricks place these two principles in serious jeopardy, and it intends to use its powers of persuasion as well as its powers of enforcement to correct that problem.

The SEC has noted that the fast pace of today's technology-driven market and the market's unforgiving attitude toward failed earnings expectations have combined to cause a "gradual, but noticeable erosion in the quality of financial reporting." Outright fraud is not the only problem, according to the SEC. Rather, all too often, corporations and their accountants are exploiting the flexibility of accounting rules to "manage" their earnings and obscure real-life financial volatility in order to satisfy market expectations. Operating in this "gray area between legitimacy and outright fraud," as the SEC's Chairman has remarked, "jeopardizes the public trust" and threatens to undermine the public confidence that gives the country's markets their stability, not to mention their prosperity.

The SEC's Chairman has focused much of his energy on encouraging the private sector to take an active role in revitalizing financial accounting and disclosure practices, but the SEC is not waiting for the problem to correct itself. The SEC's Director of Enforcement has made combating financial fraud the division's "number one priority." He has warned that the more than 800 members of the Enforcement Division—the part of the SEC that has the power to investigate and litigate against possible wrongdoers—have been directed to focus on financial fraud cases. Because this will result in an increase in the number of SEC investigations that involve accounting and financial disclosure practices, it is important to understand how the SEC conducts those investigations and how a company under investigation or in danger of being investigated should react.

Formal Orders of Investigation and Subpoena Powers

Under the guidance of the Director of Enforcement, the Division of Enforcement monitors the activity and disclosures of public companies; fields complaints from whistle-blowers, investors who have been burned, and anonymous sources; and makes recommendations to the SEC Commissioners as to who should be punished and how severely.

At the outset of an inquiry, the staff members of the Division of Enforcement can informally request information from issuers falling under the SEC's jurisdiction. The staff can also ask that the SEC issue what is known as a *Formal Order of Investigation* if the division believes that there may have been violations of the federal securities laws. The process of seeking and securing a Formal Order of Investigation does not involve the issuer or anyone outside the SEC; it is handled exclusively internally at the SEC, and the company has no right to appear during the process to argue that a Formal Order should not be issued.

The Formal Order itself can be obtained from the SEC by the issuer or subpoenaed parties, but it is not terribly informative. It generally identifies the issuer involved (e.g., In re Newco Corporation), the office handling the investigation (e.g., Washington, New York), the possible securities law violations at issue, and the staff members who will be working on the investigation. Most importantly, once a Formal Order of Investigation has been issued, the Division of Enforcement has the power to subpoena evidence and witnesses. The subpoenas may be enforced by the federal courts and failure to comply can lead to fines and other punishments.

Fighting SEC subpoenas on the grounds of irrelevance or harassment almost never succeeds. The staff of the Division of Enforcement, however, will narrow the scope of requests if the company's counsel can convince it that the request is too broad and will require a great deal of time and effort that will likely yield little useful information. As a general matter, the staff's willingness to narrow requests and extend due dates varies directly with the company's level of cooperation with the investigators.

Penalties and Sanctions

If, after its investigation, the Division of Enforcement believes that it can make a case against a company or its representatives, the staff can seek authorization from the SEC to begin administrative or judicial proceedings. At this point, the company and its targeted employees can file a *Wells Submission*, in which they can argue that, as a matter of policy, fact, or law, the SEC should not authorize the commencement of any proceeding.

If the staff of the Division of Enforcement gets authority to proceed and settlement talks lead nowhere, a hearing will follow. Administrative proceedings take place before an administrative judge (who also happens to be an SEC employee). Judicial proceedings occur before federal court judges. Although the money penalties that the SEC can impose often are not as high as civil damages (the SEC is limited in non-insider trading cases to $500,000 or the amount of financial gain realized by the offending party), the SEC has other remedies available to it. It can obtain an injunction against future violations, on penalty of contempt of court, against individual wrongdoers. It can also get "equitable" relief, such as forcing a wrongdoer to undo a transaction made possible or profitable by the fraud. It can prohibit a wrongdoer from ever again serving as an officer or director of a registered company. It can censure, suspend, or bar professionals (including lawyers and accountants) from ever again practicing before it. If the SEC determines that the misstatement was intentional, it also can refer the matter to the United States Department of Justice for criminal prosecution, as discussed in Chapter 10.

Regaining Credibility with the SEC: Fight or Acquiesce?

The premise of this book is that a company has uncovered accounting irregularities and must therefore restate its historical financial numbers. That premise dictates a course of action centered on cooperation with the SEC and conciliation. A different set of problems and a different strategy may arise, however, when the SEC is investigating an ambiguous set of facts: where there are errors but possibly no irregularities; where large reported numbers are involved but possibly not material amounts; where aggressive accounting treatment was employed but possibly not improper accounting; or where the problem is potentially serious but narrowly confined. In such situations, there may be no audit committee investigation, or, if there is one, the company and its lawyers may conclude in the face of ambiguous evidence and a disbelieving array of regulators that there have been no violations of the federal securities laws. Although confession and contrition can be cleansing, sometimes they are inappropriate.

Thus, a company frequently has defenses against charges of securities fraud, and counsel may seek to advance those defenses zealously in any proceeding before the SEC or the courts. In such situations, questions about whether to retain special counsel to do an internal review, to provide a written report to the SEC, to maintain or waive the attorney-client privilege, and to settle or fight become more complicated and more challenging.

On other occasions, an acknowledgment of past sins and contrition are appropriate, and the uncovering of financial fraud and the restatement of a company's historical financial statements usually presents just such an occasion. In its worst light, a company with restated financial statements has told the world that the numbers that it has been putting out for years were false and that some people at the company knew that they were false. The company, under such circumstances, must purge itself of earlier wrongdoing and rebuild trust. We turn to that process now.

Cooperating with the SEC

A company in the throes of an accounting irregularities crisis wants to minimize the penalties that the SEC will seek to impose against the company and its innocent agents. It is also in the company's best interest for its officers and directors (at least those not implicated in wrongdoing) to have the opportunity to clean up the company on their own, without SEC prodding. An intense investigation by the SEC, filled with detailed document requests and an avalanche of subpoenas calling for testimony, is one of the last things that a company's executives need when trying to reestablish credibility with investors, sources of capital, suppliers, and customers. It's hard enough to rehabilitate and run a company under such circumstances without the distractions and overhang of an active SEC investigation.

What should a company do to achieve a quiet regulatory environment and a favorable settlement with the SEC after admitting to a major accounting problem? To begin, the company must know what the SEC expects from management when an accounting irregularities crisis erupts. Although the SEC has not provided a checklist to public companies, experience tells us that the SEC will consider the following questions in deciding how closely it will investigate a company, and what it will do to the company and its management, after the discovery of accounting fraud:

- Has the company acted promptly and responsibly to correct previously inaccurate disclosures?
- Has the company taken steps to remove (through suspensions or terminations of employment) the individuals who initiated or advanced the accounting irregularities?

- Is the company undertaking a prompt, thorough, and credible review of its financial statements to determine the extent of the problem? Is that review being undertaken by experienced professionals who have the requisite independence from the company?
- Will the company share with the SEC the results of its internal review, even if that review is otherwise "privileged" and outside the subpoena power of the SEC?
- Has the company taken steps to ensure that accounting irregularities will not be a part of its future?

To answer these questions, the SEC will observe and evaluate the company's conduct in the weeks and months following the discovery of the fraud.

Initial Contact with the SEC

When accounting irregularities first surface, the board of directors may wonder whether it should affirmatively contact the SEC before disseminating the first press release. (If the company has uncovered a significant fraud, it can rest assured that the SEC will almost inevitably be calling on the company's officers and lawyers.) A tangible benefit to calling the SEC first is to begin the process of restoring credibility at the earliest possible moment. Of course, the company may not have a good handle on the severity of the problem on "day one," and any call may be premature. In addition, for lesser problems of questionable materiality, a call might not be warranted at all. Where a massive accounting irregularities problem has surfaced, though, a preemptive call will frequently be advisable. The call can be made to a known branch chief in the Division of Enforcement to brief the individual on what is happening at the company just before the issuance of the first press release.

Early Communication with the SEC

Once lines of communication have been opened with the SEC, the principal contact point typically will be one or more staff members in the Division of Enforcement (who no doubt will be identified in the Formal Order of Investigation). The staff members will want to know what the company is doing to quantify and remedy its problems and to whom subpoenas should be sent seeking the production of documents, the identity of witnesses, and the scheduling of testimony.

In pursuit of the twin goals of rebuilding trust and avoiding a full-scale investigation, counsel for the company should assure the staff of the Division of Enforcement that the SEC will get the company's full cooperation. Counsel should assist the staff in locating former employees and arranging for interviews as they are requested. Counsel should also identify the experts that the board of directors has retained to address the accounting problems, the role of the audit committee in overseeing the internal investigative process, and the actions it has taken against responsible agents.

The staff will want to know the expected timetable for the completion of the internal review and restatement of past financial statements. As a general matter, and subject to exceptions, the Division of Enforcement will allow a company to conduct its own internal review without immediate SEC intervention if the staff of the Division of Enforcement concludes that the review will be thorough and unbiased, that it will be conducted expeditiously, and that its results will be made available to the staff promptly after the review is complete. The company should address these concerns honestly and identify realistic timetables that will not have to be repeatedly extended.

Responding to SEC Subpoenas and the Representation of Witnesses

Even though the company is undertaking a thorough internal investigation, the SEC may simultaneously subpoena documents and take testimony of a variety of former and current company representatives to determine what went wrong. (The more high profile the case, the more likely the SEC will proceed on a faster and more active track.) From the company's perspective, the best course is to have one law firm representing as many individuals as possible. A single counsel increases the likelihood of a coordinated response, enables the company to keep track efficiently of what is going on, and minimizes the financial costs of representation. Under such circumstances, the lawyers for the audit committee usually do not represent the company or its officers and directors (other than audit committee members), but instead focus on conducting and completing the internal review. Company counsel typically represents the company in responding to document subpoenas, as well as the individual employees, officers, and directors who are not implicated in any wrongdoing.

In many situations, it may be impossible or inappropriate for the same company lawyers to represent all who are called by the SEC to testify. As a matter of the rules of ethics—which vary from jurisdiction to jurisdiction—an attorney generally may not jointly represent parties if they are adverse to one another or if they have sufficiently differing interests such that counsel's ability to represent zealously each client would be impaired by a joint representation. Moreover, joint representations are not appropriate when the parties have significantly differing interests, unless each party agrees to the joint representation after full disclosure of the facts. Former employees may not want to be jointly represented by company counsel, even if the company offers to pay for such counsel. (In fact, the company may be required to supply separate counsel under applicable indemnity obligations.)

If multiple counsel are to be involved, it may be advisable for counsel to enter into a *joint defense* or *common interest agreement*, pursuant to which the parties can exchange information and analyses while maintaining an attorney-client privilege, thereby increasing the data available to all.

Turning Over an Investigative Report to the SEC

On more than one occasion, the SEC will likely make clear that the Division of Enforcement will expect to receive from the company a copy of the final investigative report that the special committee's lawyers and accountants prepared for the committee. The Division of Enforcement staff may also request all interview memoranda, notes, and supporting materials gathered or prepared in connection with the completion of the report. Although a commitment to turn over such material is usually the linchpin in restoring credibility with the SEC, the disclosure of the report is not without a potential cost: The disclosure will give the plaintiffs' lawyers a strong argument that the report and its backup are no longer privileged and are therefore "discoverable" in the class action litigation. In fact, the plaintiffs' lawyers will argue that, if the audit committee and the company intended all along to provide the SEC with a copy of the report, then it was never meant to be a confidential communication between a client and a lawyer and therefore was never privileged to begin with.

Although the risk of losing the "privilege" is a real one and that risk may prevent a company from disclosing privileged material to the SEC in many situations, a company that has conceded accounting irregularities and has restated its financial statements will frequently have less to lose and more to gain by providing the requested materials to the SEC. Often, the materials are produced in such cases.

Counsel, however, can take steps to protect the materials, even though the report is eventually produced to the SEC. Under current law, the report and underlying data *may* continue to be protected after such a disclosure if the SEC agrees to maintain the confidentiality of the produced materials. In the recent past, the SEC has agreed to do so if the company can demonstrate the reliability of work that was done (i.e., no whitewash) and can identify the benefits that the SEC will receive by entering into such an agreement. In support of the request for confidentiality, therefore, company counsel should be prepared to:

- Demonstrate the independence of the audit committee members and their professionals, the complete access to information afforded those professionals in their investigation, and the breadth of the subjects under review.

- Advise the SEC that the company will invoke the attorney-client privilege and work product doctrine and decline to produce the report in the absence of a confidentiality agreement. In this way, the SEC will only receive the benefit of the materials if they agree to maintain them in confidence.

- Specify the extent of the effort undertaken in generating the report (e.g., boxes of documents reviewed, number of employees/witnesses interviewed, hours of lawyer and accountant time expended in analyzing materials and preparing the report). The SEC will thereby be given to understand that it gets the benefit of all that effort without governmental cost.

Making Peace with the SEC

Ultimately, probably the best the board of directors can hope for is a negotiated resolution with the SEC. The SEC has a powerful arsenal of weaponry at its disposal. Through a negotiated resolution, those involved may avoid some of the more onerous punishments the SEC might otherwise seek to impose.

In all likelihood, such a negotiated resolution will involve different penalties for different people depending upon their status and complicity (see Exhibit 9–2). Senior executives who were knowingly involved in deliberate wrongdoing can expect severe punishment. Penalties may include insistence by the SEC on removal from the company, a bar against further service as an officer or director of a public company, an injunction against further violations of the securities laws (which would be punishable by a finding of contempt), and a stiff fine. The SEC may also refer the matter to the U.S. Attorney's Office for criminal prosecution.

For those who were not deliberate wrongdoers but merely negligent, the SEC may seek penalties that are less severe. These might include a cease-and-desist order against further violations.

A difficult issue is presented to the SEC by lower-level employees who were pressured into participation by more senior executives. Such individuals obviously are in a sympathetic position insofar as their complicity may, at the outset, have been entirely inadvertent. Even knowing participation may have resulted from the need to hold on to their jobs. Still, informal statements by members of the Division of Enforcement suggest that the SEC will not permit lower-level employees to escape remedial mechanisms entirely. To be sure, it is the senior executives who will be made to suffer the most severe consequences. Nonetheless, representatives of the Division of Enforcement have been crystal clear that "there is no such thing as a good soldier." As one Division of Enforcement staff member has put it, wrongdoers will be pursued "up, down, and sideways." Penalties may include fines, injunctions, cease-and-desist orders (for conduct not warranting an injunction), and insistence by the SEC that the employees be discharged.

For CPAs involved in accounting irregularities, the SEC has an additional series of punishments owing to its ability to proceed pursuant to a rule known as Rule 102(e). This is the rule by which the SEC brings proceedings against wrongdoing professionals, and the consequences for a professional can be serious. Among the frequently employed remedies of the SEC is a permanent or temporary ban from public practice before the Commission. For many professionals, such a penalty can effectively end their careers.

As to the company itself, the penalties resulting from a negotiated resolution with the SEC may include many of those mentioned earlier—

including an injunction and a fine. Almost inevitably, though, the remedy sought by the SEC will be supplemented by a dramatic corporate-governance component. Among other things, the SEC may insist that the company bring in additional outside directors, reconfigure its audit committee, hire a new CFO, substantially reorganize its internal-control systems, and remove wrongdoers.

As a general matter, the SEC will seek to understand the facts and circumstances of a particular situation and try to use its enforcement

Exhibit 9–2. SEC Penalties

COMPANY	EXECUTIVE	PENALTY
Sensormatic	CEO	Injunction & $50,000 fine
Sensormatic	VP-Finance	Injunction, $50,000 fine & five-year bar from appearing before SEC
Bausch & Lomb	Sales Director	Injunction & $10,000 fine
Information Management	CEO	Injunction, $50,000 fine & permanent bar as officer/director
Structural Dynamics	CEO	Injunction, $100,000 fine & five-year bar as officer/director, disgorgement of trading profits
Automated Telephone	Audit Committee Member	Injunction & $15,000 fine
Paracelsus Healthcare	CEO	Injunction & $100,000 fine
Paracelsus Healthcare	CFO	Injunction, $50,000 fine & three-year bar from appearing before SEC
Paracelsus Healthcare	VP-Operations	Injunction & $75,000 fine
Paracelsus Healthcare	Controller	Injunction, $25,000 fine & three-year bar from appearing before SEC

mechanisms to fashion a result that creatively fits its perception of the underlying problem. Many of its penalties may seem harsh. Almost always, though, they will be preferable to a prolonged battle with the SEC.

Dealing with Self-Regulatory Organizations

The SEC isn't the only regulator that companies need to worry about after the discovery of accounting irregularities. The stock exchanges and associations on which companies' securities are traded also have the power to investigate and to punish. Companies must be mindful of what these self-regulatory organizations (SRO) can do to, and what they expect from, companies that restate their earnings.

What "SROs" Are and What They Do

SROs are national securities exchanges, securities associations, or clearing agencies that are registered with the SEC. There are eight active securities exchanges that are so registered: the American Stock Exchange (AMEX), the Boston Stock Exchange, the Chicago Board Options Exchange, the Chicago Stock Exchange, the Cincinnati Stock Exchange, the New York Stock Exchange (NYSE), the Philadelphia Stock Exchange, and the Pacific Stock Exchange. The National Association of Securities Dealers, Inc. (NASD) operates the Nasdaq Stock Market, Inc. (Nasdaq), which is the regulatory body responsible for over-the-counter securities.

The stock of most public companies is bought and sold over one or more of these exchanges. It is important for public companies to be listed on an exchange. The exchanges see to it that there is a liquid market for their listed companies' stock, that the execution of trades occurs quickly, and that the process of buying and selling the stock of listed companies is handled fairly, honestly, and efficiently.

By getting listed on an exchange—particularly the NYSE or the Nasdaq—companies add credibility to their stock and generally experience a higher stock price. The price of admission, however, is that companies must meet specific financial and other requirements to get listed and, to stay listed, companies must maintain defined financial levels and demonstrate good corporate governance. These requirements give rise to a potential problem: Companies suffering from accounting irregularities may be unable to meet the criteria for continued listing and may find themselves the subject of delisting proceedings. But before turning to those standards and the process and effect of a delisting hearing, let's review some important background on the national stock exchanges.

SROs and the SEC

SROs were created by the same New Deal securities legislation that gave birth to the SEC. Rather than impose direct federal regulation of securities exchanges and brokers' associations, Congress decided to allow the exchanges to regulate themselves under the SEC's watchful eye.

In order to qualify for registration with the SEC, an exchange must meet certain organizational requirements specified under law. Broadly speaking, an exchange must have the capacity to enforce compliance by its members with applicable law, to manage fairly its membership and collect membership dues, and to provide an effective and adequate disciplinary procedure. The rules of an exchange must be "designed to prevent fraudulent and manipulative acts and practices, to promote just and equitable principles of trade," and to facilitate a free, open, and competitive market.

The SEC's oversight of the rules and operation of an exchange is perpetual. Since 1975, all proposed changes to the rules of an SRO have been subject to approval by the SEC, and the SEC even has the power to impose new or amended rules. Likewise, a company or individual punished by an exchange typically has a right of appeal to the SEC, and then from the SEC to the federal courts.

An important point to remember is that, if the SEC believes that violations of securities laws or exchange rules are occurring, the SEC has the power to conduct its own investigation, even if the exchange is also conducting an investigation at the same time.

In addition, the SEC can investigate the exchanges themselves if the SEC believes the exchanges are not doing a good job of ferreting out and punishing improper conduct. The SEC exercised this power in 1996, for example, when it issued findings strongly criticizing certain Nasdaq trading practices, including anti-competitive pricing. The SEC and the NASD ultimately arrived at a settlement that required the NASD to allocate significant additional resources to enforcement of its rules and to take specific steps to prevent the criticized trading activity, which led to a major restructuring of the NASD.

Listing Requirements

Subject to approval from the SEC, the exchanges have the authority to determine for themselves which securities qualify for listing. When a company applies to have its securities listed on an exchange, it will have to comply with listing requirements for initial entrance. If the company meets those requirements and the exchange agrees to list its securities, the company must sign a *listing agreement* that will obligate the company to comply with continued listing requirements for as long as its securities are listed on that exchange.

Some of the listing requirements are financial—e.g., minimum market value, minimum number of shares and shareholders, minimum revenues. The exchanges typically refer to these standards as *quantitative listing requirements*. These standards vary widely from exchange to exchange, and if a company (particularly a start-up company) finds the requirements too stringent, it may have to apply for listing on a less desirable exchange.

In addition to setting financial standards, most exchanges also impose *qualitative listing requirements*, which include mandatory standards of corporate governance. Corporate governance standards involve critical subjects such as public disclosure of financial and other material information, the independence of directors and auditors, the existence and configuration of audit committees, voting rights, and preemptive rights. For years, these standards were basic and general, but more recently they have become more specific and pointed—with the trend toward tighter corporate governance standards being expected to continue.

Largely through corporate governance standards, the exchanges are playing an active role in the prevention and detection of financial fraud. Perhaps the most basic corporate governance requirement is that a listed company promptly disclose to the public any information that "might reasonably be expected to materially affect the market for its securities." The NYSE in fact advises that this disclosure requirement is "one of the most important and fundamental purposes of the listing agreement." A company that has discovered a serious accounting irregularity must consider whether it has violated this rule, either because the irregularity prevented accurate disclosure of material financial information or because the irregularity itself, once discovered, was not promptly reported to the public.

Enhanced Exchange Requirements

Accounting and auditing standards are being tightened further. As mentioned in Chapter 2, in late 1998 the NYSE and the NASD convened a Blue Ribbon Committee on Improving the Effectiveness of Corporate Audit Committees. The Blue Ribbon Committee recommended that the NYSE and the NASD:

1. Codify a specific definition for "independent" directors.
2. Require all listed companies with a capitalization greater than $200 million to have an audit committee comprised solely of "independent" directors.
3. Require all listed companies with a capitalization greater than $200 million to have a minimum of three "financially literate" (as defined by the Blue Ribbon Committee) directors on every audit committee.
4. Require the audit committees of all listed companies to adopt a formal, written charter for the audit committee and to review that charter on an annual basis.
5. Specify in the charter the accountability of the company's outside auditor to the board and to the audit committee.
6. Specify in the charter that the audit committee must ascertain and evaluate all relationships between the outside auditor and the company to ensure the auditor's independence.

Given the composition of the Blue Ribbon Committee (it included the chairmen of both the NYSE and the NASD), it is not surprising that the NYSE and the NASD have adopted new rules consistent with the Blue Ribbon Committee's recommendations. (See Chapter 11.)

These new requirements are designed to promote transparency and to prevent financial fraud. However, along with other listing requirements (including quantitative requirements), they also can serve as grounds for an SRO to suspend or remove the securities from the list of

---

Exhibit 9–3. New York Stock Exchange Delisting Procedures

The NYSE would consider delisting a security of a company in the event of:

- A failure to maintain certain quantitative criteria established by the NYSE
- Reduction in operating assets or scope of activities
- Bankruptcy and/or liquidation
- Authoritative advice to the NYSE that the security is without value
- A registration that is no longer effective
- A failure to solicit proxies for all stockholder meetings
- Violation of agreements with the NYSE
- Operations contrary to the public interest
- A failure to maintain an audit committee in conformity with NYSE requirements

If a decision is made to delist a security, written notice shall:

- Set forth the basis for such decision
- Set forth the specific policy or criterion under which such action is to be taken
- Inform the issuer of its right to a hearing

If the issuer does not request a hearing within 20 days after receiving notice, the NYSE staff will submit an application to the SEC to strike the security. If the issuer requests a hearing, the hearing will be held before a committee of the board of directors of the NYSE.

---

securities traded on its exchange—known as a *delisting*—if a company violates the requirements. (See Exhibits 9–3 and 9–4 for the delisting procedures of the NYSE and the NASD.) As listing requirements become more specific and numerous, the grounds upon which an SRO can initiate delisting proceedings in the event of an accounting irregularity will likely expand.

Exhibit 9–4. Nasdaq Delisting Procedures

Delisting is to occur when:

- The company falls below certain quantitative criteria established by the NASD
- The company fails to meet the NASD's corporate governance requirements
- Any event or circumstance "exists or occurs that makes initial or continued inclusion . . . inadvisable or unwarranted, even though the securities meet all enumerated criteria for . . . inclusion in Nasdaq"

If a decision is made to delist a security, notice shall:

- Describe the grounds for the determination
- Identify the quantitative standard or qualitative consideration that the issuer has failed to satisfy
- Inform the issuer of its right to a hearing

If the issuer does not request a hearing within seven days of the determination to delist, the determination will take immediate effect. If the issuer requests a hearing, the hearing will be held before a Listing Qualifications Panel, and delisting will be stayed pending a written determination by the panel.

Preventing and Handling Delisting Proceedings

In considering how to deal effectively with a company's stock exchange, we look back again to the first day of an accounting irregularities crisis. The board of directors is meeting to determine how to respond. Crisis-response assignments are being distributed. One assignment will be to investigate any potential effect that the irregularities might have on the company's ability to continue to trade its securities on the exchange where the company is listed. The goal, of course, is to prevent a delisting. The mission to accomplish that goal is to take every possible step to provide adequate and proper disclosure of the company's financial position, to rectify past violations of the exchange's listing requirements, to prevent future violations as events unfold, and to meet the ongoing financial standards.

Early Dialogue and Suspension of Trading

As soon as practical, the company should open a dialogue with the responsible listing official of its exchange. Ordinarily, this contact should be made as soon as the irregularities have been discovered. If the company does not have a handle on the magnitude of the problem, the first step usually recommended by the exchange and accepted by the company is to suspend trading in the company's stock.

This interim step often makes sense. The company at this point knows of a real problem with its financial statements but doesn't yet know how big the problem is. A suspension of trading prevents investors from buying or selling based on false financial information and eliminates liability to people who otherwise would have bought stock before a major dip in price. Suspension of trading also gives the company time to straighten out its public disclosures in a non-trading environment.

In dealing with the stock exchange, the company must be careful not to make promises it cannot keep or to misstate either the extent of its understanding of the problem or the problem itself. At the same time, the company should act expeditiously. Although exchanges have listing requirements and other standards, they also have a fair amount of discretion as to how their rules are interpreted and enforced. The rules of most exchanges contain a provision to the effect that the exchange is not bound by the specific, enumerated listing criteria and it can assess suitability for continued listing even though a security meets or fails to meet them. The bottom line is that the company should do what it can as soon as it can to persuade the exchange that, despite whatever violations the company may have committed, it is in the best interest of the exchange and the company's public investors to keep its securities listed.

The company must analyze the facts as it understands them in light of its listing agreement and the applicable listing requirements. It should attempt to identify violations that already have occurred and violations that may occur in the coming weeks and months as a result of the company's (and the market's) response to the problem. Examples of violations that already may have occurred include a failure to disclose information that has a material effect on the market (namely, the true financial picture of the company), an improper or insufficient outside audit program, or a significant conflict of interest that caused inadequacies in financial reporting. Violations of listing requirements that may occur after the irregularity has been discovered might include the failure to disclose promptly all material facts related to the irregularity, the failure to correct deficiencies in the company's accounting system that were identified in the process of handling the crisis, and the sustained devaluation of the company's stock to a level that fails to satisfy the exchange's quantitative listing requirements.

Corrective Measures

As the company continues its investigation of the accounting irregularities crisis, it will have identified one or both of two possible categories of listing violations: those that the company can prevent or correct and those that the company cannot prevent or correct. Violations that can be prevented or corrected should be. The other violations should be identified, assessed, and mitigated to the extent possible. If the company identifies a serious violation that it cannot correct, particularly a violation of the exchange's quantitative listing requirements, it should begin to explore the possibility of listing its securities on a different exchange that may have quantitative or other criteria that the company can meet.

A Two-Pronged Approach to Delisting Proceedings

Despite the company's best efforts, the exchange may nonetheless move to delist the company's securities. If that happens, and if the company believes its securities should continue to be actively traded, the company will probably want to explore two alternatives. If it hasn't already, the company may want to look into the possibility of listing its securities on another exchange. If the company can reach an agreement with another exchange, in all likelihood it will be possible to withdraw its securities voluntarily from the old exchange and list them on the new one, although even a voluntary withdrawal from listing may require that the company demonstrate to the exchange and to the SEC that its decision to withdraw will not unduly harm investors.

The company's second alternative is to prepare to defend its right to continue to be listed on the current exchange. All exchanges have codified some form of delisting procedures. Typically, the applicable procedures require the exchange to provide the company with written notice of its intention to delist the security and the grounds upon which it has tentatively made that decision. The company then has the right to request a hearing before an administrative panel established by the exchange as a tribunal for such matters, and often it must exercise that right within a prescribed period. (Some exchanges also provide another level of discretionary review by the exchange's board of directors or governors.)

If there is a case to be made, it is critical that the company be ready to put into evidence all relevant facts and to present its best case to the exchange's hearing panel. The main reason is that the company may never get another chance to present factual evidence for adjudication. The company can appeal the decision of a hearing panel to the SEC, and the SEC rules give the SEC the ability, in its discretion, to conduct a second hearing, but the SEC is not obligated to conduct a second hearing for the company. And there is no guarantee that the SEC will exercise its available discretion to see that a second hearing is held.

An additional reason to ensure an effective presentation in the hearing before the exchange is that, although the SEC on appeal would normally take an independent look at the factual record created in the initial hearing, it is likely to give significant weight to the exchange's interpretation of its own rules. Although an SEC decision can be appealed to the United States Court of Appeals, that court almost certainly will apply a standard of review that requires deference to the administrative decisions of the exchange and the SEC. In short, the company's best chance to convince a tribunal that the exchange should not delist its securities is usually at the initial administrative hearing, so the company should make the most of that opportunity.

CHAPTER 10

CRIMINAL INVESTIGATIONS

Benito Romano

It is an exceedingly unfortunate consequence of accounting irregularities that the resulting investigative proceedings may not be limited to civil class action litigation (see Chapter 7) or regulatory proceedings (see Chapter 9). Rather, where accounting irregularities have surfaced at a public company, in all likelihood federal criminal laws, as well as state criminal laws, have been broken (see Exhibits 10–1 and 10–2). Where accounting irregularities have surfaced, therefore, it may be that all other aspects of the problem will need to take a back seat to one that becomes paramount: the commencement of a criminal investigation.

In the federal system, the decision to start a criminal investigation is entirely within the discretion of the United States Attorney in each federal district, who may act merely on the basis of an allegation or a suspicion that a federal crime has been committed. As a result, a criminal investigation of accounting irregularities can originate in all sorts of ways. An investigation may be initiated because of an anonymous tip, information supplied by a conscientious or guilt-ridden employee, or facts discovered in the course of a routine audit of the company's financial statements. The company's public disclosure of financial misstatements may itself lead to the commencement of a criminal investigation.

If anything, recent trends suggest a reallocation of resources by federal prosecutors to accounting irregularities and an increased willingness to investigate and prosecute wrongdoers. This trend may be fueled in part by increased SEC activity in the area: a primary catalyst for a criminal investigation is a referral from the SEC. But the trend may also be fueled simply by increased stock ownership among the citizenry and prosecutorial awareness of the calamitous consequences for the everyday investor of financial misreporting. Indeed, U.S. Attorney's offices

Exhibit 10–1. Securities Act of 1933

Section 24. Any person who willfully violates any of the provisions of this title, or the rules and regulations promulgated by the Commission under authority thereof, or any person who willfully, in a registration statement filed under this title, makes any untrue statement of a material fact or omits to state any material fact required to be stated therein or necessary to make the statements therein not misleading, shall upon conviction be fined not more than $10,000 or imprisoned not more than five years, or both.

Exhibit 10–2. Securities Exchange Act of 1934

Section 32. (a) Any person who willfully violates any provision of this title (other than Section 30A), or any rule or regulation thereunder the violation of which is made unlawful or the observance of which is required under the terms of this title, or any person who willfully and knowingly makes, or causes to be made, any statement in any application, report, or document required to be filed under this title or any rule or regulation thereunder or any undertaking contained in a registration statement as provided in subsection (d) of Section 15 of this title or by any self-regulatory organization in connection with an application for membership or participation therein or to become associated with a member thereof, which statement was false or misleading with respect to any material fact, shall upon conviction be fined not more than $1,000,000, or imprisoned not more than 10 years, or both, except that when such person is a person other than a natural person, a fine not exceeding $2,500,000 may be imposed; but no person shall be subject to imprisonment under this section for the violation of any rule or regulation if he proves that he had no knowledge of such rule or regulation.

have even shown a willingness to undertake a criminal investigation where enforcement activity by the SEC has been nonexistent.

Whatever its origins, responding to a criminal investigation will almost always have to take priority over everything else. The government's powers to investigate are broad, and a prosecutor, informed of a potential massive fraud at a public company, will likely make the investigation a high priority. Indeed, from the prosecutor's perspective, a massive accounting irregularity problem potentially involves just the sort of dishonesty, deception, and concerted activity that fits neatly into already-tested theories of criminal liability. If a prosecutor has been following reports of accounting irregularities in the financial press, he may even have been looking for such a case in order to make a public example out of an improperly acting company. (See Exhibit 10–3.)

Still, even where the existence of accounting irregularities has been conceded, it will be far from clear to a prosecutor that a criminal prosecution should be commenced. Rather, the prosecutor will try to resolve a number of issues bearing on the extent to which an indictment of the company or any executive would be justified. Among these issues may be the following:

- The magnitude and nature of the financial misstatements, both in terms of their quantifiable materiality and whether they involved the fabrication or destruction of documents
- Whether any employee was in good faith mistaken about the relevant accounting rules
- Whether any employee had sufficient knowledge of the entirety of the scheme to justify the conclusion that the suspected perpetrator's conduct was willful and he acted with criminal intent
- Whether any employee personally benefited from the misstatements, or acted primarily to benefit the company, or acted to carry out the instructions of a superior
- Whether the company had in place a system to detect and deter the conduct under investigation, and whether the failure of that system was reasonably foreseeable
- Whether the absence of an effective system of internal control was reckless or deliberate

Exhibit 10–3. Criminal Sentences

COMPANY	EXECUTIVE	SENTENCE
Leslie Fay	CFO	Faces 115 years
Donnkenny	CFO	Faces 5 years
Livent	CFO	Faces 5 years
CUC International	CFO	Faces 10 years
SSM unit	CFO	7 years, 3 months
Bennett Funding	CFO	30 years
Health Management	CEO	9 years
Centennial	CFO	1 year, 3 months of community confinement and 3 years of supervised release
Lumivision	Accountant	10 years
Bernard Food	CFO	6 years
Ferrofluidics	CFO	5 years, 3 months
BroMenn Healthcare	CFO	1 year, 6 months
Empire Blue Cross	CFO	1 year, 6 months
A.R. Baron	CFO	5 to 15 years
Cableco	CFO	1 year, 3 months
National Grocers	CFO	5 years, suspended, and 15 years probation
Astra USA	CFO	2 years probation, the first 3 months under house arrest wearing electronic monitoring device
Financial News	CFO	1 year, 6 months (plus 2 years supervised release)
Star Clippers	CFO	2 years, plus 6 months in a controlled release program and 10 years probation
Miniscribe	CFO	2 years
Phar-Mor CFO		2 years, 9 months

Chapter 10 examines the role of prosecutors in ferreting out financial fraud involving public company accounting irregularities. First, it describes the several phases of a typical criminal investigation and possible company responses at each phase (see Exhibit 10–4). Then it turns to the responsibilities of the company to gather information in order to comply with the demands of the government, to monitor the progress of the investigation and evaluate the company's exposure to criminal prosecution, and, ultimately, to present its best case to avoid indictment. It also discusses plea negotiations and considerations as to potential sentences. Finally, it addresses briefly the interplay of the criminal investigation and related civil proceedings and the difficulties of responding effectively in such parallel settings.

The Initial Grand Jury Phase

Typically, a company first learns that it is involved in a criminal investigation when it receives a grand jury subpoena, in most instances a "subpoena *duces tecum*," compelling the company or its employees to furnish documents to the grand jury. In an investigation of accounting irregularities, such a subpoena for documents may encompass all the files underlying the company's publicly disseminated financial information, including the records underlying the transactions at issue.

For a company and its executives, the need to respond to the subpoena presents both an opportunity and a dilemma. The opportunity stems from the company's ability, in responding to the subpoena, to learn about the investigation—an education process that will be critical to a success-

---

Exhibit 10–4. Phases of a Criminal Investigation

- Grand jury subpoena

- Initial contacts with prosecutor

- Production of documents

- Grand jury testimony

- Plea negotiations (if necessary)

- Trial (if necessary)

---

ful criminal defense. The dilemma stems from the need to assess the extent to which active and complete cooperation should be pledged to the prosecutor at the outset. The formulation of a response to a criminal subpoena, therefore, constitutes a critical point in the investigatory process. And those involved are thereby placed in the position of needing to make important decisions at an early stage that can have lasting and significant effects.

Once an initial review of the subpoena and its underlying substance is complete, one of the first steps in formulating a response is often for company counsel to make a phone call to the prosecutor to make appropriate introductions and, to the extent possible, to seek background information regarding the investigation. In this initial contact, the prosecutor will be understandably guarded. Nonetheless, some useful information will frequently be shared. A general impression may be gained about the scope and focus of the investigation and the timing of additional subpoenas and testimony. Thereafter, it is not unusual for some kind of initial meeting to be arranged to discuss in greater detail the company's response. One benefit of such a meeting is that some level of additional information may be forthcoming.

It is thus that, from the outset, company counsel will be undertaking a process that is vitally important and that will be ongoing throughout the entirety of the criminal proceedings: learning as much as it possibly can about the prosecutor's case. The reason is that, unlike a civil case, in which broad principles of discovery enable the defendants basically to learn the complete details of the adversary's evidence, a criminal investigation is shrouded in a much greater level of secrecy and complete knowledge of the evidence is not usually available pursuant to the procedural rules. Less formal methods of learning the details of the prosecutor's case, therefore, are critical.

In these initial contacts, the establishment of a sound foundation for the company's dealings with the prosecutor is an additional, critically important aspect of the investigation that will also permeate the entirety of the investigative process. To state it simply, those dealings must be premised upon a foundation of absolute candor. Although it may be appropriate at various stages to decline to discuss sensitive matters, whatever counsel elects to address, counsel should avoid making a factual statement on any subject about which it suspects it may be incompletely or inaccurately informed. This admonition applies to subjects such as the existence and location of files, the burden of producing documents, and the availability of witnesses. It also applies to more substantive matters bearing upon guilt or innocence, although such subjects are unlikely to come up except in the context of a presentation late in the investigation or in discussions of the propriety of extending immunity to a particular witness. An important part of a successful criminal defense is the availability of relevant information. To that end, a relationship with the prosecutor based on trust and confidence is key.

The dilemma posed in these initial contacts—involving the issue of cooperation with the prosecutor—is a difficult one and, unfortunately, no single approach can be devised that will fit every investigation. The basic issue is whether the company should adopt a cooperative or an antagonistic stance. Among the disadvantages of cooperation is the fact that, should the company decide to cooperate fully, it may give up opportunities to assert important privileges that it might otherwise raise. Moreover, complete cooperation with the government serves to educate the government about the company's position. For example, if the company has already completed an internal investigation, it may be asked to waive any applicable privileges and to make a resulting report available. Unlike in a civil proceeding, where cooperation with regulatory authorities (such as the SEC) is almost always the preferred approach, the decision to cooperate with the government in a criminal investigation may be much more difficult, insofar as a subsequent effort to oppose the government (should such a change of heart be necessary) would be impeded by the loss of a significant tactical advantage—the loss of surprise. In criminal cases, the government is not afforded the same broad rights of discovery available in civil proceedings. It is entirely possible for a prosecutor to have no significant knowledge of the defense position until after the start of the trial.

On the other hand, the privileges that the company may assert are limited. There is, most importantly, no Fifth Amendment privilege against self-incrimination for companies. Furthermore, almost any kind of evidence, except illegal wiretaps or privileged material, whether admissible in court or not, can be considered by a grand jury. Therefore, the company's ability to oppose a grand jury investigation is to some extent restricted, and the prosecutor may even consider the company's extensive zeal in such opposition to constitute obstruction of justice. Moreover, the prosecutor's ultimate decisions about indictment of the company may be affected by the extent of the company's cooperation. And corporate management may wish to demonstrate cooperation as a matter of policy or public relations.

One issue that will almost inevitably arise, as the company begins to wrestle with the issue of cooperation, is the extent to which it is appropriate for a public company or its executives to offer anything *other* than complete cooperation with the government. Here, it is useful for executives to appreciate the fact that the U.S. system of justice affords those being investigated certain fundamental rights, and it is not unpatriotic to take advantage of them and, accordingly, to offer a defense that is disciplined and vigorous. Among the available rights is the Fifth Amendment privilege against self-incrimination, though this is available only to individuals and not to the company. Insofar as, in fraud cases, guilt can be established through circumstantial evidence, executives frequently need to understand the importance of the Fifth Amendment privilege and the appropriateness of its assertion even in circumstances in which an executive strongly believes he acted in good faith or made a mere error in judgment. Executives will frequently need to understand that it demonstrates no lack of virtue to take full advantage of those constitutional protections designed to protect the innocent from unwarranted prosecution.

Unfortunately, many of these determinations regarding cooperation, at least as a threshold matter, must be made quickly at the outset of an investigation, at a time when the company may have very little information. Most experienced practitioners find the best stance initially to be one of courteous professionalism, in which the adversary role of counsel is recognized throughout, but in which reasonable accommodations can be extended on both sides. The company should avoid an early appearance of active cooperation, which may arouse a reaction of anger if the cooperation later needs to be withdrawn.

Producing Documents to the Prosecutor

At some point the process of assembling documents in response to the subpoena must commence, and it usually begins with the threshold question of how broad the search of the company's files should be. Typically, the subpoena will be so broad as to comprehend all files of the company relevant to the perceived scope of the investigation. Even with a more narrowly drawn subpoena, questions often arise involving whether an attempt should be made to search every file that might, in any way, bear upon the matter. For example, questions may arise as to whether to review files regarding transactions not directly relevant to the scope of the investigation, but related to it because the same executives were involved, or the same transactions or products were involved in different geographical locations. In this respect, the issues that arise out of a criminal subpoena are comparable to those that arise when a civil request for documents has been received. No single answer can be given as to how broad the scope of the search for documents responsive to a criminal subpoena should be. Overall, the operating principle should be one of reasonableness.

One issue that will frequently surface in a criminal investigation, but not in a civil investigation, arises out of individual executives who have their own files that they consider personal and therefore not called for by a subpoena directed to the company. The company must be diligent in locating such files and should recognize early on that there is no such thing as a "personal" file relating to company business. Such files almost invariably are unearthed, and, although the government attorney usually understands that an initial search will not always turn up every piece of paper, the later new documents are uncovered, the more difficult the situation becomes and the more dangerous the documents can be. For the company, the problem can be serious insofar as the company can be held in contempt for failing to produce subpoenaed documents, even if the employee with physical possession has refused to produce them to the grand jury or to the company based upon his personal Fifth Amendment privileges. Documents maintained by the company are not protected by the Fifth Amendment.

Part of the process of assembling and producing documents may involve selection of a custodian to authenticate the records before the grand jury. The custodian of corporate records may be required to testify as to the authenticity of documents produced in response to a subpoena *duces tecum* and that the documents produced are those called for by the subpoena. A custodian of corporate records may not assert the Fifth Amendment privilege on the ground that the act of production of the documents is itself incriminating, so long as the act of production is not used against the custodian in a subsequent criminal prosecution of the custodian.

If the company has a document retention program pursuant to which documents are periodically discarded or destroyed, upon receipt of a subpoena *duces tecum* the program should be stopped immediately so that responsive documents are not thereby lost. It may be possible, depending on how the document retention program is carried out, to discontinue only a portion of the program so that only documents dealing with the areas apparently under investigation (defined prophylactically in the broadest possible terms) are excepted from periodic destruction.

As noted earlier, subpoenas *duces tecum* are usually very broad—broader typically than the government actually needs for its investigation or, for that matter, usually expects to get. Thus, as soon as possible, company counsel will need to contact the government attorney in charge of the investigation to discuss narrowing the scope of the subpoena and to work out a timetable for producing the documents. The best approach in any particular case will be dictated by the circumstances, and it is for this reason that the attorney must be thoroughly familiar with the company's business and the documents, including the types, volume, and location. The government may accept a staggered production of documents in which the government will specify which categories of documents are to be produced first, with the production of other categories being reserved. It will also be necessary to determine whether the government wants the documents produced directly to the grand jury with a witness to provide authentication, or whether it would be satisfied having the documents produced to an agent of the grand jury.

Counsel should try to reach an agreement in writing with the government before documents are produced stating that, when the proceedings are concluded, the documents will be returned and, if anyone other than the grand jury requests access, counsel will be informed and given an opportunity to object. The government will usually agree to return documents and give notice of requests by third parties.

Initial Contacts with Counsel for Individual Employees

While documents are being gathered and produced to the grand jury, it usually makes sense to find out who is representing other recipients of subpoenas and contact them. In an investigation of accounting irregularities, there are likely to be any number of lower-level employees with knowledge of the situation, and it would not be surprising for some to receive personal subpoenas. If the company is taking a stance of cooperation, the identity of such witnesses may be volunteered to the prosecutor. Although a judgment must be made in each case, it is often beneficial for company counsel to share and exchange information with counsel for individual employees. A comparison of the subpoenas issued can sometimes provide leads in determining the scope and focus of the investigation. Such a comparison may also provide insight into whether there are targets and non-targets and provide a basis for predicting the government's plan. On the other hand, on occasion, the company may wish to disassociate itself completely from some executives under investigation and, therefore, may not favor a comprehensive joint defense. In these circumstances, the company may conclude that it is more important not to disclose information than to find out what others know.

To the extent a joint defense is appropriate, counsel should discuss the briefing procedures and the procedures for exchange of statements and debriefing memoranda with regard to witnesses who are later to be called to testify before the grand jury. It is generally the rule that information in documents such as debriefing memoranda prepared by attorneys and exchanged pursuant to a joint defense effort, which would otherwise be protected by the attorney-client privilege, retain their privileged character. The exchange of witness interview documents and debriefing memoranda prepared by lawyers does, though, present some risk of disclosure in discovery in a civil case and that risk must be evaluated.

The risk of disclosure in a civil case presents difficult strategic decisions. If the criminal case is more likely than not to go to trial, counsel must interview witnesses and exchange as much information as possible to enable counsel to prepare. If, however, it appears that the criminal case will not go to trial, interviews of witnesses and debriefing memoranda, if undertaken, present a risk of discovery in a civil case that may outweigh the need for the information in the context of the government investigation. If counsel does not know if the criminal case will go to trial, the safest course is probably to prepare the witnesses jointly and exchange information and memoranda. The first battle will be with the government, and the company cannot afford to be unprepared for the fight.

Employee Interviews

As in civil proceedings, the conduct of witness interviews is an important part of the formulation of a defense. In the context of a criminal investigation, though, the timing of such interviews poses a particular challenge in that the interviews usually can be conducted more effectively if documents are first reviewed, but there ordinarily is an urgent need for the results of the interviews before finalizing negotiations with the prosecutor relating to the subpoena *duces tecum* which, in turn, normally precedes a full-scale file search.

Where a criminal investigation has been commenced, therefore, it is frequently advantageous to follow a sequence in which counsel begins with one or two brief exploratory interviews of executives having general responsibility for the areas of the company's business relevant to the investigation. An experienced lawyer in these circumstances will always be skeptical about the information obtained in the early stages because it may later turn out that the information came from a tainted source, but every effort should be made to identify executives whose conduct is not likely to be the focus of the criminal investigation. These interviews can be followed by a highly selective search of files most likely to contain relevant and sensitive documents. This background helps the lawyers organize the balance of the fact-gathering process in a reasonable way since they will then have obtained a substantially complete list of significant present and former employees and will have begun the process of document examination.

As in civil proceedings, some employees may refuse to participate in an interview. Presumably, any employer may reasonably require an employee to supply information to counsel on a subject within the employee's scope of employment. If the employee refuses, dismissal is the ultimate sanction. Notwithstanding the probable power to compel an interview, though, it is by no means clear that the power should be exercised. An unwilling employee is likely to be an uncooperative interviewee, and a discharged employee might retaliate by approaching the government and ultimately rendering testimony shaded as much as possible against his former employer. In such a circumstance, outright fabrication of adverse testimony has even been known to occur. As an alternative to discharge, the company may want to consider other means of gaining the desired information. Other, more cooperative employees can provide a framework within which relevant conduct can be considered, and the worst can sometimes justifiably be assumed based on an employee's reluctance to speak.

If a reluctant employee has retained counsel, it will frequently be the case that an interview can proceed on the basis of a joint-defense agreement. As noted earlier, such arrangements can be advantageous as a means of evaluating the probable exposure to prosecution and facilitation of a defense. On the other hand, because such joint-defense arrangements require confidentiality, which can be waived only with the consent of all parties involved, the company may find itself not only associating with positions it would never endorse but also possessing information it is not at liberty to disclose, even if it should desire to take a cooperative stance with the government. For such reasons, it may be best for company counsel and the employee to confer informally before proceeding with a joint-defense arrangement.

Once the interview process has commenced, it is particularly important, in light of the criminal investigation under way, that employees understand the importance of accuracy in describing their recollection of events. The term *accuracy* implies not only truthfulness but also a critical care to convey information on the basis of *testimonial quality* knowledge—that is, based on personal observation and recollection, as opposed to speculation and surmise. Although, of course, counsel should not foreclose the opportunity to hear a witness's suspicions and guesses, it is essential that the employee understand the difference and not get into a pattern of loose talk that will serve him ill if he is eventually called into the grand jury room.

Every experienced trial lawyer has encountered the situation in which, by reason of repeated recounting of a given story by a witness, a point is reached at which the witness is no longer able to draw a cognitive distinction between what the witness actually perceived and what has been discussed on prior occasions. There is considerable propensity for that type of confusion to develop in the course of a criminal investigation, particularly where the witness is repeatedly exposed to documents in an effort to refresh his recollection and suggestions as to the explanations for a given document and alternative descriptions of a particular meeting are pressed upon him by counsel. There is an obvious tension between the desire of counsel to learn as much as possible, as soon as possible, and the vital need to avoid confusing a witness by repeated preparatory interview sessions as the information is being developed. The best interviewer of a witness would, of course, be an attorney who knew exactly what had occurred, because that attorney would be best able to probe the accuracy of the witness's recollection when it deviated from the facts the interviewer knew to be true. Although that ideal can never be achieved in a criminal investigation involving complex transactions, experience suggests the importance of care in the interviewing process, so that when the employee is finally being prepared for his grand jury testimony, counsel will be sufficiently well-informed to contribute to a grand jury appearance in which the witness testifies truthfully and accurately and does not incorrectly implicate his employer. Although counsel cannot remake the facts, careful preparation can minimize the danger that a company will be indicted on inaccuracies and speculation that should not have found their way into the record.

Counsel experienced in criminal matters is also painfully aware that full disclosure from the client is not always easy to obtain. Civil case interviewing techniques may have to be modified to elicit information from persons who believe their own conduct to be criminally suspect, particularly where the conduct involved the circumvention of internal controls or departures from well-established business norms.

As with civil proceedings, development of a relationship with a witness that will produce meaningful disclosure is, of course, a matter of personal style on the part of counsel. Despite the urgency created by the criminal investigation, everyone should recognize that the process of obtaining information may take a little time and perhaps a series of conversations. The selection of counsel to conduct the interview is obviously important. Senior executives are unlikely to "confess" to a multiperson interview team that includes youthful-looking associates. Not infrequently, the interview will have to be conducted solely by a senior member of the team, and the best disclosures have sometimes occurred in a completely informal environment.

During the interview itself, the best interviewing attorneys are respectful and explicitly disavow any function as a judge or critic of the executive's conduct. As the interview proceeds, effective counsel is also sensitive to those areas in which the witness appears reluctant or to be holding back. Counsel may find it unnecessary in a particular case to encourage a complete confession at a preliminary stage. When a senior executive admits to engaging in conduct that suggests complicity in a crime, it will be apparent that a major criminal problem exists, and at the initial stage it may be preferable to refrain from pressing hard for greater detail.

The Testimonial Grand Jury Phase

Once documents have been produced to the government, and the government has had an opportunity to review them, a criminal investigation typically proceeds into a new phase: the government's procurement of testimony. During this phase, government agents or prosecutors will either seek to interview corporate employees and other witnesses or subpoena them to testify before the grand jury. Frequently, law enforcement agents conduct an initial round of interviews, and the witnesses who are to testify before the grand jury are selected based upon those interviews. On the other hand, in some situations no preliminary interviews are conducted and interviews and grand jury testimony are pursued simultaneously, or the grand jury sessions occur before witnesses are interviewed.

Before a witness actually appears before a grand jury, careful preparation is critical. Memorializing the debriefing of witnesses who have just testified is equally important and, with diligence, defense counsel may become as knowledgeable about the government's case as is the prosecutor. Although some prosecutors may try to interfere with the counsel's debriefings, prosecutors have no right to do so. In addition, some prosecutors will seek to impose an order of secrecy upon the grand jury witness. There is no authority for preventing disclosure by the witness to his attorney.

Preparing a witness to testify before the grand jury is a significant undertaking, even if it is only for the production of documents. The witness is utterly alone in a treacherous situation where the witness must accurately answer questions posed inevitably in a leading fashion by a skeptical, and often hostile, prosecutor. The prosecutor seems irritated with certain answers—which he communicates quite effectively—and the grand jurors have blended into the furniture, save for the occasional snicker, which is produced on cue whenever the prosecutor wants to suggest to the witness that his testimony is not credible. Everything the witness says in this environment is under oath and recorded for possible use later. Anxiety is in no short supply.

And there is no quick relief. A grand jury witness does not have the same rights as someone who has been arrested and is being interrogated by the police. There is no right to refuse to speak unless the witness can assert a constitutional or other privilege. A witness has no recognized right to be advised of his Fifth Amendment privilege not to be compelled to be a witness against himself. A witness has no right to be told that he is a potential defendant or target of the grand jury investigation. A witness has no right to have counsel present in the grand jury room, although a witness may leave the grand jury room to consult with counsel. And there is no constitutional right to have counsel appointed at the grand jury stage because no criminal proceeding has yet been initiated nor is it the equivalent of a custodial police interrogation.

To a limited extent, prosecutorial policy may provide a witness with some minimal protections. For example, it has been the policy of the United States Department of Justice to advise witnesses of their Fifth Amendment privilege against self-incrimination. Similarly, it is the policy of the Department of Justice to advise a witness that he is a target, if such is the case. On the whole, though, the process of testifying before a grand jury is fraught with peril. And once the witness has entered the grand jury room, he is almost entirely on his own.

A particular challenge to the grand jury witness is the preservation of applicable privileges against testimony. These are obviously important to the company's and the witness's criminal defense. They are also important to the defense of the parallel civil litigation. Before the grand jury, four privileges in particular come into play: the Fifth Amendment privilege against self-incrimination, the attorney-client privilege, the attorney work-product doctrine, and the joint-defense privilege.

The Fifth Amendment Privilege

The Fifth Amendment privilege against self-incrimination stands out in importance in a criminal investigation. As mentioned at the outset, the privilege itself is *personal*, meaning that it applies only to natural individuals. For documents, it protects only the compelled production of self-incriminating documents that are the personal property of the person claiming the privilege or papers in the person's possession in a purely personal capacity.

A witness may assert the privilege on the basis that the answers may be incriminating under either state or federal law and may also assert the privilege on the basis that the answers may be incriminating under foreign law, although the authority for that is less clear. The privilege must be asserted in response to each individual question; a blanket refusal to answer is not adequate.

The privilege against self-incrimination can be claimed in any proceeding whether it is civil or criminal, administrative or judicial. As shall be considered later, the privilege may also be asserted at a deposition taken in a civil case. The compelled testimony must expose the witness to possible criminal prosecution. A witness may not refuse to answer because it would place him in danger of physical harm, degrade him, or incriminate a third party.

As a matter of practice, grand jury targets can usually avoid the personally unnerving experience of asserting the Fifth Amendment privilege in front of the grand jurors by providing the prosecutor with a letter confirming the witness's intention to assert the privilege. Justice Department policy states that "if a 'target' of the investigation . . . and his/her attorney state in writing and signed by both that the 'target' will refuse to testify on Fifth Amendment grounds, the witness ordinarily should be excused from testifying unless the grand jury and the U.S. Attorney agree to insist on the appearance." The company may be well-advised to utilize this procedure to avoid potential prejudice and embarrassment and to avoid the not uncommon situation in which an executive is provoked into departing from his Fifth Amendment silence and begins answering questions in the grand jury room.

When a grand jury witness, in response to a question, does not assert the privilege but instead gives an answer that may be incriminating, an express waiver will be deemed to have been made. An unintentional waiver can be exceedingly unfortunate because, once a witness voluntarily reveals incriminating facts, he may not thereafter refuse to disclose the details. Once the waiver has occurred, for each subsequent question the appropriate determination is whether a responsive answer would subject the witness to a "real danger of further incrimination."

A witness who has previously discussed facts relevant to a grand jury investigation with an FBI agent, an investigator, or a government attorney may still assert the Fifth Amendment privilege before the grand jury as to testimony concerning those same facts. Likewise, a witness who has testified before the SEC or in a civil deposition may still assert the Fifth Amendment privilege before the grand jury as to the same facts.

The Attorney-Client Privilege

As in civil proceedings, the attorney-client privilege is applicable in proceedings before a grand jury. The privilege excuses a witness from testifying about (a) a communication, (b) made in confidence, (c) to an attorney by a person who is, or is about to become, a client, (d) for the purpose of obtaining legal advice from that attorney. The privilege is available to corporate clients as well as to individuals. It applies to communications from the attorney to the client as well as those from the client to the attorney.

Of particular significance to grand jury testimony is the fact that the attorney-client privilege may be waived where there has been a *voluntary* disclosure of otherwise privileged matter. Disclosure made pursuant to court order is not voluntary. Disclosure made pursuant to grand jury subpoena *duces tecum*, in contrast, *is* voluntary, insofar as the claim of attorney-client privilege can be asserted and maintained by a timely objection to the subpoena. Accordingly, as in response to a civil document request, preservation of the attorney-client privilege before a grand jury requires a thorough review of documents to eliminate privileged materials before supplying them to the grand jury.

The Attorney Work-Product Doctrine

The attorney work-product doctrine often operates closely with the attorney-client privilege. The doctrine protects written statements, private memoranda, and personal recollections prepared or formed by the attorney "in the course of preparation for litigation after a claim has arisen." It does not cover work performed for independent reasons that may have some application to a litigation later. The privilege is a *qualified* one, meaning that, upon a showing "of undue hardship" or "substantial need," documents otherwise covered by the doctrine may be ordered produced.

Both the attorney-client privilege and the work-product doctrine are subject to an important limitation. That is the so-called "crime fraud exception." Pursuant to that exception, otherwise-privileged communications that further an ongoing or future crime or fraud are not protected as work product or, for that matter, as attorney-client confidences. To the extent that the privilege has been invoked to prevent disclosure of communications with counsel regarding ongoing misreported items in the company's financial statements, the privilege's applicability may be challenged.

The Joint-Defense Privilege

The joint-defense privilege, already mentioned earlier, is applicable when otherwise-privileged information is disclosed to actual or potential co-defendants in the course of a joint defense. The privilege applies, at its broadest, to any exchanges made for the purpose of a common defense. These might include discussions between a potential defendant and counsel for other potential defendants, disclosures to agents retained by counsel for purpose of pursuing a common defense, and possibly even to discussions among potential co-defendants themselves.

For reasons discussed earlier, the joint-defense privilege is particularly important in the context of a criminal investigation arising out of accounting irregularities, given the usefulness of communications among those involved as a means of learning the focus and scope of the investigation. It is therefore of great importance that, in such a criminal investigation of accounting irregularities, a sufficient *community of interest*, at least among some of those involved, will frequently exist so that the joint-defense privilege may be properly invoked. The joint-defense privilege applies even if those sharing the information are not allies in all respects as long as the information disclosed is in furtherance of some common interest. Ordinarily, subjects and targets of a grand jury will have a sufficiently common defense interest so that their disclosures will be covered by the privilege.

The joint-defense privilege cannot be waived by disclosure to third parties without the consent of all parties who share the privilege. Such a disclosure by a member of the defense group would waive the privilege only as it applied to that party. As a practical matter, this may limit the advisability of the company entering into a joint-defense arrangement insofar as nondisclosure might violate otherwise applicable disclosure responsibilities or render any cooperation with the government less valuable.

Two additional points should be made regarding the joint-defense privilege. First, although the privilege applies to communications between various clients and counsel involved in joint-defense efforts, it is in practice inadvisable for executives themselves to attend all joint-defense meetings. Executives attending such meetings may come away with information they did not know before, and such information can influence the executive's memory of events or may convince the executive to make a proffer with the required information. It is possible that a nervous executive will inadvertently disclose joint-defense material during an interview with the government or in grand jury testimony, and such disclosure can waive the privilege as it applies to that executive. The more prudent approach is to limit the group to defense attorneys and for each attorney to relay joint-defense information to the executive when the attorney feels it appropriate.

Second, any joint-defense group member may waive his right to invoke his privilege by compromising the confidentiality of the information shared, even though such a waiver does not waive the privilege for all participants. Because the attorney-client privilege may be waived even through inadvertent disclosure, it is important to keep tight control on the dissemination of the information to ensure that it not reach parties beyond the joint-defense group. A joint-defense agreement that binds the participants to strict confidentiality should be drafted.

Prosecutorial Status and Immunity

The government divides witnesses into three categories: targets, subjects, and witnesses. A *target* is a putative defendant, someone as to whom the government has information that at least currently suggests that this person will likely be indicted. A *subject* is a person about whom the government is not sure. This person could possibly have criminal liability or could be merely a witness. His status could also change during the course of the investigation and frequently does. A person who is a *witness* is one who the government believes has no possible culpability but who is simply asked to give testimony because he or she happens to have some knowledge that would further the investigation. For example, a secretary who might be called to testify that she typed a particular document for her boss would almost certainly be regarded as only a witness. An employee who can supply background information as to the identity of individuals with various responsibilities or the nature of certain corporate procedures would also be a witness.

For those called upon to give testimony to a grand jury, one issue of the utmost importance involves the grant of *immunity*. As a general matter, absent a Fifth Amendment claim of privilege, the duty to give testimony to the grand jury is absolute. However, because it is only from the mouths of those having knowledge of the conduct under investigation that the facts can be ascertained, the government often has no choice but to take evidence from those who would be implicated by what they have to say. Under such circumstances, the government must provide immunity to those whom it compels to testify if such testimony would incriminate the witness. Unless immunity is granted, such testimony will be suppressed along with its fruits if it is compelled over a valid claim of Fifth Amendment privilege.

Two broad categories of formal immunity are recognized: transactional immunity and use immunity. *Transactional immunity* precludes the government from prosecuting a witness for any offense (or *transaction*) related to the witness's compelled testimony. *Use immunity* precludes the government from using directly or indirectly a witness's compelled testimony in a prosecution of that witness. In the federal system, a grand jury witness who is faced with a Fifth Amendment problem may be accorded statutory use immunity in return for testifying. Formal transactional immunity, in contrast, is not available in the federal courts, but can be obtained by an agreement with the prosecutor in the form of a promise not to prosecute. Use immunity is not available to a company because it is contingent upon an assertion of the Fifth Amendment privilege that the company does not have.

Informal immunity, as opposed to the statutory use immunity described above, is sometimes provided by the government. *Informal immunity*, sometimes known as *letter immunity*, is often used to permit an interview of a witness outside the grand jury, frequently as a step in a process resulting in an agreement to cooperate with the investigation.

Prosecutors regard the use of informal immunity as a tool to enhance the effectiveness and efficiency of an investigation and curtail the use of grand jury time. Informal immunity is not governed by statute but is essentially a matter of contract. A witness who has been granted such immunity sometimes later enters into a non-prosecution agreement, essentially conferring a form of transactional immunity whereby, if the witness fully cooperates and testifies truthfully pursuant to the terms of the agreement, the government promises not to prosecute him for the crimes about which he has testified. This promise is generally binding only in the district in which it is made; unlike formal immunity, it may not apply in other federal districts or in state courts. It is not as safe a guarantee for the witness, not only because it is not binding in other districts, but also because a failure by the witness to abide by the agreement's terms may enable the government to prosecute the witness, using the information the witness has already provided. When formal immunity is granted, the government can never use the testimony against the witness, except as part of a prosecution for perjury.

Informal immunity is almost always conferred by a letter addressed to the witness and signed by the prosecutor or his supervisor. Most typically, the letter will recite that the government agrees to forbear from making direct or indirect use of the witness's statements in any subsequent criminal proceeding involving the witness for violations of specific crimes that are then under investigation arising out of the witness's conduct within a specific geographic area or during a specific period of time. The letter typically will also provide that the statements of the witness in the interview may be used against the witness to impeach the witness's testimony in any subsequent proceeding, including a subsequent prosecution of the witness, and either for impeachment or substantive evidence in any subsequent case against the witness for perjury or making false statements under oath. The informal letter will also make explicit that no other agreement exists between the witness and the government.

Because obtaining statutory immunity is a somewhat elaborate internal process within the Department of Justice, informal immunity in the form of an agreement not to prosecute is granted much more frequently, particularly when time does not allow for the more elaborate process to be used.

Corporate Criminal Liability for Employee Actions

Employees who seek to advance the interests of a company in ways that are criminal may cause the imposition of vicarious liability on the company. A criminal investigation of a company's accounting irregularities, accordingly, inevitably poses the risk of criminal liability for the company. Indeed, as the investigation proceeds, the company's liability may be so thoroughly established that the company's stance, to the extent it has been adversarial, will shift to one of cooperation and possibly plea discussions.

Theoretically, a corporation's ability to disassociate itself from the criminal acts of its employees should be aided by the principle of *vicarious liability*. Under that principle, corporate liability for employees' criminal acts is limited to those instances in which the criminal acts were undertaken within the scope of an employee's authority. But what falls within the scope of an employee's authority is interpreted broadly, so broadly that even if an employee acts contrary to instruction or policy, the corporate employer may still be liable. Moreover, the law often imposes on an employer the duty to supervise and control the actions of an employee performing almost any job-related activity. Failure to control an employee's conduct can suggest that the employer *adopted and ratified* the conduct. Or an employee's action may be found to be within the scope of his apparent authority.

It is no impediment to vicarious corporate liability that the offense required a culpable mental state, such as intent or knowledge. For corporate liability to be so imposed, however, the wrongdoing employee must have acted with an intent to benefit the company. This intent-to-benefit rule avoids the anomaly of imposing liability on a company that is the victim, rather than the putative beneficiary, of its employee's criminal conduct. Depending on the particular circumstances, the conduct involved in a deliberate misstatement of a company's financial statements, if serious enough to be the subject of a criminal prosecution, may be found to have been undertaken to benefit the company.

Ironically, a company can also be held accountable for a crime when there is no single employee that could be convicted. This is the result of the *collective-knowledge doctrine*, pursuant to which knowledge can be imputed to a company based on the aggregate knowledge of its employees as a group. Therefore, a company may be found to have knowingly engaged in a crime based on evidence that one employee knew the facts relating to one element of the offense and a second or third employee knew facts relating to additional elements.

Corporate Indemnification for Counsel Fees

Every state (including Delaware and New York, home to a large number of public companies) has legislation providing for corporate indemnification of expenses (including legal fees) of directors, officers, and sometimes other corporate personnel in defending legal action brought against them in their official capacities. These statutes vary but, generally, in order to be eligible for indemnification, the executive must have acted in good faith for a purpose he believed to be in the best interest of the company. When there is a criminal proceeding, an executive normally must have had no reasonable cause to believe that his conduct was unlawful. However, indemnification may be appropriate even if the executive is convicted. And in Delaware and New York, as well as some other states, if the executive is successful on the merits, the law requires that he shall be indemnified. Authorization for indemnification is generally made by the board of directors, provided that the directors are not parties; by the board upon the written opinion of independent legal counsel; or by the shareholders. Notice to the shareholders is sometimes required. Frequently, advance payments are authorized, with the proviso that the executive must undertake to reimburse the company if it is ultimately determined that he is not entitled to indemnification.

Where the executive is designated a *target* of the investigation, the company may generally withhold advancements of counsel fees and ultimately have no obligation to pay these expenses. The company may nevertheless choose to advance these expenses on the basis of the presumption of innocence unless and until the executive is indicted or persuasive evidence of guilt is developed. The same considerations arise when the executive is designated a *subject*, although here the company may conclude that it has a greater obligation to pay attorneys' fees. In either case, the company may want to require an undertaking that it will be reimbursed in the event that it turns out that the executive is culpable. As with any undertaking, if enforcement appears likely to be problematic, adequate security can be arranged.

There may be instances in which the prosecutor or an investigator seeks to obtain the cooperation of a corporate executive by encouraging the company to discipline executives who do not cooperate. For example, if an executive indicates that he intends to assert his Fifth Amendment privilege against self-incrimination, the investigator might ask the company to coerce him into testifying. Similarly, for its own policy reasons the company may wish to dissuade an executive from asserting the Fifth Amendment privilege. There are considerable reasons to resist the pressure to do so. To begin with, there may be some danger of liability if the company fires or disciplines an executive for exercising a constitutional right. Second, the imposition of such discipline implicitly reflects a judgment that any executive who refuses to testify is necessarily guilty. It may well be that the executive is being advised by his attorney not to cooperate without immunity, not because the attorney thinks the executive has any liability, but because the attorney is simply being appropriately cautious.

If the government appears to be proceeding on a theory that the company is a target and the executive is also a target or a subject of an investigation because he furthered the company's interest by criminal means, the company will frequently advance payment of the executive's legal expenses. Particularly at the outset of an investigation, when the executive has not even been formally accused, much less convicted of a crime, allegations that he has furthered the company's interest by illegal means indicate that his need for an attorney arises out of his employment by the company. Under these circumstances, the company may justifiably conclude that it is obligated to pay his legal expenses.

Depending on his level of seniority and the extent of ostensible wrongdoing, a company's refusal to pay an employee's legal expenses in these circumstances can have a serious effect on the morale of its workforce and might be viewed by many as fundamentally unfair. An employee could complain that he got into trouble because he was trying to help the company and, even though he has not been formally accused, the company is refusing to back him up. On the other hand, there may be circumstances where refusal to pay attorneys' fees is appropriate. For example, if it seems clear even at the outset that the employee is guilty and if the employee has violated company rules or policy designed to prevent the company from getting into criminal trouble, then the company may understandably determine not to pay for his representation.

With respect to witnesses, it is normally appropriate that a company pay for their representation by outside counsel. The one factor important to emphasize is that, in this circumstance, it must be clear to the witness and to the attorney that the attorney is representing the witness and not the company. A company that is a target may have interests that conflict with the interests of employees who are witnesses. If an employee decides that he does not wish his attorney to report to the company about the information or testimony the employee has provided the government, the attorney must honor that wish and the company must understand it. An attorney who represents the company as well as the witness will ordinarily not want to accept such a condition.

Separate Counsel for Targets and Subjects

When a criminal investigation has a number of subjects or targets, as will frequently be the case where a criminal investigation has been commenced as a result of accounting irregularities, those involved will often be tempted to seek common representation. The temptation is understandable. Lawyers are expensive. More than that, inefficiencies in communication and work can seemingly be limited when one lawyer is doing the work for several executives at the same time.

Nonetheless, separate counsel for each executive who is the focus of an investigation is often the better course. A lawyer who represents two or more targets or subjects, including a lawyer who represents an individual target and a corporate target, may have an inherent conflict of interest, and the simultaneous representation of such potential defendants is fraught with danger. For example, it may be in the interest of one of the lawyer's clients to cooperate and testify against the other, but the lawyer cannot recommend that course to his client without violating the interests of the other. Moreover, even if the lawyer should withdraw from the representation of the client in whose interest it is to cooperate, the lawyer may put himself in a situation where at trial he has to cross-examine a former client from whom he has received confidential and privileged information. The lawyer cannot do so and his only course may be to withdraw from the representation of both clients.

Nor does a client "waiver" of a conflict necessarily solve the problem. Recent court opinions allow judges to disqualify lawyers who represent more than one person even if both clients waive any conflict. This means that if a lawyer represents more than one person and a conflict develops, a judge may disqualify the lawyer from representing either person even if both provide a waiver.

Even beyond the dangers posed by the potential for conflicts of interest, a hazard arising from the simultaneous representation of several executives in a criminal investigation results from the possibility of allegations of obstruction of justice. When one lawyer represents several individuals, he is fully aware of what each of the targets or subjects is doing and saying with respect to the investigation and he is able to alert someone in the event that a target or subject begins to implicate others. It is unethical, and indeed potentially illegal, for a lawyer to do so, and when one lawyer represents several targets or subjects and the government is making no headway in the investigation, a frustrated prosecutor may look at the lawyer and the company and the possibility of obstruction-of-justice charges. Indeed, there are times when the government is unable to prove the actual offense it is investigating but manages to bring an indictment nonetheless because the target of the investigation has either committed perjury or obstructed the investigation in some way.

Plea Discussions and Sentencing Considerations

In many conspiratorial offenses, the government makes a deal with one of the conspirators and offers him leniency for his testimony against others, including the company. Sometimes this leniency may be immunity from prosecution; at other times it may be a plea bargain to reduced charges, structured in such a way as to lessen the risk of incarceration or, at least, the length of any incarceration. A lawyer who seeks to negotiate with the government on behalf of a subject or target hopes his client will be treated as a witness and not a defendant. Preferably, in exchange for testimony, an executive would receive some form of immunity along the lines discussed above.

If, however, the government is unwilling to offer the executive immunity and the case against the executive is strong, the executive may have no choice but to enter a plea agreement. This also is an arrangement with the prosecutor that is a matter of contract and the terms may vary. A typical plea agreement would be one in which the executive pleads guilty to fewer crimes than the government can readily prove and may include an agreement to cooperate fully with the government. Such a plea agreement is not available in every case. In some instances, the executive will be the ultimate target and there will be no one of significance for him to testify against.

The ability of an executive to obtain formal immunity, a non-prosecution agreement, or a plea bargain varies with the strength of the government's case, the executive's perceived culpability, the government's need for his testimony, and the executive's qualities as a witness. Therefore, a lawyer faced with the task of getting the best possible terms for his client will have one important objective in mind: convincing the government that, to pursue whatever it is seeking to prove against others, the government absolutely must have this particular executive's testimony.

The process by which the lawyer tries to so persuade the government is known as a *proffer*. The lawyer generally finds out from the prosecutor in what areas the prosecutor is looking for testimony and attempts to obtain a promise that, if the executive can provide that testimony, then he will be immunized or some other deal struck. The lawyer then makes representations about what the executive can testify to, but the lawyer tries to be as general or hypothetical as possible so as not to give the prosecutor anything specific enough as a lead. Throughout the process, the lawyer is walking a tightrope. The lawyer must try to give the prosecutor enough to keep him interested, but not so much that the prosecutor can obtain the evidence without the executive's assistance.

Sometimes this is not enough and the prosecutor will want to talk to the executive personally. Before this is done, the executive will request informal immunity by means of the letter agreement described earlier. This is frequently referred to as an *off-the-record discussion* or *proffer discussion*. If these discussions prove fruitful and the prosecutor finds the executive to be a valuable and credible witness, then the prosecutor may offer the executive immunity or a plea agreement.

In the federal system, plea discussions will focus extensively on possible sentences under the Federal Sentencing Guidelines. For most defendants found guilty of a crime (whether by plea or verdict after trial) under these guidelines, the judge has exceedingly limited discretion in imposing sentence. A sentencing range is computed by starting with the *offense level* (a number assigned to each federal offense), to which one adds *points* reflecting the defendant's criminal history, certain aggravating factors particular to the offense (including, for example, enhancements for "more than minimal planning" or "breach of trust") and, for offenses involving fraud (such as accounting irregularities), the points corresponding to the amount of loss. For example, a typical corporate executive convicted of a single count of mail fraud in a scheme resulting in an aggregate loss to shareholders of $2.5 million will, in most cases, be sentenced in the range of 37 to 46 months of imprisonment. If the loss were $10 million, that defendant's sentence would be increased to a range of 46 to 57 months. A corporation convicted of the same offense (assuming it has 200 employees and a member of senior management participated in the scheme) will receive a base fine of $2.5 million, subject to multipliers, resulting in a fine range of $4 million to $8 million. The company may also be ordered to pay restitution and a remedial order may be entered as a condition of the company's probation to address the harm caused by the offense or to prevent its recurrence. The sentencing judge can mitigate the sentence by crediting the defendant with points, but only in a narrowly circumscribed manner. For example, a defendant's sentence can be reduced up to three levels for "acceptance of responsibility" by a guilty plea.

The fact that the sentencing guidelines result in an increased allocation of points corresponding to the amount of loss is, in this context, unfortunate and potentially unjust. At best, calculating shareholder losses resulting from accounting irregularities is a highly imprecise science. Making it all the more so, the main theories for estimating damages have been devised by plaintiffs' experts in civil litigation whose ostensible objectives included exaggeration of such losses to increase shareholder recoveries and, correspondingly, plaintiff attorneys' fees. To the extent that shareholder losses factor into the sentencing guidelines, therefore, the consequences can be devastating. In one case, the CEO of a drug distribution company was sentenced to nine years. In another, a senior executive was sentenced to what, for him, amounted to life in prison: 30 years. Both executives were non-violent, first-time offenders.

For a corporate defendant, the potential sentence can be mitigated by up to three levels if, prior to the offense, the corporation had an effective compliance program (see Exhibit 10–5). Using the earlier example, the fine could be reduced to a range of $2.5 million to $5 million. According to the Federal Sentencing Guidelines:

An "effective program to prevent and detect violations of law" means a program that has been reasonably designed, implemented, and enforced so that it generally will be effective in preventing and detecting criminal conduct. Failure to prevent or detect the instant offense, by itself, does not mean that the program was not effective. The hallmark of an effective program to prevent and detect violations of law is that the organization exercised due diligence in seeking to prevent and detect criminal conduct by its employees and other agents. Due diligence requires at a minimum that the organization must have taken the following types of steps:

1. The organization must have established compliance standards and procedures to be followed by its employees and other agents that are reasonably capable of reducing the prospect of criminal conduct.

2. Specific individual(s) within high-level personnel of the organization must have been assigned overall responsibility to oversee compliance with such standards and procedures.

3. The organization must have used due care not to delegate substantial discretionary authority to individuals whom the organization knew, or should have known through the exercise of due diligence, had a propensity to engage in illegal activities.

4. The organization must have taken steps to communicate effectively its standards and procedures to all employees and other agents, e.g., by requiring participation in training programs or by disseminating publications that explain in a practical manner what is required.

5. The organization must have taken reasonable steps to achieve compliance with its standards, e.g., by utilizing monitoring and auditing systems reasonably designed to detect criminal conduct by its employees and other agents and by having in place and publicizing a reporting system whereby employees and other agents could report criminal conduct by others within the organization without fear of retribution.

6. The standards must have been consistently enforced through appropriate disciplinary mechanisms, including, as appropriate, discipline of individuals responsible for the failure to de-

tect an offense. Adequate discipline of individuals responsible for an offense is a necessary component of enforcement; however, the form of discipline that will be appropriate will be case specific.

7. After an offense has been detected, the organization must
have taken all reasonable steps to respond appropriately to
the offense and to prevent further similar offenses—including any necessary modifications to its program to prevent and detect violations of law.

A federal sentencing judge has no discretion to impose a sentence below
the guidelines-sentencing range. Any such sentence can be challenged by
the government in an appellate court and such sentences have been routinely corrected. The only permitted exception occurs when the defendant
renders significant cooperation to the government, which permits the government (and only the government) to apply to the court for an order
allowing a downward departure from the guidelines range. For most defendants this is a critical juncture in the process, because it is the only
practical way to avoid a sentencing range that requires the imposition of
a jail sentence. And because possible sentencing outcomes in the federal
system have been narrowed and are often reasonably predictable, that critical juncture can arrive early and become dominant in discussions between
counsel and the prosecutor.

Other Responsibilities of Counsel for a Target Company

As a criminal investigation progresses, the company's attorney must
continue to monitor its progress, primarily by interviewing witnesses
called before the grand jury. Witnesses should be promptly and thoroughly debriefed by counsel after their testimony. Debriefing should
be done immediately after the testimony is completed—even a few hours
delay can result in significant memory loss. Efforts should be made to
learn from counsel for other witnesses, pursuant to the joint-privilege
doctrine, the nature of their testimony. Debriefing should include questions about the number of jurors present and the conduct of the proceedings, both to prepare future witnesses and to discover any improprieties that may undermine the validity of any indictments.

In many cases, information about an ongoing investigation is leaked
to the press by witnesses or by the government. Counsel must coordinate

responses to press inquiries so that any statements are consistent with its defense strategy. This is often a tricky problem because the company and its employees will be tempted to respond to all inquiries, but by doing so, they may say something that discloses strategy secrets or that constitutes an admission that the government can use as evidence.

Counsel may also have to respond to additional subpoenas for documents. As the outline of the government's case becomes clearer, he must put together a defense case. Except in the most hopeless of cases, the lawyer's goal will be to persuade the government to decline an indictment. In most instances, the lawyer will make written and oral presentations to the prosecutors and, where necessary, to the prosecutors' superiors. It is almost always possible to get a hearing within the Department of Justice or the U.S. Attorney's office at supervisory levels, and it is sometimes possible to meet with the Assistant Attorney General or U.S. Attorney ultimately responsible for the case.

Many cases are successfully resolved by persuading the government that its case is not likely to succeed at trial or that it should exercise prosecutorial discretion not to seek an indictment. The prosecutor obviously recognizes that no indictment should be recommended unless the prosecutor is personally convinced that the defendant's guilt can be proven beyond a reasonable doubt. In the context of a prosecution of the company arising out of its accounting irregularities, at this late stage the inaccuracy of the financial statements may be assumed and all of the discussions may be centered on whether any single employee acted with the willfulness required for a criminal charge. If no single employee can be charged because of a failure of evidence, the company's position in opposition to an indictment is strengthened.

But even if an executive is likely to be charged, the company may still have arguments against indictment. If the conduct at issue can credibly be characterized as aberrational or if it involved extraordinary efforts to circumvent sound internal controls and compliance procedures, the company may present itself as a victim. The company's early cooperation may be pointed to as evidence of its decision to disassociate itself from the errant executive and as the best argument to avoid indictment. Indeed, there have been apparently hopeless cases in which, because cooperation was begun early—sometimes even before the criminal investigation was commenced by the company's voluntary disclosure—indictment was avoided.

Exhibit 10–5. Federal Sentencing Guidelines: An Effective Program to Prevent and Detect Violations of Law

The precise actions necessary for an effective program to prevent and detect violations of law will depend upon a number of factors. Among the relevant factors are:

1. *Size of the organization*—The requisite degree of formality of a program to prevent and detect violations of law will vary with the size of the organization: the larger the organization, the more formal the program typically should be. A larger organization generally should have established written policies defining the standards and procedures to be followed by its employees and other agents.

2. *Likelihood that certain offenses may occur because of the nature of its business*—If because of the nature of an organization's business there is a substantial risk that certain types of offenses may occur, management must have taken steps to prevent and detect those types of offenses. For example, if an organization handles toxic substances, it must have established standards and procedures designed to ensure that those substances are properly handled at all times. If an organization employs sales personnel who have flexibility in setting prices, it must have established standards and procedures designed to prevent and detect price-fixing. If an organization employs sales personnel who have flexibility to represent the material characteristics of a product, it must have established standards and procedures designed to prevent fraud.

3. *Prior history of the organization*—An organization's prior history may indicate types of offenses that it should have taken actions to prevent. Recurrence of misconduct similar to that which an organization has previously committed casts doubt on whether it took all reasonable steps to prevent such misconduct.

An organization's failure to incorporate and follow applicable industry practice or the standards called for by any applicable governmental regulation weighs against a finding of an effective program to prevent and detect violations of law.

Other factors may influence a prosecutor's charging decision. For example, it may be that by this stage all related litigation has been resolved and the victims of the company's accounting fraud have been made whole by settlement or otherwise. Since one of the purposes of a criminal conviction of the company in the federal system—restitution to victims—has already been accomplished, arguably an additional financial penalty in the form of a criminal fine will be borne by innocent shareholders. In other cases, discussion may center on whether there is a strong prosecutorial interest at stake, such as whether a prosecution of the company serves the goals of specific or general deterrence, or whether other mechanisms, such as enforcement by the SEC or private litigation, are sufficient.

Only if all these efforts prove fruitless and the case cannot be disposed of does a trial become necessary.

Parallel Proceedings

A company caught up in a federal criminal investigation arising out of accounting irregularities must always be alert to the existence of parallel proceedings. These might include state criminal investigations, administrative proceedings, class action litigation, tax investigations, or even congressional hearings. The existence of such parallel proceedings adds still more complexity to the company's problems.

Because of the dual-sovereignty doctrine, it is possible for the federal government and a state to prosecute separately an executive or the company for exactly the same conduct. Double jeopardy prevents the federal government from trying a person twice for the same conduct, but the federal government can try a defendant for the same conduct for which he has been previously tried by a state. Thus, for example, an employee of a public company who causes the dissemination of false and misleading financial statements might be charged by the state with violations of the state laws against the creation of fraudulent business records and might also be charged by the federal government under similar statutes that apply to interstate communication facilities, the mails, or the purchase or sale of securities.

The Department of Justice has a rule that, in normal cases, it will not prosecute a defendant for conduct for which he has previously been prosecuted by a state. But there are exceptions. Moreover, the rule does not apply to state prosecutors. And state prosecutors, who frequently are elected political officials, may feel impelled to bring a parallel prosecution, particularly if it is a case that is likely to generate favorable publicity. Therefore, a lawyer who negotiates with a federal prosecutor on behalf of his client must bear in mind the possibility that he may have a problem with the state prosecutor and must make sure that any agreements with the federal government do not come back to haunt him in negotiating with the state.

Of considerable concern to the company and its officers and directors will also be the civil class action litigations. The existence of this parallel litigation is particularly troublesome during the pendency of a criminal investigation insofar as the defense of one may compromise the defense of the other. For example, it may be important to the defense of the criminal proceeding for a particular executive to assert his Fifth Amendment right against self-incrimination. However, unlike in a criminal proceeding, the assertion of that Fifth Amendment right in a civil proceeding may be used as the basis for a negative inference against the defendant. More than that, a civil jury of normal temperament may be expected to have a severely negative reaction to an executive who so declines to testify before it. As a practical matter, an optimum defense to both the civil and the criminal actions may be impossible.

In a ranking of difficult choices, the company will likely conclude that preserving defenses to criminal charges by having innocent executives assert their Fifth Amendment rights is far preferable, even at the risk of a weakened position in civil litigation. Hence, a settlement of the class action litigation becomes all the more desirable. It may be of some consolation that, while settlement of such litigation in the wake of accounting irregularities is frequently painful, restitution to shareholders may operate to the advantage of those involved in the criminal investigation in negotiations with the prosecutor.

CHAPTER 11

WHAT'S AN AUDIT COMMITTEE TO DO?

Michael R. Young

*Cleopatra: Horrible villain! or I'll spurn thine eyes
Like balls before me; I'll unhair thy head:
Thou shalt be whipp'd with wire, and stew'd in brine,
Smarting in lingering pickle.*

*Messenger: Gracious madam,
I that do bring the news made not the match.*

*Cleopatra: Though it be honest,
it is never good to bring bad news.*

—Antony and Cleopatra, Act II, Scene v

Begin with a proposition: An ounce of prevention is worth a pound of cure. In few other business contexts is that as true as in the context of accounting irregularities. The costs arising out of the discovery of accounting irregularities are extraordinary. Once irregularities have surfaced, a Securities and Exchange Commission (SEC) investigation is all but inevitable. A multimillion dollar settlement of the class action litigation is a given. Delisting by the National Association of Securities Dealers (NASD) or the New York Stock Exchange (NYSE) is foreseeable if not likely. The costs include the possibility of a criminal investigation and, in serious cases, senior corporate executives going to prison. According to one report, once accounting irregularities have surfaced, it is more likely than not that the company will soon be undergoing a bankruptcy or other major structural change.

There are, therefore, compelling reasons for a board of directors to take every reasonable measure to prevent accounting irregularities from occurring in the first place. Here's another one. At its most basic level, the installation of a system to prevent accounting irregularities involves the enhancement of the organization's systems of communication, its flow of information, and its institutional level of integrity. Such improvements will do more than help prevent accounting irregularities. They will also help the bottom line.

Chapter 11 explores the development of a system of corporate governance and financial reporting directed to the prevention and early detection of accounting irregularities. In other words, it explores primarily the configuration and operation of the audit committee. The topics addressed are these. First, the chapter reviews briefly the role of the audit committee in overseeing the integrity of financial reporting systems. Second, the chapter proposes a somewhat new approach to audit committee oversight including, in particular, the identification of just a handful of key objectives. Third, the chapter goes on to discuss the configuration of an audit committee; systems to provide for the flow of information to the audit committee; and, in particular, the audit committee's interaction with senior management, the outside auditor, and internal audit. Finally, the chapter gives some practical advice on maximizing the effectiveness of audit committee oversight.

Financial Reporting and the Audit Committee

The audit committee has not always been viewed as a keystone to a successful financial reporting system. Thirty years ago, the notion of an active audit committee was referred to as not much more than a "concept" worthy of debate. Responsibility for financial reporting, much like every other aspect of corporate conduct, was viewed as falling primarily on senior management.

More recently, however, perceptions of corporate governance have taken into account the following. No matter how good its intentions, senior management will always be subject to pressure for performance. The pressure will come from shareholders. It will come from creditors. It will come from financial analysts. A viable system of financial reporting has to accept the reality that such pressure will exist.

While it is incumbent upon senior management to strive to the utmost for integrity in financial reporting, the evolving view is that senior management therefore needs support. That support is to come from the board of directors. It is increasingly the view that it is a board function to see that the fundamentals of a working financial reporting system are in place and that those fundamentals will act as a check and balance on management to keep the pressure from getting out of hand.

An entire board of directors, of course, is too clumsy to effectively fulfill this objective. It is thus that serious responsibility for integrity in financial reporting is being placed upon a committee of the board—the audit committee. Hence the increasing attention given to the audit committee's responsibility in overseeing management's installation of a financial reporting system that minimizes the risk that accounting irregularities will occur. As summarized by former SEC Chairman Arthur Levitt in his seminal September 28, 1998, speech, "qualified, committed, independent and tough-minded audit committees represent the most reliable guardians of the public interest."

Checklists, Checklists, Checklists

For an audit committee seeking to fulfill this objective, one thing is for sure. It will find no shortage of checklists of tasks for the audit committee to undertake. Checklists for audit committees have been published by virtually all the national accounting firms in their audit committee how-to books. Checklists have been published by the AICPA. Checklists regularly appear in newsletters, articles, and committee recommendations. Checklists are seemingly everywhere.

There is just one problem. If audit committee members were genuinely to undertake all of the tasks listed on the checklists, they would have little time for anything else—like their day jobs. One representative audit committee checklist lists 36 different time-consuming tasks.

Checklists are certainly a handy reference tool, but they carry with them dangers even beyond the need of individual audit committee members to hold a full-time job. One is the danger of what might be referred to as a "checklist mentality"—a mindset that dutifully marching through a checklist will necessarily lead to a successful financial reporting system. The audit profession periodically has to remind itself that a checklist mentality simply does not work. There's no reason to think that such an approach would work any better for an audit committee.

Another weakness with excessive fidelity to a checklist is the danger that, when marching through the checklist, an inclination will exist to give everything equal time. That is to say that a checklist of 36 separate items contributes little to an understanding of those two or three that are critical as compared to others that may be merely important or not really important at all. The critical, the important, and the unimportant all tend to get equal treatment.

Still another problem with a focus on checklists stems from their unhelpfulness in establishing the correct allocation of responsibility between the oversight function of the audit committee and the hands-on responsibilities of those whom the audit committee is to oversee—such as the internal audit department and the outside auditor. For example, one checklist establishes as a supposed duty of the audit committee to "review filings with the SEC and other published documents containing the company's financial statements and consider whether the information contained in these documents is consistent with the information contained in the financial statements." Can we realistically expect an audit committee to do that?

An Approach to Audit Committee Oversight

Let us consider a slightly different approach. It starts with the premise that an audit committee, in seeking to develop a system directed to the prevention and early detection of fraudulent financial reporting, should at the outset establish no more than a handful of key objectives. The audit committee should then—through the use of company employees and outside professionals—put in place a system so that those key objectives are fulfilled. The audit committee should then—again through the use of company employees and outside professionals—monitor the financial reporting system so that the fulfillment of the key objectives is maintained.

A good set of key objectives with which to start might be the following:

- Seek to establish the proper tone at the top
- Be satisfied as to the logistical capabilities of the financial reporting system
- Put in place a system for the immediate detection of financial misreporting

Let's spend a moment on each.

The Tone at the Top

If the audit committee is to accomplish nothing else, it should first and foremost strive to establish the right tone at the top. If the appropriate tone at the top is established and communicated, every division, department, and individual within the organization will be pulling in the same direction. Without the appropriate tone at the top, you haven't got a chance.

What is the appropriate tone at the top? It involves an unrelenting insistence upon accuracy in financial reporting. It involves an unrelenting insistence that numbers are not to be massaged. It involves an unrelenting insistence upon truthfulness as the foremost objective of the corporate enterprise. It is a tone that makes financial misreporting unthinkable.

How does such a tone get established? The obvious place to start is with management. Senior executives must be vividly aware of the unacceptability of massaged financial results. This is a battle for a certain type of corporate culture, and therefore both big and small things mean a lot. Among the big things, the audit committee chairman should emphasize unequivocally and often the dual predicates of truth and transparency as the bases for financial reporting. It is a message that has to be explicitly or implicitly omnipresent in every matter to be addressed.

It is also a message that must be reinforced, and that takes us to small things. Remember that financial misreporting starts out small and in those hazy areas where individuals think they are still being honest. Accordingly, when dealing with senior management, audit committee members must be attentive to any indication of a desire to improperly influence reported results in order to attain performance objectives. Unrelenting vigilance is key. Any senior executive who slips into one of the telltale signs of managed earnings—contrived revenue enhancement, unjustified modification of reserves, even obsessive fidelity to the attainment of quarterly analyst expectations—must be corrected swiftly and unequivocally. Battles for corporate culture are the toughest battles to win.

That effort does not, however, stop with the senior executives. The audit committee must then seek a vehicle for communication of that message down the ranks through the lower levels of the enterprise. For example, those within the sales department must be given to understand that contrived methods to increase reported sales—side letters, quarter-end telephone calls to friendly customers, last-minute discounting that is not revealed to the accounting department—will not be tolerated. Analogous contrivances, such as quarter-end accelerated shipping or, worse, a failure to close the quarter-end books, are to be viewed as forbidden. At all levels of the enterprise, both egregious and subtle manipulations of the numbers are to be perceived as unacceptable.

One obvious vehicle of communication is a written code of conduct or mission statement, but let us candidly admit that such a written document can be almost useless at best and counterproductive at worst. It can be almost useless because a written document doesn't stand a chance against a corporate culture that goes the other way. It can be counterproductive when the chasm between the written document and the corporate culture becomes so wide that it suggests that the document's authors are somewhere between out of touch and evil.

How to get the word out? There really is little choice but to rely on the senior executives. They have the day-to-day contact with the lower levels, and they have to be the ones to see that an appropriate tone is communicated and reinforced. That objective, therefore, should be plainly understood. Where infractions occur—and they will—the audit committee should satisfy itself that the response was swift and unequivocal.

Key to maintaining the tone at the top will be sensitivity to pressure. Again, financial misreporting doesn't start with dishonesty—it starts with pressure. The audit committee, therefore, should try to be sensitive to the enormous pressures to which senior executives may be subject. Where necessary, the audit committee should be prepared to act as a counterbalance to that pressure and support senior management in the face of outsiders who would place numerical performance objectives above everything else. That does not mean that management's numerical performance does not matter. It means that the only numerical performance that matters is numerical performance that captures the truth.

More than that, the audit committee will want to be on its guard to keep the board of directors from inadvertently adding to the pressure. The audit committee should keep in mind that compensation systems may inadvertently create undue pressure for ostensibly splendid but substanceless performance. The audit committee should stay on guard for indications of overly aggressive budgets and sales targets. The board will get what it measures, so it has to make sure it measures what it wants. If the board measures only reported earnings, it will get reported earnings. But it may get them at the expense of truth.

Logistical Capability

Desire is one thing, attainment another. Establishment of an appropriate tone at the top, therefore, does not by itself ensure reliability in financial reporting—though it is probably 80% of the battle. The next step is to strive for a financial reporting system that is logistically capable of doing what everybody in the company now wants.

This is not a battle for corporate culture but a battle for staffing and computer systems and, therefore, infinitely easier to deal with. The obvious starting place is to look into whether the accounting department is adequately staffed and supervised. Inquiry should be made as to the adequacy of management information systems. In this area, useful information should not be too difficult to get. If staffing or systems are not adequate, the CFO would probably be pleased to have the opportunity to let the audit committee know.

A system that is adequate in one month, though, may not be adequate in the next. That is particularly so where the corporate enterprise is changing—for example, if it is growing through acquisition. The audit committee of a company that is in transformation, particularly where it is growing through the acquisition of others, should therefore remain sensitive to the effects of change on accounting capabilities and personnel. Frequently, the accounting systems of acquired companies will not be compatible with the accounting system of the acquirer, but the problem will be put off due to the press of events as the next acquisition candidate appears. A conglomerate of newly acquired accounting systems that together function as a Tower of Babel is a recipe for disaster—without even getting to the corporate cultures of the new personnel who have been acquired in the process. Asking about the accounting systems of acquired companies should not be too far down on the audit committee's to-do list.

Immediate Detection of Financial Misreporting

It is a mistake to think that things will always work the way they should. That doesn't mean the audit committee isn't doing its job. It just means that no financial reporting system will ever be completely free from defects. Therefore, it is not enough to establish an appropriate tone at the top and to ensure logistical support consistent with that tone. The audit committee has to assume that, from time to time, things will go wrong. It has to assume that, from time to time, the organization will slip into some level of financial misreporting.

The key is to find out quickly when it happens. The audit committee therefore needs a system that will enable it to be the first, rather than the last, to know. (More about that in a moment.)

A Properly Configured Audit Committee

The attainment of these corporate governance and financial reporting objectives will present significant challenges. If an audit committee is to have any hope of surmounting these challenges, it must have the underlying capability of doing so. That is to say, the audit committee itself must be properly configured. Indeed, proper configuration of the audit committee is not simply a matter of sound corporate governance. Today, it is also a matter of law.

Historically, the configuration of a company's audit committee has been left largely to the discretion of the particular company's board of directors. Thus, the SEC, while becoming increasingly interested in the effectiveness of audit committees, for years declined to enact detailed rules on the matter, deferring almost entirely to the rules of the exchange where the company's stock happened to be listed. The NYSE, for its part, specified that companies were to establish and maintain audit committees comprised solely of independent directors but specified little else. The NASD, while requiring companies to "establish and maintain" an audit committee, did not go as far as the NYSE in requiring all members to be independent: independence was required by only a majority of the audit committee members. The rules of the NASD went on to provide that the audit committee in substance should discuss aspects of the annual audit with the outside auditor.

In December 1999, the SEC approved a new series of rules that are substantially more rigorous. Pursuant to the recommendations of the Blue Ribbon Committee on Improving the Effectiveness of Corporate Audit Committees, the new rules establish enhanced requirements for audit committee membership, independence, sophistication, diligence, and disclosure. For companies whose securities are listed on the NYSE or quoted on Nasdaq, the new rules, which were phased in over a period of 18 months following their approval, require the following. First, an audit committee is to include at least three members (see Exhibits 11–1 and 11–2). Second, with very limited exception, each member of the committee is to be independent (see Exhibits 11–3 and 11–4). Third, each member is to possess (at the time he joins the audit committee or within a reasonable time thereafter) some degree of financial literacy, with at least one member having an accounting or finance background (see Exhibits 11–1 and 11–2). Fourth, the audit committee is to have in place a written charter which is to be filed with the SEC every three years (see Exhibits 11–5 and 11–6). Fifth, the audit committee is to file with the SEC a written report that specifies, among other things, whether the committee recommended to the board of directors that the audited financial statements be filed with the SEC (see Exhibit 11–7).

In some respects, the rules are highly detailed and precise. For example, the "independence" requirements of the NASD specify that the independence prerequisite is not met by a director who was an employee of the corporation or any affiliate for the current year or any of the past three years; by a director who accepts compensation in excess of $60,000 from the corporation or any of its affiliates during the previous fiscal year (other than compensation for board service, benefits under a tax-qualified retirement plan, or nondiscretionary compensation); by a director

---

Exhibit 11–1. New NYSE Rules: Audit Committee Composition

- Each audit committee shall consist of at least three directors, all of whom have no relationship to the company that may interfere with the exercise of their independence from management and the company;

- Each member of the audit committee shall be financially literate, or must become financially literate within a reasonable period of time after his or her appointment to the audit committee; and

- At least one member of the audit committee must have accounting or related financial management expertise.

Exhibit 11–2. New NASD Rules: Audit Committee Composition

Each issuer must have and certify that:

- It has and will continue to have an audit committee of at least three members, comprised solely of independent directors, each of whom is able to read and understand fundamental financial statements, or will become able to do so within a reasonable period of time after his or her appointment to the audit committee; and

- It has and will continue to have at least one member of the audit committee that has past employment experience in finance or accounting, requisite professional certification in accounting, or any other comparable experience or background which results in the individual's financial sophistication.

One director who is not independent and is not a current employee or an immediate family member of such employee may be appointed to the audit committee, if:

- The board, under exceptional and limited circumstances, determines that membership on the committee by the individual is required by the best interests of the corporation and its shareholders; and

- The board discloses, in the next annual proxy statement subsequent to such determination, the nature of the relationship and the reasons for that determination.

---

who is an immediate family member of an individual who is, or has been in any of the past three years, an executive officer of the corporation or any of its affiliates; by a director who is a partner, controlling shareholder, or executive officer of a for-profit firm that received certain types of fees or other payments from the company in excess of a specified level; or by a director who is employed as an executive of another entity where any of the company's executives serve on that entity's compensation committee (see Exhibit 11–4). The NYSE has its own set of comparably detailed "independence" requirements (see Exhibit 11–3).

Viewed more broadly, though, the rules collectively strive for three overall objectives that are fundamental to audit committee effectiveness. These three objectives are:

- Independence
- Financial sophistication
- Willingness to work

Each is a worthy objective and warrants some discussion.

Independence

Foremost, an audit committee should be independent from the senior executives of the company. The reason is obvious. It is a fundamental function of the audit committee to lean against the wind. It is, in other words, a fundamental function of the audit committee to offer reasoned resistance against the desires of management where those desires may compromise integrity in financial reporting.

The task is not for the fainthearted. During difficult times, management itself may be under horrific pressure for bottom-line results. Absent some degree of independence, a natural inclination to sympathize with those in the hot seat might prove almost irresistible. During particularly difficult times, resistance to management's ostensible needs may be perceived as the betrayal of prior favors bestowed. At a minimum, resistance could make board meetings exceedingly awkward.

What is meant by *independence*? As mentioned above, the new rules are highly detailed and complex (see Exhibits 11–3 and 11–4). The underlying concept, though, involves the exclusion of individuals who, for whatever reason, are not in a position to stand up to the tenacious desires of determined management. Excluded from among those possessing independence, therefore, are family members of executives—it probably being no small coincidence that, where accounting irregularities have surfaced, family relationships on the board of directors have been by no means rare. Also excluded from among those possessing independence are outside professionals whose judgment may be influenced due to business relationships with the company. Also excluded are directors whose compensation at another company may be determined by executives the director is theoretically overseeing. Audit committee members should be prepared to tell management what it doesn't want to hear. Relationships that

Exhibit 11–3. New NYSE Rules: Audit Committee Independence

The following restrictions shall apply to every audit committee member:

- A director who is an employee (including non-employee executive officers) of the company or any of its affiliates may not serve on the audit committee until three years following the termination of his or her employment;

- A director (i) who is a partner, controlling shareholder, or executive officer of an organization that has a business relationship (including commercial, industrial, banking, consulting, legal, accounting and other relationships) with the company, or (ii) who has a direct business relationship with the company may serve on the audit committee only if the company's board of directors determines that the relationship does not interfere with the director's exercise of independent judgment. The board of directors should consider, among other things, the materiality of the relationship to the company, to the director, and, if applicable, to the organization with which the director is affiliated;

- A director who is employed as an executive of another corporation where any of the company's executives serves on that corporation's compensation committee may not serve on the audit committee; and

- A director who is an immediate family member of an individual who is an executive officer of the company or any of its affiliates cannot serve on the audit committee until three years following the termination of such employment relationship.

One director who is no longer an employee or who is an immediate family member of a former executive officer of the company or its affiliates, but is not considered independent pursuant to these provisions due to the three-year restriction period, may be appointed, under exceptional and limited circumstances, to the audit committee if:

- The company's board of directors determines that membership on the committee by the individual is required by the best interests of the corporation and its shareholders, and

- The company discloses, in the next annual proxy statement subsequent to such determination, the nature of the relationship and the reasons for that determination.

Exhibit 11–4. New NASD Rules: Audit Committee Independence

"Independent director" means a person other than an officer or employee of the company or its subsidiaries or any other individual having a relationship which, in the opinion of the company's board of directors, would interfere with the exercise of independent judgment in carrying out the responsibilities of a director.

The following persons shall not be considered independent:

- A director who is an employee of the corporation or any of its affiliates for the current year or any of the past three years;

- A director who accepts any compensation in excess of $60,000 from the corporation or any of its affiliates during the previous fiscal year, other than compensation for board service, benefits under a tax-qualified retirement plan, or non-discretionary compensation;

- A director who is an immediate family member of an individual who is, or has been in any of the past three years, an executive officer of the corporation or any of its affiliates;

- A director who is a partner in or a controlling shareholder or an executive officer of any for-profit business organization to which the corporation made, or from which the corporation received, payments that exceed 5% of the corporation's or business organization's consolidated gross revenues for that year, or $200,000, whichever is more, in any of the past three years; and

- A director who is employed as an executive of another entity where any of the company's executives serve on that entity's compensation committee.

may compromise the committee's willingness to do so may impair its effectiveness.

How many members should be independent? This has been a somewhat controversial issue. The new rules of both the NYSE and the NASD generally require that all audit committee members be independent (see Exhibits 11–1 and 11–2). However, in implicit recognition that sometimes a non-independent director is in the position to offer unique benefits to an audit committee, both the NYSE and the NASD include a limited exception permitting the inclusion of a non-independent director under specified circumstances (see Exhibits 11–2 and 11–3). The rules make clear, however, that the inclusion of non-independent directors is intended to be a rarity. Both the NYSE and the NASD rules, for example, provide for the inclusion of a non-independent director only under "exceptional and limited circumstances." Under both the NYSE and the NASD rules, proxy statement disclosure of the non-independent director's participation is required.

At the risk of incurring the wrath of those whose commitment to integrity in financial reporting is unimpeachable, let us pause momentarily on the possibility that, in striving to preclude the participation of non-independent directors, the new rules may have gone too far. Certainly most of the members should be independent. However, an argument could be made that the inclusion of one non-independent member could enhance committee effectiveness. While the committee must be prepared to stand against the desires of management, it must also constitute an integral part of the board and of the company's corporate governance system. The inclusion of a non-independent (i.e., management) member may give the committee important insight into the cultural underpinnings or business rationale for a particular management objective. At the same time, a committee comprised entirely of independent members might correctly or incorrectly be perceived as an inflexible naysayer, giving rise to an ultimately self-destructive mindset of "us v. them." The inclusion of a management representative—as long as he can be squarely outvoted by those possessing genuine independence—may provide management the comfort that its views are being properly considered and that, on balance, the audit committee's conclusions are for the good of the corporate whole. That is particularly so where an unpalatable decision by an audit committee possessing one management member is, nonetheless, unanimous.

Still, the configuration of the audit committee should obviously conform to the rules. Those companies whose securities are listed on the NYSE or quoted on Nasdaq will therefore generally need audit committees comprised solely of independent directors. Perhaps the input of a management representative can then be obtained by including the representative in some audit committee meetings even without formal membership.

Financial Sophistication

Even audit committee members whose hearts are in the right place need to know what they are doing. Therefore, a second fundamental prerequisite of audit committee membership should be some level of financial sophistication.

What kind of sophistication? Here, the rules are particularly vague. The NYSE rules specify only that, "Each member of the audit committee shall be financially literate, as such qualification is interpreted by the company's Board of Directors in its business judgment." The NASD rules are only slightly more informative. They specify that each of the audit committee members must be "able to read and understand financial statements, including a company's balance sheet, income statement, and cash flow statement." (See Exhibits 11–1 and 11–2.)

Broadly speaking, though, experience suggests that audit committee members should possess financial sophistication in two areas. First, audit committee members should possess some working familiarity with the rudiments of generally accepted accounting principles (GAAP) and financial reporting. That's not to say that each member must be a CPA, though at least one CPA is probably a good idea. Rather, the members should possess a basic understanding of such things as the accrual system of accounting, the extent to which (for example) operating cash flow may diverge from reported earnings, and the rudiments of SEC reporting requirements. To say it another way, the members should probably know enough to appreciate that reported earnings does not always mean cash in the bank.

But financial literacy is only the first type of financial sophistication. The second is that members should possess an understanding of corporate governance systems and, in particular, the extent to which non-optimal systems can compromise truthfulness in financial reporting. One of the key functions of the audit committee members will be to keep a sharp lookout for the telltale signs of corruption. The individual members will have to know enough to recognize them when they appear.

Willingness to Work

Audit committee members should not be expected to quit their day jobs, but they have to be willing to work. Obviously they can leverage their talents through the use of employees and outside professionals, but audit committee membership—particularly in a start-up phase, where a viable audit committee has been lacking—will require significant effort and commitment. The willingness to make the effort has got to be there.

The new rules seek to encourage audit committee willingness to make the effort in several ways, one of which is through the requirement of an audit committee "charter" (see Exhibits 11–5 and 11–6). Already in use at a number of public companies, the charter—which must be in writing—is to broadly outline the audit committee's responsibility for oversight of financial reporting. (For a sample, see Exhibit 11–19 at the end of this chapter.) Thus, the new rules of both the NYSE and the NASD provide that a company's charter must specify the scope of the audit committee's responsibilities and how those responsibilities are carried out; the outside auditor's ultimate accountability to the audit committee and the board of directors; the responsibility of the audit committee and the board of directors to select, evaluate, and replace the auditor; the audit committee's responsibility for ensuring the auditor's submission of a formal written statement delineating all relationships between the auditor and the company; and the audit committee's responsibility for engaging in a dialogue with the auditor as to any relationships that may adversely affect independence. A separate SEC rule, which requires public filing of the audit committee charter every three years, ensures that the charter's contents will be adequate to withstand public scrutiny.

Preparation of an effective charter can be something of a challenge. Key components of the charter would include the basic prerequisites of audit committee configuration and, in particular, specification that members should be both independent and financially sophisticated in accordance with the new rules. In addition, the charter should define the audit committee's purpose. In this regard, it is probably wise to avoid a description of the audit committee's purpose in terms of the company's system of "internal control" given expansive interpretations of that term that are

Exhibit 11–5. New NYSE Rules: Audit Committee Charter

Each audit committee must adopt a formal written charter that is approved by the board of directors. The audit committee must review and reassess the adequacy of the audit committee charter on an annual basis.

The charter must specify the following:

- The scope of the audit committee's responsibilities and how it carries out those responsibilities

- That the outside auditor for the company is ultimately accountable to the board of directors and audit committee of the company

- That the audit committee and board of directors have the ultimate authority and responsibility to select, evaluate, and, where appropriate, replace the outside auditor

- That the audit committee is responsible for ensuring that the outside auditor submits to the audit committee a formal written statement delineating all relationships between the auditor and the company

- That the audit committee is responsible for actively engaging in a dialogue with the outside auditor with respect to any disclosed relationships or services that may affect the objectivity and independence of the outside auditor and for recommending that the board of directors take appropriate action to ensure the independence of the outside auditor

now appearing in some of the more recent financial reporting literature. A more limited and more effective statement might define the audit committee's purpose in terms of oversight of the company's system of financial reporting.

All of this should be straightforward enough. The challenge arises from the need to specify how the audit committee is to carry out its responsibilities. In particular, the challenge is to provide some meaningful level of information while, at the same time, avoiding the preparation of a docu-

---

Exhibit 11–6. New NASD Rules: Audit Committee Charter

Each Issuer must certify that it has adopted a formal written audit committee charter. Each Issuer must certify that the audit committee has reviewed and reassessed the adequacy of the formal written charter on an annual basis.

The charter must specify the following:

- The scope of the audit committee's responsibilities, and how it carries out those responsibilities

- The audit committee's responsibility for ensuring its receipt from the outside auditor of a formal written statement delineating all relationships between the auditor and the company

- The company and the audit committee's responsibility for actively engaging in a dialogue with the auditor with respect to any disclosed relationships or services that may affect the objectivity and independence of the auditor and for taking, or recommending that the full board take, appropriate action to ensure the independence of the outside auditor

- The outside auditor's ultimate accountability to the board of directors and the audit committee, as representatives of shareholders, and these shareholder representatives' ultimate authority and responsibility to select, evaluate, and, where appropriate, replace the outside auditor

---

ment that can be unfairly used against the audit committee in the event of litigation. For this reason, too, the audit committee is wise to avoid the "checklist mentality" and to draft the charter in broad, aspirational terms rather than to allow the charter to degenerate into a laundry list of "must do" items. At the same time, it is probably useful to use the charter to remind the audit committee of the requirements imposed by law. The absence of such requirements from the charter will not make them any less applicable.

Beyond the charter, the other main vehicle to encourage audit committee diligence is a written report to be filed once a year as part of the

Exhibit 11–7. New SEC Rules to Implement the Recommendations of the Blue Ribbon Committee

- Require that companies' independent auditors review the financial information included in the companies' Form 10-Q prior to filing

- Require that companies include reports of their audit committees in their proxy statements, stating whether the audit committee has:

  - Reviewed and discussed the audited financial statements with management

  - Discussed with the independent auditors the matters required to be discussed by SAS-61 (Communication with Audit Committees)

  - Received certain disclosures from the auditors regarding the auditors' independence as required by Independence Standards Board Standard No. 1 and discussed with the auditors the auditors' independence

- Require that the report of the audit committee include a statement by the audit committee whether the audit committee recommended to the board of directors that the audited financial statements be included in the company's Form 10-K

- Require that companies disclose in their proxy statements whether their audit committee has adopted a written charter and include a copy of the charter as an appendix to the proxy statement at least once every three years

- Require that companies disclose in their proxy statements information regarding the independence of audit committee members

---

company's proxy statement (see Exhibit 11–7). No specific format for the report is mandated. However, the rules are clear that the substance of the report must include several things. First, the report is to state whether the audit committee has reviewed and discussed the audited financial statements with management. Second, the report is to state whether the audit committee has discussed with the outside auditor matters specified in Statement on Auditing Standards No. 61 (Communication with Audit Committees), which is described below. Third, the report is to state whether the audit committee has addressed with the outside auditor the issue of independence in accordance with the applicable rules. Fourth, the report is to state whether the audit committee recommended to the board that the audited financial statements be included in the company's Form 10-K as filed with the SEC. Apparently for the *in terrorem* effect, the rules provide that the names of the individual audit committee members are to appear below the required disclosures. To the extent that these requirements operate to enhance audit committee diligence, they are thus consistent with the common law which, according to one articulation, requires a board of directors to seek in good faith an adequate corporate information and reporting system (see Exhibit 11–8).

Compliance with all of these requirements is going to take time, and a final note on the issue of audit committee diligence is that audit committee members should be adequately compensated for their efforts. No legitimate question exists that, at whatever the appropriate level of compensation, the company will be getting a bargain. The company's best protection against corruption of its financial reporting system is an optimally functioning audit committee. The benefits will overwhelm the costs.

Exhibit 11–8. Delaware Law

A board of directors' duty of care "includes a duty to attempt in good faith to assure that a corporate information and reporting system, which the board concludes is adequate, exists."

The information and reporting system should "in concept and design [be] adequate to assure the board that appropriate information will come to its attention in a timely manner as a matter of ordinary operations."

(*In re Caremark International Inc.*, 698 A.2d 959, 970 (Del. Ch. 1996))

Ironically, though, the board of directors should probably be on its guard against paying the audit committee members too much. At some level of compensation, audit committee membership would theoretically become an attractive perk to be held onto—thereby giving rise to a potential loss of independence. As in most compensation decisions, there thus exists a need to balance benefits and costs. In that balance, though, the actual expenditure out of the corporate coffers should not be an issue. An effective audit committee is worth it.

The Biggest Challenge: Information

Let's say that, so far, a board of directors has done everything right. Its audit committee is independent. Its audit committee is financially sophisticated. Its audit committee is ready to work, with a perfectly drafted charter firmly in place.

Such an audit committee is now perfectly positioned—to fail. That is, it is perfectly positioned to fail unless it can successfully overcome the biggest challenge. That challenge is lack of access to reliable information.

The reason may be simply stated. It is that, in a normal corporate enterprise, bad news tends not to flow up. Ever since Cleopatra struck her hapless messenger, the self-preservation instincts of even loyal subordinates have cautioned them to selectively keep bad news to themselves. The consequences of reporting bad news can be harsh and the rewards are few. Rarely does one receive stock options for reporting disaster.

The danger of the resulting "Cleopatra syndrome" is potentially the biggest hurdle an audit committee will face. At root, the problem is that the audit committee will remain in perilous danger of functioning in total ignorance. Financial reporting problems will be allowed to fester as executives seek to correct them before the audit committee is in a position to notice. Executives will not appreciate the extent to which, for the reasons described in Chapter 1, temporary bandages may only operate to make the problem worse. Gradually, the problem will grow. And the audit committee will not have a clue.

What makes this breakdown in the information flow to the audit committee ironic is that a normal corporation, no matter how infirm its systems, will ordinarily have any number of well-meaning employees who would be grateful for the chance to describe system corruption if given a non-threatening opportunity. The challenge facing the audit committee, then, is to find a way to tap into that reservoir of candid information and to install a pipeline so that it may flow upward unimpeded. Three potential sources for such information exist. They are senior management, the outside auditor, and internal audit. Not coincidentally, the "guiding principles" of the Blue Ribbon Committee focused attention on precisely these three potential information sources.

Getting Information from Senior Management

Unfortunately, a viable financial reporting system should probably accept that reliable information about system inadequacies will not be regularly made available to the audit committee by senior management. That is not to denigrate the virtue of senior executives or to suggest widespread managerial inadequacy. It is simply a recognition of human nature. Each of us has an understandable reluctance to be completely candid about our own innumerable flaws.

Some—perhaps many—senior executives would be able to rise above that. Senior executives secure with their own abilities and possessed of supreme confidence may be perfectly comfortable undertaking the laudable task of reporting to the audit committee the problems that are growing on their watch. A system that assumes such laudable candor in senior executives, though, is probably assuming too much. It is better to accept that, while striving for virtue, not everyone will achieve it.

Moreover, even secure and candid senior executives may suffer from the same problem that would plague a normal audit committee: No guarantee exists that bad news will flow up to them. A well-meaning senior executive, therefore, may be perfectly willing to share with the audit committee system inadequacies to the extent he is familiar with them. The problem may be that he doesn't fully know what they are.

The potential for managerial unfamiliarity with organizational problems is particularly acute when it comes to one of the most important aspects of the financial reporting system: the environment in which that system is to function. Management is faced with the excruciatingly difficult challenge of placing on subordinates precisely the right amount of pressure for performance: not enough, and the organization does not achieve maximum profitability; too much, and the organization is at risk that massaged numbers will slip into the reporting system. Procurement of reliable information identifying the point at which the pressure has moved from optimal to counterproductive can be difficult. Too numerous to mention are instances in which the underlying cause of financial misreporting was the pressure placed on subordinates by a CEO who would later claim total ignorance about the destructive impact his performance edicts were having.

None of this is to suggest that the audit committee should not be striving to increase senior management's candor. Nothing is ever perfect, and senior executives should be encouraged and admonished to reach into the depths of the organization and to find and report system inadequacies. Still, an audit committee has to accept that even the strongest encouragement or even the sternest admonitions will not completely overcome human nature. A financial reporting system that assumes otherwise is probably destined to fail in the long run.

Getting Information from the Outside Auditor

No financial reporting system relies exclusively on senior management. A second means of access to information about the financial reporting system exists: the outside auditor.

Meaningful, substantive interaction with the outside auditor is fundamental to effective audit committee oversight of financial reporting. If the auditor is genuinely independent and prepared to be candid, the auditor can be one of the most important vehicles for the audit committee to learn what's going on beneath the surface of reported results. Hence the emphasis in the recent literature on the need for the audit committee to ask the auditor tough, probing questions that delve into the crosscurrents of the financial reporting system. Through the outside auditor, the audit committee can learn all sorts of things that it might never get from management.

The audit committee, moreover, should take advantage of this source of information more than once a year. Indeed, under the new rules companies are now required to have their quarterly financial statements subject to outside auditor review. Correspondingly, the auditor is to engage the audit committee in a dialogue at least once a quarter (see Exhibits 11–7 and 11–12). The auditor's quarterly review, moreover, is to be undertaken pursuant to SAS-71 (Interim Financial Information), which es-

tablishes a level of scrutiny beyond the quick once-over that historically had been the convention. In conducting a SAS-71 review, the auditor may inquire into such things as significant changes in the internal
control structure, items that appear to be unusual, changes in accounting practices, and changes in business activities. A SAS-71 review is far
less than a full-fledged audit. But it can still give the auditor new insight into the company's financial reporting system.

The need for the outside auditor to conduct interim reviews thus gives
the audit committee the opportunity to inquire into financial reporting
issues that arose during the quarterly review process, and there is every
reason for the audit committee to take advantage of that opportunity. Accounting manipulations at quarter end is frequently where financial fraud
gets its start. Meaningful auditor involvement in quarterly information
gives the audit committee not only access to improved information, but
more of an opportunity to nip financial misreporting in the bud.

Of course, there is no losing sight of significant impediments to reliance upon the outside auditor for the prevention and early detection of
deliberate financial misreporting. As discussed in Chapter 1, accounting
irregularities typically start out small and well beneath the radar screen
of the materiality thresholds of a typical audit. They start with a particular type of corporate environment, and it is a type of environment to
which a normal once-a-year auditor cannot gain ready access. They start
in hazy areas of financial reporting in which much depends on the judgment of management. And, as the accounting irregularities grow over
time, a preoccupation of the participants becomes the deliberate deception of the outside auditor.

The impediments to outside auditor detection of fraudulent financial
reporting, moreover, are not merely the result of the way fraud starts and
grows. The impediments are also a consequence of the competitive environment of the audit profession and the corresponding desire by auditors to deliver what management has historically seemed to want: an unqualified audit report at the lowest possible cost. Auditors are ultimately
professionals who will seek to be responsive to the desires of their clients. Where the client has placed cost minimization above all else, the
auditors have felt pressure to oblige.

Further impeding the auditor's access to information is the fundamental reality that, no matter how hard an auditor tries, determined executives will always be able to get away with some level of deception. How-

ever deep the auditor is encouraged to probe, those within the accounting department can always take the fraud one level deeper. If the business community were to find such a situation unacceptable, it could always encourage the audit profession to abandon the audit sampling and professional skepticism approaches that constitute the hallmarks of a modern GAAS audit. In other words, a new system of audits could be installed along the lines of a fraud investigation or forensic investigation in which the auditors essentially don't believe anything anybody at the company says. That is, basically, the approach taken where accounting irregularities have surfaced, as discussed in Chapter 5. In fact, variations of this kind of approach in the context of everyday audits are active consolidation by leaders of the account by profession. One problem with such an approach, though, is timeliness—an "audit" conducted entirely along such lines would almost have to be perpetual. Another problem is cost. The forensic investigation of the books and records of one troubled public company, for example, required more than 1,000 auditors and cost more than $3 million per day.

In seeking reliable information from the outside auditor, some of these impediments an audit committee can do something about, and some it cannot. Ultimately, though, one thing will be true. The auditor, as an outside professional, will be responsive to the desires of its client. In the end, therefore, if the audit committee makes clear to the outside auditor its desire for an enhanced audit function and improved systems information, good auditors will find a way to provide the desired level of service. That is particularly so if the audit committee is willing to pay for it.

So what kinds of information should the audit committee ask the outside auditor for? Here are some possibilities:

Environmental Information

Foremost, the audit committee will want to encourage the outside auditor to do its best to seek, find, and candidly report information about the financial reporting environment. Are people under too much pressure? Are they reluctant to report bad news? Is there a danger they are camouflaging results? These are the types of questions that auditors hate to be asked. But they are also the types of questions that are fundamental to the prevention and early detection of financial fraud.

Logistical Capabilities of the Financial Reporting System

An easier issue to explore with the outside auditor will be the logistical capabilities of the financial reporting system. Both the law (see Exhibits 11–9 and 11–10) and good business sense require the company to maintain its books and records in such a way that they fairly reflect corporate transactions and events. Staffing, sophistication, computerization, software inadequacies—all aspects of the system's logistical capabilities may accordingly warrant inquiry. On this subject, the auditor's candid views should be easier to obtain. Logistical inadequacies in the accounting system only make an audit more difficult.

Exhibit 11–9. Foreign Corrupt Practices Act

"Every issuer which has a class of securities registered pursuant to section 781 of [the Securities Exchange Act of 1934] shall:

(A) make and keep books, records, and accounts, which, in reasonable detail, accurately and fairly reflect the transactions and dispositions of the assets of the issuer; and

(B) devise and maintain a system of internal accounting controls sufficient to provide reasonable assurances that:

(i) transactions are executed in accordance with management's general or specific authorization;

(ii) transactions are recorded as necessary (I) to permit preparation of financial statements in conformity with generally accepted accounting principles or any other criteria applicable to such statements and (II) to maintain accountability for assets;

(iii) access to assets is permitted only in accordance with management's general or specific authorization; and

(iv) the recorded accountability for assets is compared with the existing assets at reasonable intervals and appropriate action is taken with respect to any differences."

(15 U.S.C. § 78m(b)(2))

Exhibit 11–10. SEC Rule: Book and Records

"No person shall, directly or indirectly, falsify or cause to be falsified, any book, record or account subject to Section 13(b)(2)(A) of the Securities Exchange Act."

(17 C.F.R. § 240.13b2-1)

Managerial Bias in the Application of GAAP

Another topic that may yield useful information involves the bias of management in the application of GAAP. Is management overly aggressive? Overly conservative? Is it trying to get it right? By their nature, GAAP will probably always depend to a meaningful extent on the judgment of management in their application. A decent auditor will come to a view as to how that judgment is being exercised. The auditor should be encouraged to share it.

On this issue, the audit committee will be assisted by new amendments to GAAS that will likely operate to increase auditor candor (see Exhibits 11–11 and 11–12). Intended to cultivate an "open and frank discussion" between the audit committee and the outside auditor, the new amendments require the auditor to discuss with the audit committee "the auditor's judgments about the quality, not just the acceptability, of the entity's accounting principles as applied in its financial reporting." Under the amendments, this discussion is to include such matters as the consistency of the company's accounting policies and the clarity and completeness of the company's financial statements. In order to further foster open and frank discussion, the auditor's judgments need not be communicated in writing. The amendments also require the auditor, where appropriate, to seek to discuss such matters with the audit committee not only in the context of the annual financial statements, but on a quarterly basis as well (see Exhibit 11–12).

The Level of Cooperation and Difficulties Encountered

At bottom, the audit committee is trying to smell a rat. It is trying to get reliable, candid information about the environment or culture in which

---

Exhibit 11–11. New Amendments to Statement on Auditing Standards No. 61 (Communication with Audit Committees)

- Requires the outside auditor to discuss with the audit committee information relating to the auditor's judgment about the quality, not just the acceptability, of the company's accounting principles, including:

  — Consistency of the entity's accounting policies and their application

  — Clarity and completeness of the entity's financial statements

  — Items that have a significant impact on the representational faithfulness, verifiability, and neutrality of the accounting information included in the financial statements

- Encourages the participation of management in the discussion

- Suggests that the discussion be "open and frank"

- Does not require that written documentation of the discussion be provided to the audit committee or management

- Requires auditor presentation to the audit committee of "uncorrected misstatements"

---

financial reporting takes place, the institution's logistical capabilities to fulfill its objectives, and where things might have gone astray.

It therefore makes sense to ask the outside auditor about the company's level of cooperation during the course of the audit and the extent to which any difficult issues were encountered. Frequently, a lack of cooperation and the encountering of difficult issues will go hand in hand. Either individually or together they can be a telltale sign of a broader problem. In particular, they can suggest an attitude toward financial reporting that is not consistent with a healthy overall environment.

Exhibit 11–12. New Amendments to Statement on Auditing Standards No. 71 (Interim Financial Information)

- Clarifies that an auditor should communicate to the audit committee matters described in SAS-61 (Communication with Audit Committees) when they have been identified in the conduct of interim financial reporting

- Requires that an auditor should attempt to discuss the matters described in SAS-61 with the audit committee (or its chairman) and someone from financial management prior to:

  — The filing of the Form 10-Q, or

  — As soon as practicable if such communication cannot be made before filing

---

Unusual Revenue or Reserve Activity

Part of asking the auditor to do more than the bare minimum may involve encouraging the auditor to explore unusual patterns in revenues or reserves.

The reason for looking at revenues is that revenue manipulation is frequently where widespread financial fraud will get its start. In particular, the auditor can be asked to look out for instances in which revenue recognition patterns do not appear to match the ebb and flow of the company's normal cycle of business activity. Revenue spikes toward the end of a quarter or other financial reporting period may be a warning that something untoward is afoot.

Much the same is true of changes in company reserves. Here, the auditor might be encouraged to scrutinize the level of reserves not only at year-end but during the course of the year to look for unjustified or inexplicable reserve level changes. Unusual reserve activity that does not seem explainable by virtue of business developments here, too, should be explored. Reserves that are established or modified almost entirely based upon the judgment of management may warrant particular scrutiny.

Beyond issues of revenue recognition and the adjustment of reserves, the auditor might be asked about other aspects of the application of GAAP in which management judgment plays an important role. The audit committee should do its best to satisfy itself that adjustments are the natural consequence of business activity and not the manifestation of a desire to attain preestablished financial reporting targets.

Nonmaterial PAJEs

A recent addition to the list of issues for the outside auditor is the topic of *nonmaterial PAJEs*. This addition is the result of a somewhat controversial bulletin by the staff of the SEC.

First, a word about nomenclature. A *PAJE* is a proposed adjusting journal entry—that is to say, an adjusting journal entry that has been proposed by the auditor as a result of audit testing. If the adjustment is made, it becomes known simply as an *adjusting journal entry*. If the adjustment is not made, it remains a *proposed adjusting journal entry* (some might call it a *passed adjusting journal entry*) or a *PAJE*.

Historically, it has generally been within the discretion of management to decline to make adjusting journal entries as long as they collectively were not material. There were exceptions to that, but generally management could decline to record PAJEs collectively falling below a materiality threshold—say 5% to 10%—without running the risk that the financial statements would be viewed as *materially* misstated.

In Staff Accounting Bulletin No. 99 (see Exhibit 11–13), as mentioned in Chapter 4, the SEC has tried to change that. Apparently premised on the view that executives at some public companies were abusing the concept of materiality by declining to make "nonmaterial" adjusting journal entries to increase reported earnings, the SEC staff has taken the position that it will no longer accept purely numerical materiality analysis in assessing the fairness of financial statement presentation. In particular, the staff has taken the position that even adjustments falling below traditional numerical thresholds may nonetheless be viewed as material if, for example, failure to make the adjustment disguised a failure to meet analyst expectations, turned a loss into a profit, masked an important trend, or affected a company's compliance with regulatory requirements. In addition, the staff has suggested that a failure to make even ostensibly minor adjustments to the company's books and records may be improper

Exhibit 11–13. SEC Staff Accounting Bulletin No. 99 (Materiality)

"The staff is aware that certain registrants, over time, have developed quantitative thresholds as 'rules of thumb' to assist in the preparation of their financial statements, and that auditors also have used these thresholds in their evaluation of whether items might be considered material to users of a registrant's financial statements. One rule of thumb in particular suggests that the misstatement or omission of an item that falls under a 5% threshold is not material in the absence of particularly egregious circumstances, such as self-dealing or misappropriation by senior management. The staff reminds registrants and the auditors of their financial statements that exclusive reliance on this or any percentage or numerical threshold has no basis in the accounting literature or the law.

* * *

Among the considerations that may well render material a quantitatively small misstatement of a financial statement item are—

- whether the misstatement arises from an item capable of precise measurement or whether it arises from an estimate and, if so, the degree of imprecision inherent in the estimate

- whether the misstatement masks a change in earnings or other trends

- whether the misstatement hides a failure to meet analysts' consensus expectations for the enterprise

- whether the misstatement changes a loss into income or vice versa

- whether the misstatement concerns a segment or other portion of the registrant's business that has been identified as playing a significant role in the registrant's operations or profitability

- whether the misstatement affects the registrant's compliance with regulatory requirements

- whether the misstatement affects the registrant's compliance with loan covenants or other contractual requirements

- whether the misstatement has the effect of increasing management's compensation—for example, by satisfying requirements for the award of bonuses or other forms of incentive compensation

- whether the misstatement involves concealment of an unlawful transaction."

---

when undertaken "as part of an ongoing effort directed by or known to senior management for the purposes of 'managing' earnings." Complementing SAB 99 is an amendment to GAAS (specifically to SAS-61) which requires the auditor to inform the audit committee "about uncorrected misstatements" found by the auditor which "were determined by management to be immaterial."

No longer, therefore, can an audit committee take complete comfort that financial statement inaccuracies falling below numerical materiality thresholds need not be worried about. Now they must be. Moreover, they must be worried about in a context in which the propriety of a failure to make adjustments turns on such qualitative criteria as the perceived effect of the failure and, to some extent, the motive of management.

For the time being, therefore, the audit committee may want to explore with the outside auditor any proposed adjustments that have not been made. In the event that such adjustments exist, the audit committee may face the fairly unpleasant task of inquiring into the reason and the extent to which the failure to make the adjustment would be second guessed by the SEC or others. To avoid potential trouble, some audit committees may see fit simply to put in place a policy that, regardless of materiality, all proposed adjusting journal entries should be made.

Thoroughness of the Audit

Not all audits are created equal. True, every conscientious auditor will conduct the audit tests that GAAS require. But why would the audit committee want to stop there? The audit committee might want to explore with the auditor the extent to which the auditor has done more than meet the standard professional requirements. In particular, the audit committee might ask the auditor about those devices used to gain extra insight into the corporate environment and to root out potential causes of financial misreporting. If the committee is going to go through the trouble of hiring the auditor, it may as well encourage the auditor to do an extra good job. Useful information is so precious, it seems a shame to let the auditor get away with making a minimal effort.

SAS-61 Items

In order to conform to the new rules, the audit committee will want to make sure it has appropriately discussed with the auditor items listed in SAS-61, referred to briefly above. Neither the new rules nor SAS-61 actually *require* the audit committee to discuss with the auditor the specified items. SAS-61 actually places the burden on the auditor to undertake the communication, and the new rules only require the audit committee to disclose whether discussion of the specified items has taken place (see Exhibit 11–7). Nonetheless, given the awkwardness of a public disclosure that for some reason the specified items have not been discussed, the audit committee will want to make sure that the discussion has occurred.

Exhibit 11–14. SAS-61 Communications

- The auditor's responsibility under GAAS

- Significant accounting policies

- Management judgments and accounting estimates

- Audit adjustments

- The auditor's judgments about the quality of the entity's accounting principles

- Other information in documents containing audited financial statements

- Disagreements with management

- Consultation with other accountants

- Major issues discussed with management prior to retention

- Difficulties encountered in performing the audit

The actual list of items to be discussed pursuant to SAS-61 is extensive (see Exhibit 11–14). It includes the auditor's responsibility under GAAS; significant accounting policies; management judgments regarding accounting estimates; audit adjustments; other information in documents containing audited financial statements; disagreements with management; consultations by management with other accountants; major issues discussed with management prior to auditor retention; difficulties encountered in performing the audit; and (under the new amendments to SAS-61 discussed above) the auditor's judgments about quality, and not just the acceptability, of the company's accounting principles. Moreover, the new amendments to GAAS require appropriate discussion of SAS-61 items in conjunction with the auditor's quarterly review—not just at year end (see Exhibit 11–12).

As a practical matter, to the extent that the audit committee has already delved into the areas described above, it will likely find that it has already more than adequately addressed all or virtually all of these SAS-61 items. Nonetheless, to the extent it has not, the audit committee will want to make sure that any remaining items are appropriately considered.

Auditor Independence

No discussion of the audit committee's interaction with the outside auditor would be complete without consideration of the issue of auditor independence.

Probably one sentence can fairly capture the present state of play on the issue of auditor independence in the United States. It is a mess. Indeed, sometimes it almost seems as if everyone is disagreeing about everything. Among the subjects of discussion are: What limitations should the concept of auditor "independence" actually impose? Should the focus be on independence in fact or independence both in fact and in appearance? Can auditors be truly independent given that the audit client pays the fee? Does preservation of independence isolate auditors from critical information about the company and thereby compromise the effectiveness of the audit? Who should be writing the rules?

These and other fundamental issues continue to be the subject of earnest discussion and debate. Actually, to characterize the dialogue as "earnest discussion and debate" is probably something of an understatement. It is the kind of "discussion and debate" that takes place in a boxing ring.

In one corner of the ring is the champion of broad governmental regulation—the SEC. Faced with the statutory responsibility for protection of the integrity of financial markets, the SEC advocates bright-like regulatory constraints as the key to independence of the auditor. In the other corner are the champions of private-sector policing, which is to say the accounting profession. The accounting profession—speaking through its national association, the American Institute of Certified Public Accountants (AICPA)—insists that the objective of auditor independence and the broader goal of audit effectiveness are enhanced most effectively through private-sector policing that appropriately responds to audit-client needs.

The resulting tension between the advocates of regulation and the advocates of self-policing is not particularly new. In fact, for years it has been an omnipresent feature of the relationship between the two, though both over time managed to forge a sort of peaceful coexistence characterized by mutual respect and suspicion. In the latter part of the 1990s, however, that peaceful coexistence began to break down. Among those affected by the consequences are audit committees.

The explanation for the breakdown is complicated, but one of the biggest factors was the consolidation of the accounting profession and its expansion in the direction of non-audit services. The SEC's expressed concern focused on whether the audit service was being used by accounting firms as a loss leader to get other business. The SEC wondered about the extent to which an auditor "'low-balls' the audit fee—even offering to perform it at a loss—in order to gain entry into and build a relationship with a potential client for the firm's non-audit services." More broadly, the SEC suggested that "the rapid rise in the growth of non-audit services has increased the economic incentives for the auditor to preserve a relationship with the audit client, thereby increasing the risk that the auditor will be less inclined to be objective." Insofar as the SEC relied upon the independent audit as the backbone of integrity in financial reporting, the SEC seemed to fear that the whole system was going to melt down.

According to the accounting profession, the SEC's concerns were fundamentally misplaced. The accounting profession pointed to the increasing computerization of financial reporting and the genuine need of companies to upgrade financial reporting and management information systems which, after all, would only serve to enhance financial reporting reliability. It was, moreover, the outside auditor who was best positioned to provide the company with exactly what it needed, with the collateral benefit of enhancing both the auditor's knowledge of the company's system and the audit profession's access to sophisticated systems personnel. The accounting profession contended that, contrary to the SEC's suggestion, enhanced audit scrutiny would not be a natural consequence of isolating the auditor from what was going on.

Repeated attempts to find a middle ground ended in failure. All the while, as audit clients sought increased auditor involvement in non-audit services, the concerns of the SEC correspondingly increased. At one point, a workable solution seemed to be devised in the creation of a third body—the "Independence Standards Board" or "ISB"—whose membership included prestigious members of both the accounting profession and others. However, while the ISB managed to take significant strides forward, the SEC did not seem to feel that it was keeping up with events. Finally, in seeming exasperation, the SEC decided to take a draconian step. It unanimously voted to issue a proposed rule that would prohibit auditors altogether from providing important types of non-audit services to audit clients.

The ensuing conflagration became known as the "Auditor Independence War." It was fought in every possible theater—commission hearings, congressional testimony, regulatory rulemaking, backroom politicking, and the financial press. To a meaningful extent, the intensity of the debate was caused by the perception that the stakes were so high: The SEC seemed to believe that integrity in financial reporting was under deliberate assault, while the national accounting firms faced the prospect of dismemberment of their bodily parts. To a large extent, though, the intensity was probably explainable by another characteristic of the debate. Each side genuinely believed what it was saying.

In the end, the SEC backed down from its draconian prohibition on non-audit services and, instead, adopted an approach that placed more emphasis on disclosure. The ISB, for its part, kept its existing rules in place. And, as things turned out, several of the largest accounting firms decided to spin-off or otherwise disconnect from their consulting practices. Peace was restored.

But the fallout from the battles carries with it important implications for audit committees. For one of the consequences was to place on audit committees the burden of increased attentiveness to the issue of auditor independence. At the same time, the history of battles fought and compromises struck resulted in a regulatory framework characterized by three different, separately promulgated sets of rules which are, to a large extent, overlapping and not always intellectually consistent. Those three sets of rules are those promulgated by the AICPA, the ISB, and the SEC.

Of the three, the audit committee can probably afford to pay the least attention to those promulgated by the AICPA. They are mostly the auditor's problem. Broadly stated, the rules acknowledge the "utmost importance" of public confidence in the independence of auditors and admonish that auditors "should not only be independent in fact; they should avoid situations that may lead outsiders to doubt their independence" (see Exhibit 11–15). More detailed rules provide for auditors a specific set of do's and don'ts.

Exhibit 11–15. Auditor Independence

"It is of utmost importance to the profession that the general public maintain confidence in the independence of independent auditors. Public confidence would be impaired by evidence that independence was actually lacking, and it might also be impaired by the existence of circumstances which reasonable people might believe likely to influence independence. To *be* independent, the auditor must be intellectually honest; to be *recognized* as independent, he must be free from any obligation to or interest in the client, its management, or its owners. For example, an independent auditor auditing a company of which he was also a director might be intellectually honest, but it is unlikely that the public would accept him as independent since he would be in effect auditing decisions which he had a part in making. Likewise, an auditor with a substantial financial interest in a company might be unbiased in expressing his opinion on the financial statements of the company, but the public would be reluctant to believe that he was unbiased. Independent auditors should not only be independent in fact; they should avoid situations that may lead outsiders to doubt their independence."

(AICPA Professional Standards § 220.03)

The second set of rules—those promulgated by the ISB—require a little more audit committee attention. (See Exhibit 11–16.) In particular, ISB Standard No. 1 requires an auditor to provide the audit committee with a written description of all relationships between the auditor and the company that the auditor believes may reasonably be thought to bear on independence; to confirm for the audit committee the auditor's judgment that it is independent within the meaning of the securities laws; and to discuss with the audit committee the overall topic of the auditor's independence. The disclosures and discussion are to take place at least once a year.

The third set of rules—those of the SEC—require the highest level of audit committee attentiveness insofar as, unlike the other sets of rules, they place the onus for compliance directly on the audit committee. (See Exhibit 11–17.) The main thrust of the rules, insofar as directly relevant to audit committees, are these. First, a company's annual proxy statement (in a section entitled "Audit Fees") is to set forth all fees the company paid for its audit and quarterly review services. Second, the proxy statement (in a section entitled "Financial Information Systems Design and Implementation Fees") is to set forth all fees for specified information technology services rendered by the auditor during the year. Third, the proxy statement (in a section entitled "All Other Fees") is to set forth fees billed for all other non-audit services. Fourth, the proxy statement is to set forth whether the audit committee considered whether the auditor's provision of non-audit services was compatible with maintaining the auditor's independence.

The net effect of all this is that audit committees have been given the task of evaluating auditor independence against a backdrop of rules and regulations promulgated by three separate bodies who cannot even agree on what the concept of auditor "independence" means. Nor is it a source of much comfort that the new rules do not actually require the audit committee to disclose whether it concluded that the auditor was in fact independent. It would probably strike many as awkward for an audit committee to encounter significant evidence that an auditor was not independent and then to do nothing about it.

That leaves it for the audit committee to accomplish what the regulators and the accounting professionals cannot: Formulate a practical test for evaluating auditor independence and consider the extent to which auditor independence has been compromised in any given year. While the history of the concept suggests the task is herculean, in fact it is not. It involves simply a common sense evaluation of the audit committee's relationship with the auditor and whether the audit committee, in its judgment, thinks the auditor is willing to stand up to management and tell it like it is. An auditor unwilling to do so—an auditor who, for example, seems too ready to acquiesce in the face of managerial pressure—is an auditor whose independence may be open to question.

How to assess auditor independence while remaining attentive to the requirements of the rules? Here is a practical five-step approach (see Exhibit 11–18). First, in the context of each audit, the audit committee should receive from the outside auditor a written description of all relationships between the auditor and the company that, in the auditor's judgment, may reasonably be thought to bear on independence (see ISB Standard No. 1). Second, the audit committee should obtain a breakdown of all audit fees (including quarterly review fees), financial information systems design and implementation fees, and all other fees paid to the au-

---

Exhibit 11–16. Independence Standards Board Standard No. 1 (Independence Discussions with Audit Committees)

- Applies to any auditor intending to be considered an independent accountant with respect to a specific entity administered by the SEC

- Requires that, at least annually, such an auditor shall:

    — Disclose to the audit committee of the company, in writing, all relationships between the auditor and its related entities and the company and its related entities that in the auditor's professional judgment may reasonably be thought to bear on independence

    — Confirm that, in the auditor's professional judgment, it is independent of the company within the meaning of the Securities Acts

    — Discuss the auditor's independence with the audit committee

---

ditor over the course of the year (see the new SEC rules). Third, the audit committee members should think about, and discuss among themselves, the extent to which the relationships and fees run the risk of compromising auditor independence (see again the new SEC rules). Fourth, the audit committee should discuss with the auditor the subject of auditor independence, including any concerns about independence being compromised, and receive from the auditor written confirmation that the auditor in its judgment believes it is independent (see again ISB Standard No. 1). Fifth, the audit committee should ensure the documentation of all this by seeing to it that (i) its audit committee report states whether the audit committee has received the written descriptions regarding independence from the auditor and discussed with the auditor the subject of its independence (ISB Standard No. 1), and (ii) the company's proxy statement sets forth the requisite fee information and whether the audit committee considered whether the auditor's provision of such non-audit services was compatible with maintaining the auditor's independence (the new SEC rules). (There is an additional proxy disclosure requirement regarding audit leasing of non-audit personnel, but its significance is too limited to discuss here.)

Exhibit 11-17. New SEC Rules on Auditor Independence

- Proxy statements should disclose annual fees for audit and quarterly review services

- Proxy statements should disclose aggregate fees for financial information systems design and implementation

- Proxy statements should disclose all other fees for non-audit services

- Proxy statements should disclose the number of hours expended on an audit by leased personnel (if over 50% of hours expended on the audit)

- Proxy statements should disclose whether the audit committee considered whether the outside auditor's provision of non-audit services was compatible with auditor independence

---

This five-step approach still leaves unanswered precisely the test for when an auditor is not independent, but the audit committee can be comforted by the fact that no such test exists. In the end, it is really a matter of gut feel as to whether the audit committee can trust the auditor both to provide candid information and to stand up to management in ensuring the financial statements' adherence to GAAP. Will the audit committee's determination be second guessed by the SEC where non-audit services get too large? There is a risk. But the audit committee can seek to stay ahead of that risk by keeping in mind a series of factors (formulated by the accounting profession's own "O'Malley Panel") formulated to assist in evaluation of whether a non-audit service will enhance or impede the company's auditor relationship. These factors include:

- Whether the service is being performed principally for the audit committee
- The effects of the service, if any, on audit effectiveness or on the quality and timeliness of the entity's financial reporting process
- Whether the service would be performed by specialists (e.g., technology specialists) who ordinarily also provide recurring audit support
- Whether the service would be performed by audit personnel and, if so, whether it will enhance their knowledge of the entity's business and operations
- Whether the role of those performing the service (e.g., a role where neutrality, impartiality and auditor skepticism are likely to be subverted) would be inconsistent with the auditor's role
- Whether the audit firm's personnel would be assuming a management role or creating a mutuality of interest with management
- Whether the auditors, in effect, would be "auditing their own numbers"
- Whether the project must be started and completed very quickly
- Whether the audit firm has unique expertise in the service
- The size of the fee(s) for the non-audit service(s)

Although a consideration of such factors is obviously useful, the audit committee should not lose the forest for the trees. The key question,

---

Exhibit 11-18. A Five-Step Approach to Audit Committee Assessment of Auditor Independence

- Receive a written description of all relationships between the auditor and the company that may reasonably bear on independence

- Receive a breakdown of audit and non-audit fees

- Think about and discuss potential impediments to auditor independence

- Discuss independence with the auditor and receive the auditor's written confirmation of its independence

- Ensure appropriate documentation in the audit committee's report and company's proxy statement

---

again, should be whether the outside auditor is prepared to tell it like it is. Aspects of the auditor relationship that may impede the auditor's willingness to do so—whether they be significant consulting agreements or simply a long history of close social ties with the CEO—are factors that the audit committee will probably want to take into consideration.

All the while, though, the audit committee should keep in mind this: Pure auditor independence is probably not attainable. As long as the company retains and pays the auditor, the auditor will maintain some level of sensitivity to the company's wants and needs. The key to an effective audit function, therefore, is not to focus on the artificial ideal of pure independence. It is, rather, to use the auditor's inevitable inclination to accommodate the desires of its client to enhance, rather than to impede, the outside audit function. In other words, it should be made clear to the auditor that thoroughness, candor, zeal, and integrity are the criteria by which performance will be measured—not the minimal requirements of GAAS and the dutiful issuance of an annual audit report. The crux of the audit relationship should evolve into one in which the auditor becomes an integral part of the system pursuant to which the audit committee gains access to useful systems information.

An underlying premise of such a relationship is that it should be the audit committee, and not senior executives, that selects and engages the auditor and determines the audit fee. For the same reasons that human nature impedes senior management's desire to convey bad news about itself, human nature similarly impedes management's desire for an auditor that will expose its own inadequacies. That is not to fault management or, for that matter, human nature. It is simply to acknowledge the way it is.

As the audit committee strives for a more complete and interconnected relationship with its outside auditor, the committee should probably keep in mind the extent to which an expansion of the auditor's role will work against the auditor's culture and traditions, which have been inclined in the direction of standardized and numerically focused reports. The level of responsiveness to an expanded audit role will likely vary not only among CPA firms, but among individual practitioners within firms. Ultimately, though, auditors should come to recognize the extent to which broader auditor involvement in financial reporting information and systems will operate to the audit profession's distinct advantage. Among other things, it will reduce if not eliminate the extent to which the audit is perceived as a mere commodity, and give opportunity to individual practitioners to demonstrate the uniqueness of their own professional excellence.

Getting Information from Internal Audit

Unfortunately, even the most splendid outside auditor will suffer from one fundamental impediment to its effectiveness: By definition, the auditor is an outsider. Whether the auditor undertakes fieldwork once a year, once a quarter, or even more frequently, the outside auditor will still be conducting examinations only periodically. There is one thing, therefore, that the outside auditor may not be able to accomplish. The outside auditor may not be able to sufficiently integrate itself so that it becomes part of the fiber of the enterprise and thereby gains complete access to the all-important environment or culture where accounting irregularities have their start.

To fill the gap, the audit committee may want to consider installation of an internal audit department. In general, it would make sense to ask the internal auditors to evaluate many of the areas listed above while taking advantage of the one characteristic that gives internal audit an edge: internal auditors are there all the time.

Unlike the outside auditor, therefore, the internal auditor is in a position to participate in hallway gossip; to plug itself into the processes of forecasting, budgeting, sales, and shipping; and to develop important relationships whereby it can attain a genuine feel for the pulse of the organization. While fellow employees may never let down their guard completely, certainly there is greater opportunity for internal auditors to gain access into the workings of the enterprise than for somebody whose principal function is to remain as an outsider.

A hot topic of debate is whether an audit committee should "outsource" the internal audit—that is, turn over the internal audit function to the outside auditor. There are both pros and cons, but one question is whether an outsider can effectively plug himself into the culture of the organization in the same way as an employee. It may be that creative and zealous outsourced internal auditors would be able to overcome that impediment. It is a subject of legitimate debate.

Installation of an effective internal audit function, whether outsourced or not, will not necessarily be easy. One reason is that here, too, the audit committee—insofar as it seeks touchy-feely information about the corporate environment rather than crisp statistics on the reliability of numerical data—will to some extent be working against the traditions of the audit profession insofar as internal auditors are, after all, still auditors. Even internal auditors who are admonished to seek and report candidly both statistically derived and gut-level information about the workings of the financial reporting system may find themselves inclined to prefer the former at the expense of the latter.

A single anecdote will illustrate the challenge. One audit committee of a public company was fortunate to have as its chairman an individual who had not only served as CEO of several companies but who possessed extraordinary expertise in corporate governance and, in particular, in the ways that financial reporting systems can break down. This audit committee chairman undertook, as one of his top priorities, the installation of an effective internal audit capability. The structure of the reporting relationship was exactly right: the internal auditors were encouraged and admonished to look for problems. They were instructed to report all problems to the audit committee directly.

Over time, the chairman got a sense that the environment was not quite right and might be conducive to problems. He shared his concerns with the internal auditors, who were admonished to look harder. Alas, the internal auditors reported that they didn't see a thing. To them, everything looked just fine.

As it turned out, things were not fine. The company did indeed suffer from an environmental problem, and the internal auditors had either not been sufficiently skilled or sufficiently zealous to plug themselves into it. The true depth of the problem became known only after a significant change in the senior management ranks.

The point of this anecdote is this. In today's world of financial reporting, audit committees are facing an extraordinary challenge. They are being asked not only to assume significant oversight responsibility for the prevention and early detection of fraudulent financial reporting. They are being asked to do so through the use of tools, such as the outside auditor and internal audit, that will themselves have to undergo some degree of cultural evolution before they are in a position to provide the kind of information a modern audit committee will want to have. Even sophisticated and diligent audit committee members will no doubt find the task exceedingly frustrating, and probably few, if any, audit committees so far have managed to install an optimum system. At root, the challenge is to reconfigure the way people think about corporate governance and financial reporting. Theoretically, the tools are there. But some modifications will be necessary before they can be made to work.

Making the Tools Work

How can the audit committee maximize the effectiveness of the tools at its disposal? In other words, how can the audit committee most effectively use the outside auditor and internal audit to trigger a cascade of information and, in particular, to enable bad news to flow up? Here are some ideas.

More on the Tone at the Top

To get the tools to work, it will be critical for the audit committee to set the right tone. If one wants to encourage the flow of bad news, then the flow of bad news must be rewarded. At the same time, the audit committee should zealously guard against the natural inclination of human nature to recoil and punish bad news. It didn't work for Cleopatra. There's no reason to think it will work any better for a modern audit committee.

As a practical matter, this translates into insistence on complete co-operation by employees and executives with both the internal and the outside audit functions. Officers and employees must be made keenly aware that truthfulness and candor are the orders of the day and, correspondingly, that attempts to obfuscate, disguise, or dissemble are absolutely forbidden. Once again, it is a battle for the culture of the organization.

At the same time, the audit committee should appreciate that the auditors must not be too heavy-handed. The auditors' mission is a delicate one and must be approached with an appreciation for the subtleties of human nature and the completely understandable reluctance of others to report bad news. At some point, the task becomes less an exercise in the application of GAAP and more an exercise in the sociology of organizations and the foibles of human nature. Auditors who appear to go about their task with any level of arrogance, swaggering boastfulness, or lack of appreciation for the sensitivity of their positions must either be admonished to change or, more likely, moved to another position. The audit function is not one in which heavy-handedness will get results.

One particularly difficult issue the audit committee will likely face, moreover, is senior-executive insecurity arising out of enhanced and expanded internal and outside auditor functions. Senior executives will no doubt appreciate that they are supposed to know what's going on within the company they are running. An understandable reaction on their part would be a level of insecurity verging on paranoia. At a minimum, the installation of enhanced internal and outside audit functions would seem to do nothing to foster a sense of trust in senior executives or their integrity.

For reasons so eloquently explained by John O. Whitney in his management text *The Economics of Trust*, a sense of mistrust must not be permitted to creep into the relationship between the audit committee and senior management. Trust is critical, and without it the installation of enhanced audit functions could end up proving counterproductive. That sense of trust must be maintained through the recognition, explicitly shared with senior executives, that nobody is perfect, no enterprise is perfect, and that, simply by virtue of its position, the audit committee may have access to information that even the most well-meaning and effective senior executives may not. That information will not be used against the executives, but, rather, will give them a heretofore unavailable opportunity to gain new insights into their company and enhance its operations. The information is not being obtained to be used against anyone. It is being obtained so that everyone may benefit from its revelation.

Will some senior executives nonetheless try to exact revenge from an employee who has spilled the beans? It is almost inevitable that the ranks of senior management will include executives who would so foolishly react. That is, therefore, still another thing for which the audit committee will want to keep its eyes open. If it learns of an executive seeking to so stifle truthful information, the committee's reaction in most instances should probably be unequivocal and swift. Such an executive in all likelihood does not know how to get information or how to use it when it's available. Who knows what's been happening in his department? He inevitably doesn't. A direct communication with the executive is probably in order. Also in order may be his removal.

Minimize Reliance on Paper

For some reason, almost anyone within an organization is drawn to demonstrate his or her diligence through the generation of paper. That is particularly so when people are not quite sure what they're supposed to be doing. As an audit committee undertakes to improve financial reporting, therefore, an inclination may exist for those involved to generate written reports—inspection reports, exception reports, reports consolidating reports—all accompanied by the normal barrage of memoranda, correspondence, and (today) e-mails.

In many areas of corporate endeavor, the mindless generation of paper merely wastes time. In the context of corporate governance and financial reporting, it can actually be counterproductive. The reason probably stems from the underlying reluctance of individuals to write with the same candor that they speak—particularly when the topic is criticism of the organization or, more frightening, their own superiors. A resulting loss of candor would be particularly unfortunate in the transmittal of information to the audit committee insofar as some of the most important information involves subtle aspects of the corporate environment and tone. Such information can be difficult to quantify and document, and exclusive reliance on written reports may cause such information to be lost completely. Human resource directors are familiar with a phenomenon in which the performance evaluations of individual employees tend to improve when, having been presented orally, they must then be reduced to writing. There's no reason to think that the phenomenon will not occur where the evaluations are of corporate rather than individual performance.

To the full extent possible, therefore, the better approach may be to minimize the use of paper and to gain access to information through direct face-to-face meetings. In that way, the true richness of feedback can be explored and the participants can be made to feel more at liberty to convey potential problems before they would seem to warrant documentation. Feelings, concerns, gut-level instincts—all of these would likely be more forthcoming if they could be presented orally rather than on paper. Presumably for such reasons, the new amendments to GAAS decline to require the auditor's written communication of certain kinds of information (see Exhibit 11–11).

An additional reason exists to minimize the generation of paper, though one is loathe to acknowledge it. The reason stems from the disadvantage of unnecessary documentation in the event of litigation. While written reports might be used affirmatively in litigation to demonstrate the diligence of audit committee members, the reports might also be taken out of context to show supposedly unpardonable flaws in the financial reporting system. The minimization of written reports reduces the risk.

It is probably too much to ask that an effective communication system be entirely paper-free. After all, there will be a lot to keep track of. Nonetheless, even under the best of circumstances, the efficiency of an organization is probably inversely proportional to the amount of paper it generates. That may be particularly so when it comes to perpetual evaluation of the corporation's financial reporting system and, in particular, the corporate environment.

Learn the Business

To "learn the business" does not mean to study the most recent Form 10-K. Nor does it mean rote memorization of product lines, divisions, or facility locations. What the audit committee really wants to understand is how the organizations runs—what is the system by which the company conceives, creates, sells, and publicly reports. A significant underlying objective in understanding the system is development of an appreciation for those aspects of the system (e.g., budgeting, sales, shipping) in which vulnerabilities leading to potential breakdowns in financial reporting are most likely to occur.

That kind of information is not available from audited financial statements. It is more readily unearthed, rather, through one-to-one contact with executives and operating personnel. At one public construction company, for example, the audit committee chairman arranged for a series of half-day meetings with executives in five separate areas (finance, construction, human resources, bidding, and estimates) to develop a meaningful understanding of just how the company worked.

Public companies are, at bottom, simply collections of human beings trying to get along as best they can. An understanding of how individuals interact—the motivations, the pressures, the problems—can contribute mightily to an understanding of underlying vulnerabilities.

Meet with Others and Alone

The audit committee's function poses something of a dilemma. On the one hand, the audit committee consists of outsiders who, by definition, are at least once-removed from the company. On the other hand, the audit committee wants to develop an overall sense of the company's financial reporting weaknesses that is more objective and more vivid than that of almost anyone else.

A consequence is that the audit committee should have two types of meetings. One type is meetings with others. "Others" would include the CEO, the CFO, at times key operating personnel, the outside auditor, and internal audit. The purpose of such meetings (and their effectiveness may be enhanced if they are done separately) is to capture the full texture of each individual's experience and views as to what is going on and, more important, where problems may be developing.

The other type of meeting consists of meetings in which the audit committee members confer by themselves. Only in isolation can they candidly express their views as to the strengths and weaknesses of individuals, company systems, and the company as a whole. That is not to say that each meeting must adhere to a rigid agenda—first the CEO, then the CFO, then the internal auditor, then ten minutes for private discussion. Rather, it means that, as the audit committee seeks to explore potential vulnerabilities in financial reporting, a full spectrum of meeting configurations may be useful.

Meet When Necessary

One issue that seems to have attracted more than its share of regulatory attention is the frequency with which audit committee meetings should be held. Should they be held once a year? Once a quarter? Once a month? Before each board meeting? On an ad hoc basis?

No rule or regulation definitively answers the question, though former SEC Chairman Arthur Levitt made clear his disdain for an audit committee that presumed to fulfill its functions while meeting "only twice a year before the regular board meeting for fifteen minutes." At the other end of the spectrum, Arthur Levitt has presented to the business community his Platonic ideal of an audit committee that "meets twelve times a year."

Here is a common sense suggestion. While it sounds almost too obvious to mention, a good approach would be to hold audit committee meetings as often as necessary. For example, an audit committee just getting started or at a company whose financial reporting system suffers from a history of problems might want to meet as often as every two or three weeks. As appropriate systems are put in place, once a month or, later still, once a quarter may be just fine. The point is that the frequency of meetings should be driven by the needs of the company—not by a self-imposed edict or by the desire to create an appearance of diligence. Good judgment is probably the best guide.

Use Good Judgment

The importance of good judgment brings to mind one final point. All organizations are different. They have different histories. They operate in different industries. They have different cultures. What works for one company may not work for another. It is hard to conceive of a single set of guidelines for effective audit committee oversight that would work optimally at all companies across the board.

Perhaps the most important guideline an audit committee might use to accomplish its objectives, therefore, is simply the good judgment of its individual members. In the end, the audit committee is trying to measure the pulse of the enterprise throughout the trials and tribulations of its corporate life. The overriding goal is to isolate the financial reporting system from the inevitable pressures that result when things don't go exactly as desired. No regulation, charter, checklist, mission statement, or corporate resolution can effectively guide the audit committee as it seeks to fulfill that goal. The best tool, rather, is the informed good judgment of the individual committee members.

Exhibit 11-19. Sample Audit Committee Charter

Organization

There shall be an audit committee of the board of directors composed of three directors, selected by the board, each of whom shall be independent of management and free of any relationships that, in the opinion of the board, would interfere with the member's exercise of his or her independent judgment. Each member of the audit committee shall be financially literate (as defined in the applicable rules), and at least one member shall have past employment experience in finance or accounting, requisite professional certification in accounting, or some other comparable experience or background that demonstrates that individual's financial sophistication and expertise. The chairperson of the audit committee shall be selected by the board of directors. The audit committee shall meet at least four times a year and more often when the circumstances so require.

Purpose

It shall be the fundamental purpose of the audit committee to assist the board of directors in fulfilling its responsibility to oversee the company's system of financial reporting.

Responsibilities

In performing its oversight function, the audit committee shall undertake those tasks that, in its judgment, would most effectively contribute to the effectiveness and integrity of the company's financial reporting system. In so doing, the audit committee shall:

1. Encourage within senior management a corporate environment or "tone at the top" that strives for integrity in financial reporting.

2. Make appropriate inquiry into the logistical capabilities of the financial reporting system.

3. Make appropriate inquiry to assess the ability of the financial reporting system to prevent financial misreporting and to detect financial misreporting should it occur.

4. Possess, along with the board of directors, ultimate authority and responsibility for the selection, evaluation, and, where appropriate, replacement of the outside auditor of the company's financial statements, so that the outside auditor shall ultimately be accountable to the board of directors and to the audit committee.

5. Inquire into the independence of the outside auditor; receive from the outside auditor a written statement, consistent with Independence Standards Board Standard No. 1, delineating all relationships between the auditor and the company that in the auditor's judgment may reasonably be thought to bear on independence; receive from the company a description of aggregate annual fees paid to the auditor for audit, financial information systems design and implementation, and other non-audit services; engage in dialogue with the auditor and, to the extent appropriate, the board of directors, with respect to any disclosed relationships, services, or fees that may affect the objectivity and independence of the auditor; receive from the outside auditor written confirmation that the auditor in its judgment is independent; and take, or recommend that the board take, appropriate action to ensure the independence of the auditor.

6. Determine that the outside auditor, in addition to being engaged to perform annual audits of the company's financial statements, has been engaged to perform quarterly reviews of the company's Forms 10-Q.

7. Discuss with management, the company's chief financial officer, the outside auditor, the director of internal audit, and/or others (as the committee believes appropriate), the company's financial statements and financial reporting

system, including potential weaknesses in the system, with such discussion to take place jointly and/or separately depending on the committee's judgment.

8. Discuss with the outside auditor, to the extent appropriate, the items identified in Statement on Auditing Standards No. 61 (including the auditor's judgment about the quality, not just the acceptability, of the company's accounting principles), with such discussion, to the extent it takes place in conjunction with quarterly information, to take place prior to the filing of each Form 10-Q or, if such discussion cannot reasonably take place prior to filing, as soon as practicable thereafter.

9. Make a recommendation to the board of directors as to whether the company's audited financial statements should be included in the company's Form 10-K.

10. Prepare an annual audit committee report, to be included in the company's proxy statement, stating whether the committee has:

    - reviewed and discussed the audited financial statements with management;

    - discussed with the outside auditor the matters required to be discussed by Statement on Auditing Standards No. 61;

    - received appropriate disclosures from the outside auditor regarding the auditor's independence as required by Independence Standards Board Standard No. 1 and discussed with the auditor the auditor's independence;

    - recommended to the board of directors that the audited financial statements be included in the company's Form 10-K.

11. See that the company's proxy statement includes a statement that the company has adopted this charter, that the company's proxy statement includes information regarding the independence of audit committee members, that the company's proxy statement includes information as to audit and non-audit fees and the audit committee's consideration of whether the auditor's provision of non-

audit services is compatible with maintaining auditor independence, and that a copy of this charter is included as an appendix to the company's proxy statement at least once every three years.

12. Investigate any matter brought to the audit committee's attention within the scope of its duties which, in its judgment, warrants investigation, and possess the power, without the consent of the board of directors, to engage outside professionals for that purpose.

13. Review and assess the adequacy of this charter on an annual basis.

CHAPTER 12

DUE DILIGENCE

Michael R. Young

This is a chapter for investors. It is also a chapter for lenders, investment bankers, venture capitalists, financial analysts, insurance companies, and anybody else who has reason to steer clear of companies that are particularly vulnerable to accounting irregularities. The earlier chapters have suggested that accounting irregularities can surface almost anywhere. The objective of this chapter is the identification of those kinds of companies where accounting irregularities may be most likely.

Looking at the Numbers

For fun, let's start with some financial statements. Set forth below are the balance sheet and income statement of a public company in the drug distribution business. Take a look at them. The question when you are through will be: Do you see any indication of an accounting irregularity? (Here's a clue: At least one of the numbers is fraudulent.)

April 30,	1995	1994
Assets (Note 3(a))		
Current:		
Cash and cash equivalents	$ 4,562,712	$13,495,480
Accounts receivable, less allowance for doubtful accounts of approximately $3,898,000 and $2,206,000	35,883,354	22,257,279
Inventories	9,833,853	2,341,488
Other receivable (Note 1(d))	-	1,444,426
Deferred taxes (Note 4)	1,575,300	617,000
Prepaid expenses and other	1,163,541	71,811
Total current assets	53,018,760	40,227,484

Improvements and equipment, less accumulated depreciation and amortization (Notes 2 and 3)	2,488,307	1,456,557
Excess of purchase price over net assets acquired (Note 1)	35,464,260	10,319,317
Other	1,275,775	414,746
	$92,247,102	$52,418,104

Liabilities and Stockholders' Equity		
Current:		
Accounts payable	$11,843,944	$ 5,237,210
Accrued expenses	1,009,694	1,070,075
Income taxes payable	-	1,759,590
Current maturities of long-term debt (Note 3)	3,135,267	147,416
Total current liabilities	15,988,905	8,214,291
Long-term debt, less current maturities (Note 3)	23,191,123	108,311
Total liabilities	39,180,028	8,322,602
Commitments and Contingencies (Note 5)		
Stockholders' equity (Note 6)		
Preferred stock - $.01 par value - shares authorized 1,000,000; issued and outstanding, none		
Common stock - $.03 par value - shares authorized 20,000,000; issued and outstanding 9,316,017 and 9,104,431	279,481	273,133
Additional paid-in capital	38,019,510	35,953,281
Retained earnings	14,768,083	7,926,153
Unearned restricted stock compensation	-	(57,065)
Total stockholders' equity	53,067,074	44,095,502
	$92,247,102	$52,418,104

Year ended April 30,	*1995*	*1994*
Revenues	$89,297,547	$44,249,516
Cost of sales	60,353,291	28,643,460
Gross profit	28,944,256	15,606,056
Operating expenses:		
Selling	2,898,208	1,847,197
General and administrative	14,542,488	7,209,342

Interest	269,316	88,215
Total operating expenses	17,710,012	9,144,754
Income from operations	11,234,244	6,461,302
Interest income	333,077	290,341
Income before income taxes	1,567,321	6,751,643
Income taxes (Note 4)	4,725,391	2,750,685
Net income	$6,841,930	$4,000,958

Earnings per share of common stock		
- primary	$.73	$.54
- fully diluted	$.73	$.53
Weighted average shares outstanding		
- primary	9,408,300	7,383,040
- fully diluted	9,420,816	7,593,465

Did you find it? Don't feel too bad. The auditors didn't either.

The company is (actually, was) Health Management, Inc., the subject of the first trial of an accounting irregularities class action pursuant to the new securities laws of the mid-1990s. By the end of the trial, the evidence demonstrated that these financial statements had been infected by at least 14 separate instances of fraud. The fraudulent numbers included accounts receivable, inventories, cost of sales, gross profit, and all types of expenses. The fraud was perpetrated by no fewer than a half-dozen employees, ranging from the CEO (who was sentenced to nine years) to a lowly truck driver who had driven a truck containing what turned out to be fictitious inventory. The fraud was supported by false schedules, forged documents, and a network of fabrications and lies. It took an investigation spanning years before the details were finally known.

Were the auditors at fault for missing such a massive fraud? A federal jury didn't think so. After a four-week trial, the jury exonerated the auditors of any professional wrongdoing whatsoever.

The normal reaction to such a scenario—massive accounting fraud and a failure of auditor detection—is: How can that be? Surely, many presume, the standards of the accounting profession are sufficiently rigorous that massive fraud should not go undetected. And it strikes many as peculiar that a team of certified public accountants could both fulfill their responsibilities under generally accepted auditing standards (GAAS) and still not catch the fraud.

So let's not let these auditors off so easily. Instead, let's put their work under a microscope and second guess the jury as to whether the auditors were at fault. For this purpose, we will select just one aspect of the fraud— relating to what turned out to be fictitious inventory. The question is: Were the auditors at fault because they didn't look or, if they did look, didn't dig deep enough?

Here were the circumstances. During the course of the audit, the auditors learned that a portion of the company's inventory had been in transit between company warehouses at the time of the year-end inventory count. By this point in the audit the inventory would have been sold, so the auditors could not simply confirm its existence by looking at boxes on the shelves. Instead, they had to come up with investigative techniques probing into the circumstances of the transfer, the surrounding documentation, its purpose, and the explanations of those involved. Here is what they did. First, they went into the company's records and retrieved the inventory transfer documentation and saw to it that it corroborated corporate records located elsewhere and was properly executed by the transferring executives. They then cross-checked the transfer documentation with the inventory records of receipt. They then met with the CFO. They met with the controller. They mathematically determined that the inventory had, in fact, been purchased before the shipment. They corroborated their mathematical analysis through an evaluation of gross profit margins. They even met with the truck driver and checked his expense report and receipts.

Why did the auditors miss the fraud? Because, as it turned out, it was all an elaborate lie. The transfer documentation had been forged. The receiving documentation had been forged. The CFO had lied. The controller had lied. Even the truck driver (whose expense report had been carefully fabricated to match the actual tolls on the Pennsylvania turnpike) had lied.

The point of this anecdote is this. Accounting fraud can be excruciatingly difficult to dig out. Even an outside auditor on the specific lookout for fraud may not find it. And that auditor may have inspected questionable transactions, sought corroborating information, cross-examined executives, conducted statistical tests, and performed a top-level "analytical review" to assess whether numerical correlations made sense. But it is an unfortunate aspect of financial reporting that determined management can almost always stay one step ahead of the outside CPAs. However deep the auditors dig, determined executives can almost always take the fraud one level deeper.

For those on the outside hoping to sidestep companies particularly susceptible to accounting irregularities, this is not good news. The logical implication is that, once the fraud has gotten past the auditors, there is little realistic hope that any outsider—be it an investor, lender, investment banker, insurance company, or whatever—is going to find it through his or her independent examination. And anyone hoping to uncover fraudulent financial reporting simply through study of a company's financial statements ought to give up. It's not likely to happen.

Now it is true that some would contend otherwise. Some would contend that careful scrutiny of the results and accompanying notes will bring to the surface potentially fraudulent financial reporting. And, once a fraud has been publicly exposed, there is ordinarily no shortage of sincere and well-meaning professionals who, with the benefit of hindsight, can point to this or that numerical anomaly in the financial statements which, they will contend, should have clued in everybody else to the fraud. But it's one thing to find numerical anomalies once a fraud has been revealed, and quite another to uncover fraud as it lies undetected beneath layers of deceptive entries, forged documents, and lies. The overwhelming experience is that public exposure of fraud seems to take pretty much everyone by surprise.

Looking at the Environment

Acknowledgement of the difficulty of uncovering financial fraud does not mean that we are reduced to simply hoping for the best. Although an outsider cannot reasonably expect to uncover financial fraud, an outsider can, based on an understanding of the root causes of financial fraud and the experience of those companies that have been afflicted, seek to develop a set of criteria focusing on the common characteristics of those companies where financial fraud is most likely to occur. An understanding of such telltale criteria can help prudent investors and others avoid those public companies most at risk.

The key to the development of such telltale criteria is to go back to square one—where fraudulent financial reporting gets its start. That takes us back to Chapter 1, and the fact that fraudulent financial reporting gets its start with a certain type of corporate environment. To reiterate briefly, it is an environment in which corporate activity is driven forward by an unhealthy combination of two things: (1) overly aggressive targets for performance, and (2) a "tone at the top" which views a failure to attain those targets as unforgivable. In other words, fraudulent financial reporting gets its start in an environment which places individuals under undue pressure to fudge—a little at first, worse later on—financial results. In the first instance, companies falling prey to that kind of environment may be companies for outsiders to avoid.

But this recognition immediately leads to a host of frustrations by outside evaluators of financial performance. One source is the recognition that the kind of pressurized environment that can give rise to financial misreporting in many respects will not look that different to an outsider from a financial reporting environment that can lead to spectacular success. True, aggressive targets and significant pressure can give rise to fraudulent financial reporting. But they can also give rise to heroic endeavor and phenomenal results. How many successful businesses can there be in which the corporate generals did not subject the troops to some blend of both carrot and stick? And how do we tell when the corporate environment is just right or, in contrast, when it is a petri dish for fraud? Sometimes even the CEO himself might not know.

There is an additional layer of frustration beyond the similarities between corporate environments that lead to success and corporate environments that lead to fraud. That frustration stems from the inability to gain insight into the nature of the environment to begin with. The processes of budgeting, establishing forecasts, and holding executives accountable to them are almost entirely internal processes far removed from the ultimate results reported to the public. Contrast those processes with the resources available to a typical investor who realistically is not going to have the time, money, or ability to evaluate a potential investment based on anything other than publicly available paper—which will say little about the financial reporting environment. Even those with greater access, such as lenders and investment bankers, may find their ability to probe into the soul of the company somewhat constrained, even assuming they have the know-how to probe in the right places, which they may not.

No one, therefore, should operate under the delusion that familiarity with the telltale signs of corruption will allow even cautious investors to step around accounting land mines waiting to explode. Just as likely, they will lead knowledgeable investors to throw up their hands in exasperation and to put all of their money into CDs.

Still, for those willing to take on the task, there is one attribute of financial reporting systems working in their favor. That is, quite simply, that executives in public companies—particularly accountant-types—are not easily corrupted. Experience suggests that the level of pressure to which executives must be subject in order to cross the line into financial misreporting is almost overwhelming. In searching for the wrong kind of environment, therefore, one is not simply searching for an environment characterized by modestly aggressive targets or the heavy weight of pressure. One is searching for an environment in which the targets are close to absurd and the pressure is almost unbearable. In other words, one is not simply searching for a bad environment. One is searching for a bad environment in the extreme.

How bad does the environment have to get? Here is a real life example. Judged purely by its numerical results, the experience of Leslie Fay during the early 1990s would have seemed extraordinary. The company was led by a hard-driving but well-regarded CEO who knew in intimate detail the intricacies of the garment industry. The senior executive staff enjoyed the talents of an aggressively hands-on CFO who seemed to have memorized every nook and cranny of the financial reporting system. Throughout the organization were hard-charging heads of the company's various divisions, all seeming to demand of themselves and their staffs the most exemplary performance that was humanly possible.

However, beneath the surface, things had gotten out of hand. Being charitable, the CEO's demands were too aggressive and disconnected from the operational impossibility of the targets he was establishing. Beneath the CEO, the hands-on CFO turned out to be a tyrant. An unhealthy combination of intolerance, obsession for control, and lack of empathy placed lower-level executives in an environment in which the CFO reportedly obsessed over such things as cash in restroom vending machines, employees' lunches in the executive refrigerator, and the number of family photographs on employees' desks. In this environment, meetings to establish the next year's budget became screaming matches. Once established, budgets were viewed as commitments (they had to be physically signed by the responsible executive), and actual results below budget were not tolerated.

The result was not an environment in which executives were simply subject to pressure. The result was an environment in which they were subject to intellectual mind games and torture. When what would turn out to be one of the then-largest accounting frauds in history publicly surfaced, one executive was found to have to described the corporate environment like this:

> Presently, Divisional management receives the budget package (history) and develops what they believe to be, from their frame of reference, reasonable goals. From their first proposal, they probably hear the words "not good enough" at least four or five times. Each critique and set of reviews precipitate dozens and dozens of man-hours of effort for accounting, division heads (who are primarily sellers) and planners. During this process, the morale of all starts to wane. The adopted budget, which was intended to be a tool and bench mark, becomes an unconditional surrender to what is perceived by many as an insurmountable mountain with intermittent punishment along the road.

After the fraud unraveled, justice was done—but not before the company had gone bankrupt and investors had lost millions of dollars. An extensive outside investigation resulted in a massive corporate housecleaning. And the CFO was criminally convicted.

That's the kind of environment that can lead to fraudulent financial reporting. And that's the kind of environment outsiders want to avoid. How to find it? Insight into the wrong kind of environment can be gleaned through consideration of six things. They are:

- The CEO
- The CFO
- The audit committee
- The industry
- The growth history
- The economy

Each is considered in turn.

The Chief Executive Officer

One of the hardest things for an outsider to assess but, alas, also one of the most important in assessing the financial reporting environment, is the style of a company's management. The central question is: How does management manage? By intimidation? By absurd targets? By unjustified optimism? Or by a realistic assessment of potential opportunities and how they might be pursued?

The place to start for the answer is with the CEO. More than any other single force, the CEO will set the "tone at the top" and establish priorities for everyone. If his first priority is the integrity of the organization, it will be shared by others. If his priorities include a properly functioning accounting department, that priority will be shared as well. If, however, the CEO's overriding objective is aggressive growth toward the construction of a corporate empire, that objective will dominate everyone else's agenda.

Unfortunately (at least from the perspective of financial reporting), fairly rare is the CEO who builds a company into a spectacular success by focusing primarily on the accounting department. The path to greatness, rather, frequently lies with some kind of strategic vision and the implementation of an aggressive program to pursue it. The much-sought skills in a CEO thus include supreme confidence, entrepreneurial courage, the ability to inspire workers, and a capacity for raising cash. Somehow a proclivity for accounting systems seems to get less emphasis.

Right away, therefore, almost any company setting out to pursue greatness (which is to say, almost every company worth investing in) has a built-in bias in favor of visionary expansion with less emphasis on the more mundane mechanics of financial reporting. While the company is still small, a make-do accounting department installed almost as an afterthought might work just fine. But that can change when the CEO gets what he is seeking—success. As the company grows, so do the demands on its financial reporting system as additional capital is raised, new products or services are created, revenues increase, facilities expand, employees are added, and expenses mount. Also accompanying success may be increased pressure—pressure to match the triumphs of previous quarters with even bigger triumphs in the present one. Gradually at first, and then with increasing velocity, increased pressure can result in a financial reporting environment that becomes dominated by an unfortunate combination of stretched systems, exhausted accounting staff, inadequate computerization, never-diminishing outside expectations, and corresponding internal demands. Soon, the financial reporting system, no longer as reliable as when the company was starting out, may start producing information of questionable veracity or, even worse, may become a vehicle through which executives seek temporary numerical enhancements to compensate for momentary operational or economic difficulties. The CEO's interest in the integrity of the system—perhaps never very great to begin with—may decline as operational and performance issues demand ever-increasing attention. All it takes is a small bump in the road for the entire structure to collapse into its own internal hollowness.

What is the lesson here? Foremost, it is the exercise of caution when evaluating a company run by a CEO possessed of supreme vision and energy but little ostensible attentiveness to the discipline of financial reporting. Sure, we all want to invest in a CEO who aspires to greatness. But an optimal CEO will also possess a healthy respect for the importance of operational infrastructure and, in particular, for the quality of the information the organization produces. Growth is critical, but financial reporting infrastructure is critical too. The former without the latter is a monument built on sand.

The Chief Financial Officer

A key player in balancing the pursuit of growth with a sound financial reporting infrastructure is the individual who runs the system: the CFO. In particular, those seeking to evaluate the company's financial reporting environment are looking for a CFO who functions on at least two levels. The first is the level of infrastructure. More than any single individual, it is the CFO's responsibility to see to the installation of a viable financial reporting system and, after that, to its expansion in accordance with the needs of a growing enterprise. That means that the CFO has to be an advocate—an advocate for staffing, computer systems, and money. He must be intolerant of temporary Band-aids and the unwillingness of his CEO to be distracted by the needs of the back-office accountants.

But that is only the first level on which the CFO must operate. The second is that the CFO must operate as the frontline guardian of integrity in financial reporting. This is not an issue of infrastructure, but an issue of corporate governance and backbone. In today's volatile stock market, the pressure on a CEO for short-term financial performance can be somewhere between excruciating and intolerable. The CFO must understand that. But, at the same time, he must not give in to it. He must be prepared to tell the CEO what he does not want to hear—"This quarter we're not going to make it." He must be politically sensitive to CEO attempts to override financial controls through the exploitation of the judgment calls inherent in GAAP and the perceived flexibility in the financial reporting system. He must be sensitive to—and prepared to defend against—aggressive budgets and the intolerance of others for failure to attain targeted results.

Why? Because an overly aggressive CEO and an overly compliant CFO can operate in tandem to create a "tone at the top" that all but guarantees some level of financial misreporting. Even ascribing to the CEO and the CFO wholesomeness of motive, the combination of a CEO's aggressiveness with a CFO's compliance can subject underlings to unfiltered insistence upon unreasonable demands in a context in which a champion for financial reporting integrity is lacking. The pressure can increase exponentially as unreasonable demands are passed down the chain of command. With no place to turn, executives at all levels do what it takes to comply. Where the demands are impossible to fulfill honestly, executives explore the only available alternative.

Worse than an overly compliant CFO, the CFO may himself become a collaborator in the CEO's unreasonable demands for performance and a contributor to the pressure placed on underlings. The effect is the same, only now the pressure has increased beyond even the unreasonable demands of the CEO. The risk of financial reporting corruption increases.

At a still more dangerous level, the CFO himself becomes a knowing participant in corruption of the system. Arm in arm with the CEO, or perhaps with the CEO's explicit awareness, the CFO himself exploits judgment calls under GAAP and flexibility in the system as he fundamentally comes to view the accounting department as the facilitator of the CEO's financial reporting needs. The system, accordingly, becomes disconnected from its purpose of reporting the results of operations and, instead, becomes nothing more than a means to an end—the end being the fulfillment of investor expectations. Not only does system integrity lack a champion: the would-be champion is himself a contributor to the system's corruption.

So any effort to understand the all-important financial reporting environment must include significant emphasis on the CFO. Technical skill, sophistication, operational experience—all of these are important. But also important are intestinal fortitude, strength of character, and unrelenting commitment to integrity in financial reporting. Those seeking to evaluate the environment of an organization must accept today's reality of the horrific pressures to which the CEO will be subject. A key question is the CFO's ability—notwithstanding that pressure—to keep the financial reporting system on the straight and narrow path. A company with such a CFO has a good chance of avoiding the small pitfalls that can evolve into big ones.

The Effectiveness of the Audit Committee

Now we come to what many would call the star of the show. That is the board's audit committee.

Ideally, an audit committee would not be needed at all. A company with a properly balanced CEO and a rock-solid CFO would seem to make an audit committee entirely redundant. What purpose is to be served when both the CEO and the CFO are each doing exactly the right thing?

Fair enough. But let's get serious. In how many companies can we expect the CEO to remain equally attentive to both financial performance and the soundness of accounting systems? And in how many companies can we expect a CFO to be steadfastly resistant to the earnest desires of his or her boss? That is to say, in few companies can we expect to find the CEO and the CFO doing their jobs exactly right. More likely, the CEO will place disproportionate emphasis on financial performance and the CFO will not be completely impervious to the priorities of the boss. The system to that extent will be vulnerable to corruption.

There is, therefore, a role for the audit committee, and it is a vital one. It has been discussed at length in the preceding chapter, but can be briefly summarized here. It is to oversee the financial reporting system with particular sensitivity to its vulnerabilities and the need for early detection should financial misreporting take place. The question for an evaluator of the financial reporting system is whether the audit committee's oversight role is being fulfilled.

What is the evaluator looking for? Start with independence. (See Exhibit 12–1.) An evaluator wants to see an audit committee sufficiently independent from the CEO to be able to perform its critical function of telling the CEO what he does not want to hear—that he is being too aggressive, that his financial reporting system is not up to snuff, that his "tone at the top" is not right. If the audit committee is not sufficiently independent, then it may prove no more effective than an overly compliant CFO. The financial reporting system, now at the board level, will lack the requisite champion for integrity in financial reporting, and the system will be at risk that any corruption will grow unimpeded.

In this regard, the investor has a friend in the new rules of the New York Stock Exchange and the NASD, discussed in detail in the preceding chapter. To reiterate briefly, those rules seek to impede audit committee participation by those whose exercise of independent judgment would be compromised by relationships with executives. Specified as among those lacking independence are employees of the company, directors receiving compensation from the company in excess of acceptable levels, immediate family members of executives, those individually or through their firms maintaining significant business relationships with the company, and those whose compensation at another company might be determined by an executive of the present one. A cautionary note, though, is that technical compliance with the rules may not be enough. The rules are a good starting point, but interpersonal relationships can compromise independence in a way that no rule can completely guard against. The underlying objective is not merely compliance with the technical rules, but the existence of genuine independence from corporate executives, which involves a more nuanced and subtle assessment of interpersonal relationships.

Here, an evaluator's understanding can potentially be enhanced by disclosures provided to the SEC. Biographical information in Form 10-K

Exhibit 12–1. An Effective Audit Committee

- Independent
- Financially sophisticated
- Diligent

and proxy statements can be scrutinized for ties with management which, while not breaking the rules, nonetheless suggest relationships by which genuine independence may be impeded. For example, business relationships controlled by the CEO may exist between an audit committee member and the company which, while not large enough to violate the rules, nonetheless provide a meaningful incentive for the audit committee member to stay on the CEO's good side. Or it may be that, while not possessing any formal relationship, an audit committee member and the CEO have been best friends for years.

Of course, effective audit committee oversight does not stop with independence, and the next step is to evaluate the members' financial sophistication. Here, again, the evaluator is assisted by the new rules which mandate some level of financial sophistication in each of the audit committee's members, but now the problem with the rules stems from their understandable inability to define exactly what financial sophistication means. Going beyond the vague admonitions of the rules, an evaluator of audit committee effectiveness may want to be particularly sensitive to whether any member possesses sophistication not simply in the technical requirements of GAAP but in corporate governance and, in particular, in the ways that financial reporting systems can be corrupted. Is there anything in the members' backgrounds to suggest they understand the importance of the "tone at the top?" That financial fraud starts with a certain type of environment? That overly aggressive targets and an unforgiving environment can be the death knell of integrity in financial reporting? It is not enough to have some technical knowledge in accounting—after all, the company has a CFO and an entire accounting department for that. The audit committee's function is to keep a diligent watch for corruption in the system itself.

An additional place to gain insight into the audit committee's level of sophistication may be the audit committee charter now required to be appended to the company's publicly filed proxy statement at least once every three years. No aspect of a typical audit committee charter can be expected to substantively address the sophistication of the audit committee members—aside from some obligatory preamble which (in deference to the new rules) may recite that the audit committee shall include "financially sophisticated" members. Nonetheless, insight into the committee's sophistication may be gleaned by reading between the lines and scrutinizing the thoughtfulness with which the charter appears to have been formulated. For example, the previous chapter highlighted the audit committee's critical role in overseeing financial reporting and seeking to ensure the right kind of environment or "tone at the top" in the financial reporting process. Are those aspects of the audit committee's function specified in the charter? Or does the charter seem to miss the forest for the trees, plunging right away into a checklist of mind-numbing activities ("review with the auditor the scope of the audit"), without any indication that the committee itself understands the handful of key objectives to which its energies should be primarily directed? Even worse would be a charter that reads like an instrument whose principal objective is to provide the audit committee with cover by emphasizing the financial reporting responsibilities of everyone (management, the outside auditor, the internal audit department, the CFO, etc.) but itself.

What kind of audit committee members does an investor want to see? There is no single answer, but it would seem to behoove a modern audit committee to include at least one member who has served as an auditor at an accounting firm. To its credit, the accounting profession has subjected its members to a barrage of educational programs directed at corruption in financial reporting, and few accounting firm partners could have remained impervious to the onslaught. This does not mean, obviously, the inclusion of someone—even a retired someone—from the company's outside accounting firm; that could potentially give rise to a whole host of independence issues and interconnecting relationships that would be impossible to unravel. Rather, a retired partner from one of the competing accounting firms might in many respects seem close to ideal.

That, in turn, takes us to that attribute of audit committee oversight which evaluators might find most important: the diligence with which members pursue their financial reporting responsibilities. Here, the evaluator is blessed with some useful disclosures in the Form 10-K and proxy statement. Foremost is the disclosure of the number of times the audit committee met over the previous year. If the number of meetings is one or two, the evaluator should consider whether an audit committee exists in little more than name. It is questionable whether an audit committee can provide meaningful financial reporting oversight when it meets only an average of once every six months.

Of course, the mere recitation that an audit committee "met" more than a couple of times a year does not in itself guarantee audit committee diligence. Beyond the potential for draftsmen to stretch the word "meeting" beyond the boundaries of normal English usage, the mere occurrence of a meeting in no way guarantees that the meeting was productive or focused on the right things. Hence, there is another reason to explore the biographies of the audit committee members and make a common sense assessment as to whether the members' positions and responsibilities would allow time for active audit committee participation.

For example, one might infer that a retired CPA would be almost ideally positioned to devote substantial effort to audit committee activities. Indeed, audit committee participation might even give such an individual an outlet for energies and skills that would otherwise go to waste. But the same cannot necessarily be said of a 45-year-old investment banker at the height of his career, dashing from city to city, making money hand over fist with each new client that goes public. Such an individual may bring extraordinary experience and depth to the board, but it may be worth wondering whether he's prepared to make the time commitment that diligent audit committee participation would require.

This is not, one should hasten to add, to criticize audit committee participation by investment bankers, lawyers, or other busy professionals. Nor is it to suggest that a retired accounting firm partner will always be best. The point, rather, is the usefulness of considering the members' backgrounds in evaluating the diligence with which the audit committee can be expected to oversee the financial reporting process. (See Exhibit 12-2.) For audit committee members, there is rarely an instant payoff, and busy professionals being pulled in different directions may feel the need to allow audit committee participation to receive a lower priority.

An additional resource to assess audit committee diligence may, again, be the audit committee charter. Here, too, one trying to size up committee diligence will need to probe between the lines, but clues may be discernible. For example, what exactly does the charter say about the level of audit committee activity? Does the charter specify a requisite number of meetings per year and, if so, how many? What does the charter say about the extent to which the audit committee is to meet collectively and privately with key executives and other providers of information, including the outside auditor and the director of internal audit?

Exhibit 12–2. Public Sources to Evaluate Audit Committee Effectiveness

- Proxy statements

- Forms 10-K

- The audit committee charter

Overall, an optimal charter should read like a document thoughtfully prepared by a committee that is ready to take on its oversight function. Less than optimal would be a series of mind-numbing paragraphs of lawyers' gobbledygook, presumably approved with little thought shortly before the SEC-mandated deadline.

A New Industry

Up to now, the potential indicia of a dangerous financial reporting environment have been limited to those within the company. Now we broaden the scope of the evaluator's analysis and consider the age of the company's industry. The point here is to use extra caution when the industry is new.

The reason is this. If a CEO, CFO, and audit committee are suboptimal, their coexistence in a new industry can maximize the opportunity for financial reporting weaknesses to develop. In old, established industries, the basics of accounting to a large extent are hemmed in by well-worn conventions and benchmarks in which fuzzy areas are few and numerical anomalies quickly stand out. In a new industry, in contrast, management is by definition blazing a new trail. The conventions of accounting are far from established, and a disconnect between the company's accounting and the underlying business reality may not be apparent until after the collapse. (See Exhibit 12–3.)

To begin, consider in an old, established industry how little mystery is left. The business's product line or service is pretty much established. The level of demand is largely fixed. Pricing is confined to very narrow parameters. Competitors are known. Expectations for return on investment can probably be measured in basis points. True, such a business is

---

Exhibit 12–3. "New Industry" Problems

- Expenses unknown

- Revenues unknown

- Return on investment unpredictable

- Unjustified expectations

- Entrepreneurial accounting

- Accounting judgments unguided by operational track record

---

always trying to elbow its way ahead of similarly entrenched competitors. But, overall, the thrill of the unknown is gone.

In a cutting-edge industry, in contrast, everything is up for grabs. Companies that did not exist yesterday are leapfrogging ahead of each other in the creation of new products or services. Demand is perceived to be somewhere between anybody's guess and infinity. Pricing is a total unknown. Investment returns are estimated to be somewhere north of those from the California gold rush. To look at it another way, jump-starting an innovative business in a new industry provides the opportunity for man's boundless capacity for optimism to expand unimpeded by experience. Unfortunately, things do not always work out as hoped.

For that matter, the path from cradle to accounting disaster in a new industry can be surprisingly predictable. It starts with a new product or service (waste management, health care, the internet, tulip bulbs) and a self-selecting group of competing entrepreneurs with enough vision, energy, and persuasiveness to raise enormous amounts of cash. Once raised, the cash must be immediately put to work, and research and development begins, employees are hired, facilities established, and advertisement commences. In the start-up phase, some things can get overlooked. One is expense. Nobody is quite sure how much all this is going to cost. Another is revenues. They are simply unknowable. Another is whether revenues less expense will satiate investors' elevated expectations of return on investment. In truth, nobody really knows what "the vision" can generate because it has never been done before. All that anyone knows is that it is certainly going to be Big.

In this quest for the next big thing, therefore, the seeds of its own destruction are potentially sewn. For there is no opportunity for a careful correlation of revenue, expense, and return on investment—beyond the immutable belief that the first and the third will be big and that the second, therefore, doesn't matter. The problem begins when expenses are higher than expected and revenues less, but the surrounding hype precludes business community recognition that, at a purely economic level, things aren't going so well. The consequence can be investor demand for a level of performance that the fledgling business simply cannot meet.

Accounting irregularities begin with pressure, and the need to fulfill unrealistic expectations in a new industry can be a prime source. Now the fact that the industry is a new one creates two problems: the absence of conventions in the application of accounting principles and the absence of operating history to guide accounting judgments as to what may be expected to go wrong.

The former stems from the fact that generally accepted accounting principles turn in part on exactly that—accounting that is "generally accepted"—and, in a new industry with untried business models, that which is "generally accepted" has yet to be established. In the absence of clear rules and well-worn conventions, a company's application of accounting principles can become as entrepreneurial as everything else it does. As new competitors enter the fray, the innovative accounting of one may start to imitate the innovative accounting of another, and the "generally accepted" norm may evolve into an accounting approach that, in truth, may not fairly capture the underlying business reality. Businesses in such an industry may report fabulous returns for a time, but at some point the more objective views of disinterested members of the financial community—academics, the financial press, FASB, the SEC— may intervene. If the accounting has become too entrepreneurial, prior-reported results may have to be revised downward.

The other problem with accounting in a new industry—the lack of an operational track record—is a consequence of the need to look into the future in reporting the results of today. The most obvious example is the need to establish present-day reserves for upcoming events such as a failure to collect receivables, future obligations of the business growing out of present-day sales, or anything else that fairly ought to be considered before reporting the bottom line. When an established track record exists, the determination of such future amounts can be almost automatic. In a new industry, it can be little more than an educated guess. Again, therefore, the opportunity exists to exploit uncertainty in accounting to enhance today's results.

Do the resulting accounting problems involve the kind of deliberate misstatements that qualify as accounting "irregularities"? It depends. It depends in part on whether the misapplication of accounting principles or incorrect estimates resulted from a good faith but mistaken judgment or a deliberate desire to camouflage the truth. The more fundamental point, though, centers on the extent to which growth in a new industry may carry with it the potential for unjustified pressure for performance and an accounting methodology which can become a vehicle to assist in seeing that unjustified expectations are fulfilled.

What are some examples of industries where these elements have come together to disastrous effect? There are a number. They include, for example, the waste management industry in which increased environmental sensitivity and new federal regulations combined to create a new industry of technological landfills in which pricing skyrocketed and then collapsed—with multitudinous allegations of accounting fraud following quickly behind. They include the health care industry which, for analogous reasons, followed a similar pattern. They include the telecommunications industry. And they include, of course, the new industries created by the internet where companies seemed to go through the entire cradle-to-disaster cycle almost in a matter of months. For those willing to go back further, they also include the railroads, automobiles, aviation, and radio.

For one seeking to undertake due diligence, the ultimate lesson is not to avoid new industry start-ups. It is to be aware. From a perspective of solid accounting, a new industry start-up can bring out the worst. Rather than blind faith in reported earnings, a degree of skepticism is in order.

An Aggressive Growth Program

It is unfortunate that the characteristics described above frequently go hand in hand with companies that aggressively pursue growth. And if a financial reporting environment is already lacking—with an overly aggressive CEO, a compliant CFO, an ineffective audit committee, and new industry entrepreneurial accounting—a program of aggressive growth is sure to test its weaknesses. Indeed, it is often a CEO's aggressive pursuit of growth that gives otherwise small accounting problems the opportunity to become truly monumental disasters.

Some of the biggest problems from growth occur when a company tries to make incremental leaps forward through acquisition, and one of the most obvious is that, in acquiring another business, you can never be sure what you're getting. Acquiring a company can be exceedingly difficult—not just from the paperwork, which tends to get a disproportionate share of the attention, but from the difficulty in ascertaining whether, at bottom, the acquired business is any good. Insight into the viability of the company's customer base, revenue stream, cash flow, and business prospects often resides at levels far below the reported numbers. And the risk increases owing to a natural incentive for the seller to dress up the numbers in hopes of getting the best price. All too often, acquiring companies have taken on accounting problems that didn't surface until months or longer after the closing documents had been signed. By that point, the acquiring company's reported results themselves had become infected with fraud.

But aggressive growth creates problems for the acquiring company beyond the potential to inherit someone else's accounting manipulations. One of the most fundamental, which has already been suggested above, is simply the problem of infrastructure. The company outgrows its financial reporting staffing, computer systems, and executive capability. As the growth continues, things only get worse.

Such an overstretched infrastructure is not merely a problem in itself. For the consequences may include an inability of the system to record, process, and report financial data automatically without the significant intervention of accounting personnel to bridge the gap between incompatible or cobbled-together accounting systems. When the need for human intervention increases, so too increases the opportunity for human mistakes and, somewhat more ominous, the potential need for human discretion in the process by which final results are determined. The need for such discretion introduces the possibility that, when the going gets tough, that discretion may be abused.

A further problem from aggressive growth is its potential to disguise numerical anomalies that, in a more stable environment, might point to accounting problems. If, for example, a stable business were to generate cash flow which over a sustained period departed from reported earnings (look again at the financial statements of Health Management), the discrepancy at some point would likely trigger attention and inquiry. In a fast growing business, in contrast, a stable environment remains elusive, period-to-period comparisons are difficult, and numerical anomalies can get lost in the confusion. Beneath the surface of attractive results, accounting problems can lurk.

Still another problem with aggressive growth arises from the pressure on executives to see that it is sustained. At its simplest level, the problem is a mathematical one: 20% revenue increases are easier when revenue is $1 million than when it has already increased five hundred-fold. But beyond that, growth opportunities in any particular industry are not infinite. Once the easy opportunities have been exploited, continued growth comes only with increased difficulty and, often, at a higher price—as new entrants bid up the costs of production as they try to get in on the action.

At some point, it may make sense for the growth curve to level off, but a decision to curtail growth can be impeded by another force acting on executive judgment: hype. Surrounding a rapidly expanding company, particularly in a new industry, is almost inevitably a high profile in the financial press and a stock price that may reflect journalistic accolades more than business fundamentals. A stock price inflated thereby creates a strong disincentive to terminate a growth program that, in fact, may be objectively unsustainable. The natural desire is to keep the growth curve in place.

Putting all of these elements together, then, can result in a company that looks like this. It is dominated by a visionary CEO determined not to disappoint aggressive financial community expectations. At his right hand is a compliant CFO who, as a practical matter, cannot avoid doing what the CEO wants. The accounting staff is overworked. The audit committee is irrelevant. Industry conventions for "generally accepted" accounting are still being written. The accounting system does not work effectively even under the best of circumstances. And everyone within the company is subject to tremendous pressure to continue a growth curve that, in fact, cannot be sustained. It is a disaster waiting to happen.

An Industry Downturn

The catalyst for the disaster will often involve what, to those within the company, at first seems a momentary slump. In truth, it may be more than that: It may be the first indication of a business downturn that will end up in engulfing the industry. (See Exhibit 12–4.) At its first appearance, though, it is almost impossible to see a broader downturn for what it is.

Unfortunately, a momentary slump in the face of unrelenting pressure for expansion can make exploitation of an already vulnerable accounting system difficult to resist. Indeed, resistance can melt away if a lack of accounting convention yields the conclusion that no one is doing anything wrong. Accounting adjustments thus may take care of the problem for one quarter, but the pressure returns when, the next quarter, the business has not bounced back. More aggressive accounting follows. And so the pattern goes. The industry continues to decline. The accounting becomes increasingly aggressive. At some point, executives have crossed the line into fraud. Executives are now on the treadmill described in Chapter 1.

Stepping back, perhaps the most alarming message for outside evaluators of financial performance involves the ostensible similarities between a genuinely successful company and a company whose success is really a function of accounting manipulation. Both may be dominated by a visionary CEO. Both may be growing in a new and exciting industry. Both may be generating a sustained pattern of excellent results. And,

---

Exhibit 12–4. A Petri Dish for Accounting Irregularities

- Overly aggressive CEO

- Overly compliant CFO

- Ineffective audit committee

- New industry

- Aggressive growth program

- Industry downturn

---

without delving into what is going on beneath the surface, both may look like terrific vehicles for investment. No wonder so many have lost so much money.

The critical point is not to stuff one's money into a mattress. It is to recognize those criteria that may suggest an accounting problem and to increase skepticism accordingly. More than anything, the lesson is to look beneath the veneer of reported results.

CHAPTER 13

ACCOUNTING IRREGULARITIES AND THE FUTURE OF FINANCIAL REPORTING

Michael R. Young

We have at this point looked at the topic of accounting irregularities from almost every conceivable angle. We've looked at their origin. We've looked at the immediate aftermath of detection. We've looked at the procurement of new audited financial statements, the mechanics of an investigation, dealing with class actions, responding to regulators, and criminal implications. We've looked at prevention and avoidance. Seemingly, the entirety of the subject has been thoroughly explored.

Except for one question: Why? Why now, as we begin the twenty-first century, are we seeing such an increase in fraudulently reported financial results—particularly given the seemingly contrary trend of corporations seeking to behave like good corporate citizens? What is going on in the world of financial reporting that is giving rise to almost an epidemic of misreported financial results?

As mentioned at the outset, the underlying cause is not dishonesty. Nor is it immorality. Beyond the experience of any individual company, the cause is rooted in the fact that we are at a historic moment in the evolution of financial reporting. In particular, we are at a moment where financial market demands for information are not being met by the financial reporting system that happens to be in place. On the one hand, financial markets are demanding instantaneous, non-stop financial information. On the other hand, our financial reporting system is designed to provide information only periodically—once a quarter at best. The consequence is misreported financial results.

Identification of an underlying cause of accounting irregularities is an important first step. The second step is to assess the direction in which the financial reporting system seems to be evolving and the extent to which the mismatch between financial market needs and financial reporting system capability will worsen, get better, or stay pretty much the same. Here the news is good. There is every indication that the financial reporting system is evolving in a way that will eventually cause the underlying pressures giving rise to fraudulent financial reporting to dissipate. There is much reason to hope, therefore, that the present upsurge in accounting irregularities will ultimately prove to be a temporary problem rather than a long-term feature of financial reporting by public companies.

A Real-Time World

Let us first spend a moment on the demands of today's financial markets. In particular, let us first address the insatiable thirst of financial markets for nonstop information.

In substance, financial markets today are functioning in a real-time world. Innovators such as Bloomberg, Dow Jones, and any number of entrepreneurial upstarts flash financial and business information around the world the instant it's available. One such company advertises the delivery of "global financial news to 16,000 places every minute." Traveling executives increasingly find themselves transporting miniaturized communications centers—cellular phones, pagers, beepers, even fax machines—so that they may instantaneously receive, and act upon, the latest events. Anyone with access to the Internet—which is, increasingly, everyone—has ready access to financial information that, in another era, would have been available to just a highly select few.

The extent of this information revolution has infiltrated the very fiber of our culture. With many of us spending much of each day in front of a computer, it seems perfectly natural to see the latest financial statistics flashing across a corner of the screen. It seems completely normal that, while heading for a Broadway theater in Times Square, stock prices courtesy of Dow Jones are never more than a glance away. It hardly seems surprising that the telephones on airplanes (no longer are we cut off while flying) give us second-by-second financial market updates. Even more traditional businesses are transforming themselves. CBS, through its MarketWatch.com, now advertises "the hottest financial stories" and "market data in real-time" to allow all of us to "stay ahead of the market."

The impact of this onslaught of information on financial markets is nothing less than extraordinary. If something happens at the Bundesbank in Germany with the potential to influence United States financial markets, we might expect no more than 10 to 15 minutes to elapse before trading on the New York Stock Exchange is affected. Indeed, it seems that almost no corner of civilization, no matter how ostensibly isolated in locale or tradition, can escape the insatiable thirst for information of a real-time world. Even the courts, with their explicit exclusion of electronic communications devices from their hallowed halls, are not immune. When an important court decision is rendered, strategically placed individuals, through a carefully designed system of hand signals, find a way to get the information within seconds to the outside world so the information can be electronically transmitted and put to use.

A 1930s Financial Reporting System

Our financial reporting system, of course, was not designed with any of this in mind. The basics of today's system were, after all, designed in the 1930s during the Great Depression. It was a time when carbon paper was viewed as a technological innovation. The dominant concern at the time was not the speed of transmission of reliable financial information but the objective that reliable financial information be available to begin with. It was natural to assume that the information itself would be transmitted almost entirely on paper.

At the core of this Depression-era system, moreover, was the concept that financial information need be available only periodically. That is to say, no one had reason to think that some day technological innovation would collapse the time needed to assemble and report financial information to days or even minutes. The underlying concept of the 1930s, rather, was built upon the notion that the financial results of operations were to be assembled by a heavily populated accounting staff, packaged for management, and ultimately—every so often—provided to the public. The public, in turn, could make its investment decisions accordingly.

Hence, the original public reporting requirements of the Securities Exchange Act of 1934 contemplated the filing of financial information only annually. Over time, the laudable objective of encouraging efficiency in financial markets caused this requirement to be changed to semi-annually and quarterly. At root, though, the system remained a periodic one. In other words, the underlying premise of the system continued to be that financial information would be made available only periodically. Today's system is thus an anachronistic remnant of the technology—i.e., carbon paper and the printing press—that existed when the system was designed.

True to its historical underpinnings, moreover, the core of today's financial reporting system continues to be a financial report that comes out once a year. That report, of course, is the set of annual financial statements that is audited by an outside accounting firm and included with the company's annual Form 10-K.

And let's pause a moment to look at how those financial statements are put together. First, we wait for the year to end. Then we wait for another twelve weeks or more while the auditor combs through the company's books and records. Then we wait while the data is assembled, typed, delivered to a printer, and, then, given to the United States Postal Service, which ends up delivering the information on foot. By the time users of the financial information receive it, the most recent information is ordinarily three months old. It took less time for Columbus to discover America.

It is true that, under encouragement from the SEC, the financial community is trying to take big strides forward. Thus, we have the development of the Edgar system of electronic SEC filing and, increasingly, companies placing their Forms 10-K and Forms 10-Q—as well as press releases, product information, and background data—on their Web sites. Although this is a big step in the right direction, it continues to be intellectually hindered by the periodic concept of the 1930s. That is, basically all we are doing is taking periodic information from paper and placing it on the computer.

Thus, a vacuum in financial reporting exists. It is a vacuum between the real-time financial information that financial markets demand and the inability of our creaky, sputtering financial reporting system to deliver information more frequently than once a quarter.

So Enter the Analysts

It is the miracle of a capitalist system that such a vacuum does not last for long. Here, an entire population of entrepreneurs have rushed in to provide to financial markets the updated financial information they so earnestly desire. Those entrepreneurs are the community of Wall Street financial analysts.

For it is not, in fact, the case that a user of financial information only has access to financial performance once a quarter. Instead, a user has available the more up-to-date information provided by financial analysts—in the form of readily published earnings expectations. This analyst information may be right or it may be wrong, but it possesses one virtue that the official financial data does not. It is available.

It is thus that we find ourselves in the peculiar position of having in place a carefully structured and painstakingly built formal financial reporting system that is being largely ignored by everybody. And a fair argument can be made that today's system is indeed being largely ignored. The annual filing of a Form 10-K does not move financial markets. By the time the 10-K comes out, the information at best is ancient history and has been factored into the stock price for months. Many have probably heard the story of a food manufacturer which, as a test of the usefulness of its annual financial statements, offered shareholders a choice: a glossy copy of the company's annual report or a free pound of cookies. Most shareholders went for the cookies.

Although unaudited quarterly statements play a more important role, rarely do even quarterly statements move markets. That is to say, rarely do quarterly statements move markets when they are consistent with already existing analyst expectations. When they are not consistent with expectations, they can move markets quite a lot.

That takes us to the crux of the matter. What moves financial markets is not an annual 10-K or even a quarterly 10-Q. What moves financial markets is the published expectations of Wall Street analysts. In substance, the published expectations of Wall Street analysts are perceived to establish, within a very narrow margin, the parameters for the upcoming actual financial results. Analyst expectations have become, in effect, a company's reported earnings.

A Consequence Is Accounting Irregularities

What does all this have to do with accounting irregularities? The elevated importance to financial markets of analyst expectations has resulted in a financial reporting environment in which, for a number of public companies, the preoccupation of financial reporting is not accurately depicting the financial performance of the enterprise. Rather, the preoccupation of financial reporting is seeing to it that analyst expectations—one way or another—are fulfilled.

For public companies faced with this preoccupation, its fulfillment can be a nightmare insofar as no legally satisfactory way exists by which the accuracy of analyst expectations can be controlled. That is not for lack of trying on the part of analysts. Analysts earn their living, and if they're lucky get famous, providing investors with estimates of public company future financial performance. The easiest way to formaulate such estimates is to ask a company's CFO what he or she expects.

Such an analyst inquiry would seem like a golden opportunity for a CFO to get accurate information out on the street and to keep analyst expectations from varying from the truth. However, the law, as a result of its understandable paranoia about the leakage of inside information, tries to keep precisely that from happening.

So here's what can end up taking place. The analyst needs to get updated financial information. He telephones the CFO. He gives the CFO, say, his latest guess as to how the quarter is going to come out. And he asks the CFO, "Am I right or wrong?"

There is no completely satisfactory way for the CFO to answer that question. Basically, the CFO has two choices. First, he can try to "steer" the analyst into a more accurate prediction or simply tell the analyst he is right or wrong. However, the CFO himself may not have a firm sense of how the quarter is going to come out and may end up inadvertently creating an expectation that can neither be fulfilled nor easily corrected. Worse than that, providing up-to-date financial results to a single analyst creates a risk of giving out inside information. If the information is material, and it probably will be, that sets up the CFO for a subsequent charge of violating SEC regulations and being a participant in insider trading. Insider trading is a felony.

The second alternative is for the CFO to keep his mouth shut. Here, the problem is a different one. If the CFO keeps his mouth shut, and the analyst goes forward with the publication of incorrect expectations, then the actual quarterly results, when they come out (by preannouncement or otherwise), will potentially wreak havoc. If actual results exceed analyst expectations, then shareholders are all the happier and no real harm results (beyond extraordinary inefficiency in information dissemination). If, however, actual results are significantly below street expectations, the result for the stock price can be significant. So-called "momentum" investors may flee the stock. The stock price may collapse. And the company—as well as the CFO, the CEO, and any number of inside and outside directors—may very well end up defendants in class action litigation.

Either way, our hapless CFO is at substantial risk that an incorrect earnings estimate will create a street expectation that cannot be fulfilled or painlessly corrected. If an incorrect estimate takes hold, then, as quarter-end approaches—and with it the inevitable day of reckoning—the pressure mounts. And so does the incentive to exploit those hazy areas of generally accepted accounting principles (GAAP) which would allow the company ostensibly to make up for the earnings shortfall. (See Chapter 1.)

It is, therefore, the vacuum resulting from what financial markets want, which is immediate financial information, and what the present structure of financial reporting systems enable companies to deliver, which is quarterly and annual reports, that has contributed so handily to the financial reporting environment that lies at the core of the recent increase in accounting irregularities. The vacuum is filled by analysts, and analyst expectations, in turn, create enormous pressure on a company to see that they are fulfilled. Accounting irregularities, of course, don't start with dishonesty. They start with pressure.

Other Capital Market Inefficiencies

Still additional problems result from the vacuum created by the real-time demands of financial markets and today's periodic system of financial reporting.

One such problem is the resulting volatility both in individual stock market prices and in the market as a whole. The underlying causes of that volatility, of course, are numerous. A big cause, though, stems from the market gyrations that come about during "earnings season" when companies announce or preannounce quarterly results. For an individual company, the fallout can include a collapsing stock price, a demoralized work force (whose stock options may now be under water), anxious lenders, and class action litigation (even in the absence of an accounting irregularity problem). An October 1999 announcement of a weak outlook by IBM resulted in a one-day loss of market value of $39 billion. Three months later, Lucent Technologies' announcement of an anticipated failure to attain analyst expectations (it said it expected to miss them by about 15 cents) translated into a market capital loss almost twice as large—$64 billion.

But the fallout is not limited to the management and the shareholders of the particular company that happens to disappoint. When Intel preannounced disappointing earnings for the first quarter of 1998, it reportedly triggered a collapse in securities markets around the world. Unpredictable volatility in the securities markets is something that investors have just learned to live with.

But they don't live with it for free. Volatility means risk. And risk means investors want a higher return on their capital investment. An important consequence of the volatility that necessarily results from our periodic financial reporting system, therefore, is the additional premium investors require from the securities markets to compensate for the increased risk. Here, again, the cost is not limited to the company or investors of a particular company that happens to disappoint. To some extent, it is shared by the stock market as a whole.

Operational inefficiencies from a periodic reporting system follow as well. Manufacturing companies, on going public, have perceived a change in the buying patterns of their customers, owing to their customers' awareness of the manufacturers' need to attain a certain level of quarterly revenue. One such company, for example, found that, after going public, purchases by distributors tended to become clustered in the third month of each quarter. As the company went into each third month, its nervousness over a prospective failure to make its quarterly numbers led to increasing levels of discounting, which only increased the incentives for the company's customers to hold off their purchases as long as they could. After several years, the company found its assembly lines less active in the first month of each quarter and then working overtime in the third. Shipping problems developed as the physical limitations of the loading docks could not accommodate quarter-end peak demand. The problem was exacerbated insofar as other manufacturing companies in the geographic vicinity seemed to be going through the same thing and all were simultaneously seeking to line up available trucking. On top of everything else, quarter-end also presented a shortage of trucks.

Such logistical problems can lead to breakdowns in accounting systems. One representative of the SEC's Division of Enforcement encountered a public company which, he suspected, had turned back its computer clock as a result of a logistical failure to ship all merchandise during a quarter-end peak. Faced with seemingly corroborative documentation from the independent trucker showing that shipment had in fact taken place before quarter-end, the SEC official on a hunch telephoned the trucker only to learn that the trucker, at the request of the manufacturer, had back-dated the shipping documentation. Nor was the request that the trucker do so apparently at all unusual. The trucker went on to volunteer that, at the end of each quarter, he received literally hundreds of similar requests from other companies.

The problems do not stop there. Still another results from almost extraordinary inefficiency in the way that critical financial information ends up being transmitted to the public through the intermediary of financial analysts. Mechanically, the present system works something like this: The typical CFO at a public company has sitting on his desk a computer. That computer is plugged into the company's management information system, which provides information that is sufficiently reliable for the fundamental operational and financial decisions of the enterprise. It tells the CFO, and for that matter anybody who's plugged into it, financial performance to date and, by inference, to some extent where the company will be at the end of the quarter.

Now let's consider a Wall Street analyst whose office happens to be, say, in a building across the street. He has sitting on his desk a computer. It is the analyst's fundamental mission in life to find out what's on the CFO's computer and to get it into *his* computer. He'll take whatever information he can get, put it into his own computer, and thereby generate an earnings forecast.

To find out what's on the CFO's computer, the analyst uses one of the most up-to-date of technological devices—the telephone. He telephones the CFO to extricate whatever clues and insights he can gain about the company's financial performance.

For reasons already discussed, the law heavily discourages the CFO from selectively providing important information. So the two may end up speaking in code. The analyst may say something like, "I'm predicting EPS of $.32 for the quarter—how comfortable are you in that area?" The CFO, having been cautioned against expressing a view on analyst expectations, at most allows himself to talk about the past. He accordingly might respond with something like, "How can you be at $.32 when this quarter last year we came in at $.25, as we have, in fact, for the previous 17 quarters." At some point, our analyst gets the message and, sure enough, puts out his new earnings forecast: $.25. Although both possess the most efficient means of electronic communication in the history of civilization, our CFO and Wall Street analyst have digressed into a communication system of winks and nods over which cuneiform would be an improvement.

And that's without even getting to company incentives to "talk down" analyst expectations to less than actually foreseen, or to the potential incentive by analysts to issue favorable reports owing to preexisting relationships between the company and the analyst's investment bank. All of these amount to extraordinary inefficiencies in the dissemination of financial information to the investing public.

Our Depression-era periodic system of financial reporting even creates inefficiencies from the perspective of financial management. The chairman of one high-tech company once observed that his internal financial reporting systems were sufficiently sophisticated that every day he, like other senior executives, received on his e-mail a report of revenue on the previous day's shipments. It so happened that the nature of the company's business was such that its margins were fairly consistent. Thus, receipt of shipping information in terms of revenues yielded in substance daily information of earnings and, by inference, earnings per share. The information was reliable and always up to date. Unfortunately, such was the terror instilled in the chairman by virtue of the federal securities laws, that the chairman (who wanted periodically to sell a portion of his very substantial stock holdings) became paranoid about having access to such timely information when the public did not. He accordingly had himself disconnected from the company's e-mail.

There's Another Way

So that's where we are at the moment. Our periodic system of financial reporting creates enormous pressure for fundamentally honest people to perpetrate accounting fraud. It creates unnecessary volatility in the stock market. It requires rational investors to demand a premium for securities investments. It gives rise to operational inefficiencies. It results in enormous inefficiency in the transmission of information from public companies to financial markets. It even creates an incentive for corporate managers to disconnect themselves from up-to-date information.

There's got to be a better way. And, in fact, there is. Members of the financial community are increasingly acknowledging the need for an evolution beyond the financial reporting system of the 1930s into an era of non-stop information of the sort financial markets want. In other words, there was an alternative available to our chairman who disconnected himself from the company e-mail, though we can hardly blame him for not thinking of it. He could have stayed connected to his e-mail. And, in fact, he could have let the e-mail go out to the analysts and the financial community at large. That is to say, he could have reported his company's financial results on a real-time basis.

Now an understandable reaction on the part of CFOs might be unmitigated terror. Anyone familiar with the agony of putting out a quarterly press release has reason to flee from the concept of fundamentally doing so at least once a day. How would the information be checked? What controls would there be on reliability? What happens if there's an honest mistake? How can we protect ourselves from the class action plaintiffs?

Those are all good questions, and not all of them have perfect answers. But the accelerating pace of innovation in technology and financial reporting systems will make increasingly apparent the need to move beyond the periodic system rooted in the technology of the 1930s. Already the AICPA is hard at work on the development of real-time auditor "assurance services" so that users may be satisfied as to the reliability of real-time financial information without waiting for the comfort of a year-end audit. At the same time, scholars are embracing the potential for innovations in financial reporting potentially made available by the concept of computer-to-computer interaction. Experts on legal liability are fashioning new ways to manage the risk of exposure to litigation arising out of real-time financial information, including the possibility of contractual limitations to liability entered through the use of "electronic signatures" transmitted by computer. And the United States Senate, through its subcommittee on securities, has undertaken to explore a reconfiguration of 1930's era securities regulations to facilitate enhanced financial reporting systems.

At the very least, moreover, the opportunity for dramatic advances in capital market efficiency will be lost on no one. Among other things, real-time financial reporting would free corporate America from its economically nonsensical preoccupation with quarterly results. There is absolutely no economic justification for focusing upon a quarter as the economic unit in which to take stock of financial performance beyond the fact that that's what's written in the law. Making available financial information on a real-time basis would almost require users of financial information to discard the quarter as a unit of measurement and to adopt a unit that made sense for each particular business and industry. For some companies and industries, that unit might be a week, a month, a quarter, semi-annually, or a year. The point is that users would have the freedom to adopt a time period that actually made sense rather than the "one size fits all" period decreed by federal law.

A more fundamental advantage, moreover, would be the opportunity for increased efficiency in financial markets as investment would be allocated not according to quarterly results or the "best guess" estimates of financial analysts, but by reliable financial information provided directly by the company all the time. A collateral but equally significant benefit would be the decrease in stock market volatility insofar as discrepancies between market expectations and actual results would never develop or, having developed, would be corrected in modest amounts every day rather than in one large correction at the end of each quarter.

Still another advantage would be the practical elimination of the principal incentive for—and perhaps the mechanical ability to perpetrate—financial misreporting in the form of accounting irregularities. Gone would be the brooding omnipresence of quarterly analyst expectations and, accordingly, the pressure to manipulate results in order to meet them. More than that, also largely eliminated would be the mechanical ability to perpetrate accounting sleights of hand, insofar as financial information would be publicly available automatically before any of the (at least traditional) manipulations could be put in place. That is not to suggest, of course, that real-time financial reporting would eliminate financial fraud for all time. We all know better than that. But it would take us a giant step in the right direction.

None of this is to suggest that anyone is proposing that the totality of a company's internal reporting system be opened up to the outside world. Public companies will inevitably want to limit access to information that is reliable and that can reasonably be transmitted on a regular basis. In addition, the transmittal of any such information would presumably be accompanied by appropriate caveats and warnings directed to the extent of the information's reliability. Before any of this can happen, moreover, financial reporting systems would have to be improved to the point where the real-time transmission of key information were possible. Companies would have to follow the example of companies such as Microsoft, which is collapsing the time it takes to assemble and report financial results to achieve a "continuous close" where information is accurate and current every day of the month.

Nevertheless, the real-time needs of financial markets are dragging today's financial reporting system in the direction of increased frequency of financial reporting without anyone really focusing on the broader implications. An increasingly common example is the advent of earnings "preannouncements" when actual results are diverging significantly from analyst expectations. According to one survey, 72% of Fortune 500 CFOs have decided to preannounce or provide early guidance on earnings, presumably as a consequence of the downside of waiting for the end of the legally mandated quarter. Other examples of more frequent data being made available without waiting for quarter-end include companies that regularly report mid-quarter results, retailers who post on their Web sites updated sales figures, hotel chains whose Web sites include updated occupancy rates, and newspapers whose Web sites include updated circulation figures. Meanwhile, the SEC's new "Regulation FD," in clamping down further on the selective disclosure of material information to analysts, has given public companies a stark choice: make information available to everyone or keep it to themselves. Increasingly, companies are choosing broader and more frequent disclosure.

The good news, therefore, is that, although fraudulent financial reporting will never be eliminated, the pressures giving rise to the present-day epidemic of accounting irregularities will foreseeably cease. Change rarely comes easily, and we can expect earnest debate and startling innovation as financial reporting proceeds through the twenty-first century. Some will inevitably long for the days of carbon paper. But for others, a new era of financial reporting may be, at least to some extent, exhilarating.

A

Accountant, forensic, 83-84
  benefits of using outside forensic
    accountants, 100
  billing rates, 99
  coordination with outside auditor,
    116-18
  defined, 97
  evidence-gathering techniques, 104
  experience of, 102, 107
  expertise of, 98-99
  facilitation of financial statement
    restatement, 68
  immediate objectives of, 105-6
  independent forensic accounting
    team, 68
  interaction with incumbent auditor,
    68, 76, 116-17
  interaction with lawyers, 114-16
  investigation conducted by. *See*
    Investigation, forensic
  objectivity of, 101
  reasons for hiring, 97-102
  retention by outside counsel, 83-84
  retention of, 57
  scrutiny of transactions, 104, 114
  typical approach of, 105
Accounting conventions
  forensic accountant's expertise, 98
  new industry vs. old industry, 297
Accounting irregularities. *See also*
  Fraud
  defined, 3-6, 70
  discovery of, 45. *See also* Aftermath
    of fraud discovery
  D&O insurance policy and, 156-57
  errors distinguished from irregulari-
    ties, 4-5
  evolution of financial reporting
    system, 306
  examples of, 70
  fulfilling analysts' expectations,
    310-11
  increase in, 1, 3
  investigation of. *See* Investigation
  "irregularity" absent from press
    release, 56

  in new industry, 300
  nomenclature, 4
  petri dish for, 303
  start and growth in corporate
    environment, 6, 250
  surfacing of, 20
  undetected growth of, 3
  vulnerability to, 281
Accounting policies, changes in, 71, 72
Accounting systems, 87, 98-99
  of acquired companies, 233
  adequacy of, 233
  general ledger, 113-14
Acquisitions, 233, 301
Action plan by board of directors, 53-54
Adjudication
  in delisting proceedings, 189
  in D&O insurance coverage, 159-60
Adjusting journal entry, 256
Aftermath of fraud discovery, 45
  action plan implementation, 53
  auditor's upper hand, 60
  initial board meeting, 46-50
  initial press release, 54-56, 127-30
  preliminary investigation, 45-46
  race against time, 51-53
Aggressive growth, 300-2
AICPA. *See* American Institute of
  Certified Public Accountants
  (AICPA)
American Institute of Certified Public
  Accountants (AICPA)
  auditor "assurance services," 315
  auditor independence issue, 261
  auditor independence rules, 263
  new rules of financial reporting, 36
  standards for previously issued
    audit reports, 63
American Stock Exchange (AMEX),
  181
  new rules of financial reporting,
    24, 36
Analysts. *See* Financial analysts
Attorney-client privilege
  and forensic accountants, 114-15,
    117

Attorney-client privilege, *cont.*
  in grand jury testimony, 208
  interviews of witnesses, 89
  investigative report, 94-95
  limitation, 209
  waiver of, 89, 94-95, 208
Attorney work-product doctrine, 208-9
Audit committee, 16-17. *See also* Audit
    committee functions
  activating in aftermath of discovery,
    56-57
  Blue Ribbon Committee recommen-
    dations, 35-39, 234-35
  charter. *See* Charter of audit
    committee
  communication with. *See* Communi-
    cation with audit committees;
    SAS-61
  as defendants in class-action
    lawsuits, 42, 122
  forensic accountants retained by,
    97-98
  ignorance of, 17
  inadequacies of, 16-17
  inadequate configuration, 41
  independence. *See* Audit committee
    independence
  insufficiently diligent, 41-42
  internal audit functions and, 40
  key role in financial reporting,
    27-28
  Levitt initiative concepts, 34-35
  litigation risks, 43-44
  outside auditor and, 17, 40. *See also*
    Audit committee information
    from the outside auditor
  outside counsel reporting to, 83
  oversight of financial reporting. *See*
    Financial reporting, responsibility
    for
  responsibility for investigation,
    56-57, 68, 97-98
  Treadway Commission's recommen-
    dations, 27-28
Audit committee functions, 227-28
  access to reliable information,
    247-48
  active participation, 296
  assessment of auditor independence,
    265-66

battle for corporate culture, 231
charter, 235, 242-44, 295, 296-97
charter, sample, 277-80
checklists, 229-30
compensation, 246-47
configuration of committee, 234-41
CPA as member, 241, 296
detection of financial misreporting,
    233-34
diligence, 295-96
effectiveness of, 292-97
establish proper tone at the top,
    231-33, 271-73
financial sophistication, 241-42,
    294-95
good judgment, 276-77
independence. *See* Audit committee
    independence
information from internal audit,
    269-71
information from senior manage-
    ment, 248-49
information from the outside
    auditor. *See* Audit committee
    information from the outside
    auditor
key objectives, 230
learn the business, 274-75
logistical capability of reporting
    system, 233, 252
meetings, 275-76, 295-96
membership requirements, 234-35
minimize paper, 273-74
outsource of internal audit, 270
oversight of financial reporting. *See*
    Financial reporting, responsibil-
    ity for public sources to evaluate
    effectiveness, 297
purpose defined in charter, 242-43
report filed yearly with SEC, 235,
    244-46
statement of purpose, 243, 277
tools, 271
trust in senior executives, 272-73
willingness to work, 242-47
Audit committee independence, 237-41,
    293-94
  requirements, NASD and NYSE,
    235-36, 238-41
  rules prior to 1999, 234

Audit committee information from the
outside auditor, 249-51
  auditor independence, 260-69
  checking thoroughness of the audit,
    258-59
  environmental information, 251
  insufficient demands for, 42
  level of cooperation, 253-54
  logistical capabilities of financial
    reporting system, 252
  managerial bias in GAAP applica-
    tion, 253
  nonmaterial PAJEs, 256-58
  quarterly review process, 249-50
  SAS-61 items to be discussed,
    259-60
  unusual reserve activity, 255-56
Auditor. *See also* Outside auditor
  audit process during re-audit, 74-76
  benefits of retaining incumbent
    auditor, 65-67
  delicate mission of, 272
  documents requested in audit
    process, 74-75
  forensic accountants' interaction
    with, 76
  incumbent vs. new auditor, 57,
    65-67
  independence of. *See* Auditor
    independence
  inventory inspection and verifica-
    tion, 112
  mistrust of, 64-65
  new auditor reluctance, 67
  new procedures in audit testing, 74
  non-audit services, 261-62, 264, 267
  professional skepticism approach,
    68, 75, 103
  re-audit by, 74-76
  selection of, 66
  working papers of, 66-67, 117
Auditor independence, 260-69
  AICPA policy, 261
  AICPA rules, 263
  effect of lawsuits, 78-79
  five-step approach to audit commit-
    tee assessment, 265-68
  GAAS requirements, 78, 268
  ISB rules, 263, 264
  SEC regulatory concerns, 261-62

  SEC rules, 263, 264, 266
"Auditor Independence War," 262
Auditor's failure to detect fraud, 18-19,
  283-85
Auditor's Responsibility to Detect and
  Report Errors and Irregularities.
  See SAS-53
Audit process, 74-76
  evidence requested, 74-75
  misconceptions among company
    personnel, 74
  new audit team personnel, 76
  new procedures, 74
  new system conducted as fraud
    investigation, 251
  timeliness of audit approach, 251
Audit reports
  auditor's upper hand, 60
  effect on previously issued reports,
    62-64
  prior-year reports, 67
Audit sampling, 68, 104, 251
  abandonment of approach, 251
Audit testing
  GAAS audit vs. forensic investiga-
    tion, 104
  GAAS requirement, 258
  new procedures, 74
AU Section 380 (Communications With
  the Audit Committee), 38

B

Bankruptcy, 52
Banks. *See* Lenders
Barter transactions, 110
Bill-and-hold transactions, 109
Bily v. Arthur Young & Co., 32, 33
Blame for financial misreporting, 40-42
  outside auditor's role, 23-25
Blue Ribbon Committee
  formation of, 2, 35
  recommendations, 35-39, 184,
    234-35, 248
  report on corporate audit committees
    (1999), 24
  SEC rules to implement recommen-
    dations for audit committees,
    234-35, 245

Board of directors
    action plan, 53-54
    audit committee's sensitivity to
        pressure, 232-33
    auditor's recommendation to notify
        statement users, 63-64
    auditor's relationship with, 65
    crisis for, 20-21
    crisis management, 45, 47
    as defendants in class-action lawsuit,
        122
    initial meeting in aftermath of fraud
        discovery, 46-50
    insurance (D&O). *See* Insurance,
        director and officer (D&O)
    participation in fraud, 48
    role in financial reporting, 27,
        228-29
Bookkeeping, 98-99
Books and records, 252
    forensic investigation of, 251
    SEC rule, 253
Boston Stock Exchange, 181

C

Cash crisis, 51-52
Cease-and-desist orders, 179
Cendant Corporation, 1, 34
Certified Public Accountant (CPA)
    as audit committee member, 241,
        295
    punishment for wrongdoing by
        SEC, 179
Charter of audit committee, 235,
    242-44, 295, 296-97
    sample, 277-80
Checklists
    for audit committee, 229-30
    board's action plan implementation,
        53
Chicago Board Options Exchange, 181
Chicago Stock Exchange, 181
Chief executive officer (CEO)
    aggressive pursuit of growth by,
        301, 302
    as defendant in class-action lawsuit,
        122
    knowledge of fraud, 48, 117
    possible involvement in fraud, 62

    pressure for performance, 291-92
    pursuit of greatness by, 289-90
Chief financial officer (CFO)
    as defendant in class-action lawsuit,
        122
    as guardian of financial reporting
        integrity, 290-92
    information provided to financial
        analysts, 310-11, 313-14
    insurance application signed by, 162
    knowledge of fraud, 48, 117
    possible involvement in fraud, 62
    pressure to misrepresent financial
        results, 1-2
Cincinnati Stock Exchange, 181
Claim, defined, 145-46
Claims based on accounting irregulari-
    ties, 1
Claims-made insurance policy, 144-46,
    154-55
    notification requirements, 154-55
Class action lawsuits. *See* Lawsuits,
    class-action
Cleopatra syndrome, 247, 272
Collective-knowledge doctrine, 213-14
Committee of Sponsoring Organiza-
    tions of the Treadway Commission
    (COSO). *See also* Treadway
    Commission
    committee recommendations
        applicable to small companies,
        38-39
    study on underlying causes of
        fraudulent financial reporting, 2
Committee to investigate the fraud,
    56-57, 68
Common interest agreement, 177
Communications With the Audit
    Committee (AU Section 380), 38
Communication with audit committees.
    See also SAS-61
    access to reliable information,
        247-48
    from internal audit, 269-71
    from outside auditor, 249-51
    from senior management, 248-49
Community of interest, 209
Company, as defendant in lawsuit, 121,
    129

Complaint, consolidated, 124-27, 129-30

Computerized information
database retrieval, 86
general ledger system, 113
preservation of records, 106
searches of company's computer files, 104

Confidentiality. *See* Privilege

Conflict of interest, 216-17

Consideration of Fraud in a Financial Statement Audit. *See* SAS-82

Consignment sales, 109

Cookie-jar reserves, 15

Corporate criminal liability for employee actions, 213-17

Corporate environment
example of, 6-11
insight into wrong kind, 288
pressure, 11, 26-27, 286-88
start and growth of accounting irregularities in, 6, 250
start of financial misreporting in, 3, 19, 285-88
tone at the top, 27, 231, 286

Corporate governance standards, 183

COSO. *See* Committee of Sponsoring Organizations of the Treadway Commission (COSO)

Counsel. *See also* Outside counsel
class-action lawsuits, 123-24
conflict of interest, 216-17
contacts with prosecutor in criminal investigations, 196-97
counsel for target company, 221-24
employee's counsel in criminal investigations, 200-2
employee's request to have counsel present for interview, 89
indemnification for fees, 60, 214-16
responding to SEC subpoenas, 176-77

Court cases
Bily v. Arthur Young & Co., 32, 33
Ernst & Ernst v. Hochfelder, 126

CPA. *See* Certified Public Accountant (CPA)

Credibility
regaining with SEC, 173-74

restoring of, 52, 60

Criminal indictment, 222

Criminal investigation. *See* Investigation, criminal

Criminal sentences, 194
sentencing guidelines. *See* Federal Sentencing Guidelines

Crisis for board of directors, 20-21, 45, 47

Crisis in cash, 51-52

Cross-claims, 79. *See also* Lawsuits; Litigation

Customers
contacting, 53
effects of doubts about company's financial stability, 61, 65
interest in objective investigation, 101
restoring of credibility with, 60

D

Damages
estimates, 137-38
uninsurable punitive damages, 149

Damages experts, 137

Database information in investigation, 86

Day-traders as shareholders in lawsuit, 138

Debt covenant, violation of, 129
event of default, 51
lending agreement provisions, 51

Defendants in class-action lawsuits, 121-23
audit committee members, 42, 122
categories of, 128-29
company as defendant, 121, 129
discovery process, 132
insurance coverage, 128-29, 141-42, 157-61, 164
officers, 121-22
outside auditor, 123, 134-35
outside directors, 122
representation, 124
selling shareholders, 123
underwriters, 122-23

Defense costs, 59-60

Delaware Law, 246

Delisting of securities, 58, 167, 182

Delisting of securities, *cont.*
    company approach to proceedings,
        188-89
    corrective measures, 188
    effect of no audited financial
        statements, 65
    hearing request, 189
    Nasdaq procedures, 186
    NYSE procedures, 185
    prevention and handling of, 186
    suspension of trading, 187
    time pressure for investigation, 53
Depositions, 132, 136
Depression-era financial reporting
    system, 307-8, 314
Diligence of audit committee, 41-42,
    295-96
Directors
    board. *See* Board of directors
    director defined for insurance, 146
    indemnification of, 59-60
    insurance coverage, D&O policy.
        See Insurance, director and
        officer (D&O)
    insurance exclusion for outside
        directorship, 147-48
    outside directors as defendants in
        class-action lawsuits, 122
Disclosure requirements, SEC, 168-70
Discounting used for revenue manipula-
    tion, 110, 312
Discovery
    adding outside auditor as defendant,
        134-35
    depositions, 132, 136
    document requests, 132-34
    pretrial investigation, 131, 132
    process of, 132-136
Dishonesty, in fraudulent financial
    reporting, 11
Division of Enforcement of the SEC
    final investigative report, 177-78
    Formal Order of Investigation,
        171-72, 175
    initial contact by company, 175
    penalties and sanctions, 172-73,
        179-80
    shipment timing, 313
    subpoena powers, 171-72, 176-77

Document(s). *See also* Report(s)
    forensic accountant's investigation,
        103-4, 106
    procured for internal investigation,
        85-86
    produced in response to criminal
        subpoena, 198-200
    production of documents in
        class-action lawsuit, 132-34
    request by auditor, 74-75
    request in discovery process, 132-34
    search of files in criminal investiga-
        tion, 202
    securing after fraud discovery, 58
D&O insurance. *See* Insurance, director
    and officer (D&O)
Double jeopardy, 224
Downturn in business, 303-4
Dual-sovereignty doctrine, 224
Due diligence, 281-304
    underwriters' investigation of
        prospectus, 126-27

E

Economics of Trust, The (Whitney),
    272
Edgar system of electronic SEC filing,
    308
E-mail communications
    as investigative evidence, 86
    revenue reports, 314
Employee
    corporate criminal liability for
        employee actions, 213-17
    counsel for individual employees in
        criminal investigation, 200-2
    counsel provided for former
        employees, 177
    interviews in investigation. *See*
        Interviews of witnesses
    joint-defense agreement in criminal
        investigation, 203
    restoring credibility with, 60
    senior executives. *See* Senior
        executives
    termination due to involvement in
        fraud, 48-49, 91-92

welfare, corporate concern for, 3

Enforcement Division. *See* Division of Enforcement of the SEC

Environment. *See* Corporate environment

Equitable relief, 173

Ernst & Ernst v. Hochfelder, 126

Ernst & Young, 31

Errors
  defined, 4, 5, 70
  difference between irregularities and errors, 4-5
  examples of, 70

Estimates, inaccurate, 71-72

Evidence, preservation of, 106

Evidence gathering
  auditor's requests for documents, 74-75
  forensic investigation, 104
  retrieval of database information, 86

Evolution of financial reporting, 24

Exclusions in insurance policies. *See* Insurance, D&O, exclusions

Expectation gap initiative, 31

Expectation gap revision of SAS (1989), 24

Expenses, manipulation of, 112-13
  common accounting fraud areas, 108

F

FASB. *See* Financial Accounting Standards Board (FASB)

Federal criminal investigation, 191-95

Federal Sentencing Guidelines
  effective compliance program, 219-21, 223
  sentencing range, 218-21

Fifth Amendment privilege
  civil and criminal proceedings, 225
  corporate indemnification, 215
  criminal investigations, 197-98
  custodian of company's documents, 199-200
  grand jury witness, 206-8
  and immunity, 211
  waiver, 207-8

Final adjudication in D&O insurance coverage, 159-60

Financial Accounting Standards Board (FASB), 2. *See also* SAS-53; SAS-61; SAS-71; SAS-82

Financial analysts, 309
  fulfilling expectations of, 15, 109, 310-11
  identifying vulnerable companies, 281
  information from CFO to, 313-14

Financial fraud. *See* Accounting irregularities; Financial misreporting; Fraud

Financial markets. *See also* Securities exchanges; Stock market
  demand for non-stop information by, 305
  effect of analysts' expectations, 309
  inefficiencies, 311-12
  initial press release to, 54-56
  real-time demands of, 306-7, 311, 317

Financial misreporting. *See also* Financial reporting, responsibility for
  blame for, 40-42
  blaming outside auditor for, 23-25
  dishonesty not a cause of, 11, 305
  effect of quarterly expectations, 109
  elements of, 11-13
  epidemic of, 305, 317
  pressure as cause of. *See* Pressure to misrepresent financial results
  role of audit committee in detection of, 233-34
  start and growth in corporate environment, 3, 19, 285-88
  tone at the top created by CEO and CFO, 291
  Treadway Commission's study of, 25-26

Financial reporting, responsibility for, 23, 40
  allocation between management and outside auditor, 31-32
  audit committee's oversight role, 17, 27-28, 229-30, 292-97
  CEO's priorities, 289-90
  CFO as guardian of integrity, 290-92

Financial reporting, responsibility for, *cont.*
  corporate management's primary responsibility, 31
  corporate officials' expanded responsibilities, 43
  court decisions, 32, 33
  effect of Treadway Commission's report, 30
  senior management subject to pressure, 228-29
  tone set by top management, 27
Financial reporting system
  designed in 1930s, 307-8
  designed to provide periodic information, 305-6
  evolution of, 24
  evolving beyond periodic system, 306, 315
  inefficiencies of periodic system, 311-14
  logistical capabilities of, 233, 252
  real-time basis vs. periodic system, 311, 315-16
  "touchstone" principals of, 170
Financial statements
  effect on financial markets, 309
  example of fraudulent numbers, 281-83
Financial statements, new audited, 61
  auditor. *See* Accountant, forensic; Outside auditor
  effect of lawsuits, 78-79
  management representations, 76-78
  mistrust in auditor-management relationship, 64-65
  outside auditor's involvement, 61-62
  previously issued audit reports, 62-64
Financial statements, restated
  audit process, 74-76
  bottom line, 79-80
  facilitated by forensic accountants, 68
  guidelines, 70
  increasing number of, 1
  issued after completing investigation, 63
  materiality assessments, 72-74

reasons for requirement, 69-72
responsibility for, 68-69
retention of incumbent auditor, 57
Fines imposed by the SEC, 179, 180
Fines imposed in criminal prosecutions, 219
Foreign Corrupt Practices Act, 252
Forensic accountant. *See* Accountant, forensic
Forged documents, 104, 105, 106
Form 8-K, filing upon occurrence of specified events, 169
Form 10-K Annual Report, 308
  disclosures in, 295
  effect of previously issued audit reports, 62-63
  effect on stock prices, 309
  filing with the SEC, 169
  inclusion of audit committee's letter of disclosure, 37-38
  inclusion of audited financial statements, 246
  insurance application process, 162
  placing on Web sites, 308
  Section 10(b) prohibitions, 125
Form 10-Q quarterly report
  auditor review before filing, 38
  filing with the SEC, 169
  placing on Web sites, 308
  Section 10(b) prohibitions, 125
Formal Order of Investigation, 171-72, 175
Fraud. *See also* Accounting irregularities
  aftermath of discovery. *See* Aftermath of fraud discovery
  common accounting fraud areas, 108
  deliberate fraud. *See* Insurance, D&O, exclusions
  distinction between irregularity and fraud, 4
  investigation of. *See* Investigation
  new standard for use of term fraud, 4, 70
  outside auditor's failure to detect, 18-19, 283-85
  reckless fraud, 126, 157-58
  start and growth of, 11-13
  surfacing of, 20

Fraudulent financial reporting. *See* Financial misreporting

G

GAAP. *See* Generally accepted accounting standards (GAAP)

GAAS. *See* Generally accepted auditing standards (GAAS)

General ledger, 113-14

Generally accepted accounting standards (GAAP)
  appropriate reserve levels, 110
  changes in accounting policies, 71, 72
  changes in estimates, 71-72
  clarity of rules, 108
  expenditures expensed or capitalized, 112
  financial statement violations, 69
  forensic accountant's expertise, 98
  judgment in application, 107-8, 256, 291
  managerial bias in GAAP application, 253
  revenue recognition, 8, 109

Generally accepted auditing standards (GAAS)
  amendments to increase auditor candor, 253, 258, 260, 274
  auditor independence, 78, 268
  auditor's failure to detect fraud, 283
  auditor's opinion on financial statements, 76
  audit sampling approach, 68
  forensic investigation vs. GAAS audit, 102-5, 251
  inspection of inventory, 111-12
  jury's understanding of, 24
  management representations, 76-77
  management's responsibility for financial statements, 31
  materiality thresholds of GAAS audit, 18
  professional skepticism approach, 68, 103, 251
  quality of accounting principles, 37
  required audit testing, 258

Government, investigation by, 85. *See also* Federal criminal investigation

Grand jury phase of criminal investigation
  employee contact with counsel, 200-2
  employee interviews, 202-5
  initial contacts with prosecutor, 196-97
  initial grand jury phase, 195-205
  response to subpoena, 195-96
  testimonial grand jury phase, 205-12

Grand jury subpoena. *See* Subpoena *duces tecum*

Growth curve of expanding company, 302

H

Health care industry, 300

Health Management, Inc., 283, 302

I

Illegal acts, defined, 71

Immunity of witnesses, 210-12
  formal, 211, 218
  informal, 211-12, 218
  letter, 211-12
  from prosecution, 217-18
  transactional, 211, 212
  use, 211

Indemnification, 59-60
  counsel fees, 60, 214-16
  insurance coverage for loss, 148
  of underwriters, 123

Independence of auditor. *See* Auditor independence

Independence Standards Board (ISB)
  evolution of financial reporting (1997), 24
  rules on auditor independence, 263, 264, 265
  Standard No. 1 (Independence Discussions with Audit Committees), 264, 265, 266

Independent counsel. *See* Outside counsel

Indictment, 222

Industry downturn, 303-4

Information revolution, 306-7

Injunctions, 179, 180

Insider trading, 310
Institutional investors, 138
Insurance, director and officer (D&O),
    49-50, 141-42
    accounting irregularities, 156-57
    analysis of policy, 144
    application process, 162-63
    capacity requirement for insurance
        coverage, 147-48
    claim, defined, 145-46
    claims for wrongful acts, 147-50
    claims-made policy, 144-46, 154-55
    class-action defendants, 128-29,
        141-42, 157-61, 164
    Coverage A (individual side), 142
    Coverage B (company reimburse-
        ment), 142
    coverage issues, 163-65
    date of coverage, 146
    declarations page of policy, 142
    defining terms of policy, 143
    deliberate fraud exclusion. *See*
        Insurance, D&O, exclusions
    endorsements. *See* Insurance, D&O,
        endorsements
    entity coverage, 142
    exclusions. *See* Insurance, D&O,
        exclusions
    factual determination, 159-60
    imputation from one insured to
        another, 158-59, 161
    indemnification for wrongful acts,
        148
    insured, defined, 146
    insuring clauses of policy, 143, 144
    "loose cannons on the deck," 160-61
    losses, 148-49
    notice-of-claim provisions, 154-55
    prior acts date, 146
    reckless fraud, 129, 157-58
    retention and coinsurance, 156
    retroactive date, 146
    self-insurance, 156
    settlement of class-action lawsuit,
        131
    structure of typical policy, 142-43
    terms and conditions, 143
    tests of claims for coverage, 144
Insurance, D&O, endorsements
    addition of employees, 147

defined, 143
    exclusions added by endorsement,
        150
    expansive, 153-54
    outside directorship coverage, 147
    restrictive, 153
Insurance, D&O, exclusions
    added by endorsement, 150
    claims covered under other policies,
        151
    conduct, 150
    deliberate fraud, 49-50, 141
    deliberate fraudulent act exclusion
        provision, 155-56, 159
    exclusion section of policy, 143,
        150
    insured v. insured, 152-53
    interpretation issues, 151
    outside directorship, 147-48
    pending and prior litigation, 151
    prior-notice, 155
Insurance carriers, notification of, 53
Intent-to-benefit rule, 213
Interim Financial Review. *See* SAS-71
Internal audit, 17-18
    audit committee's interaction with,
        40
    communication with audit commit-
        tees, 269-71
    ineffectiveness of, 17-18
    lack of viable function, 420
    outsourced to outside auditor, 270
    recommendations of Blue Ribbon
        Committee, 36
    recommendations of Treadway
        Commission, 28
Internal control system, 242-43
Internet access to financial information,
    306
Internet companies, 300
Interrogatories, 132
In terrorem effect, 246
Interviews of witnesses
    criminal investigation, 202-5
    employee interviews, 88-90, 115-16,
        202-5
    forensic investigation, 115-16
    internal investigation, 87
    lack of subpoena power, 87-90

lawyer participation, 115-16
people to be interviewed, 87
privileged communications, 115
eluctance to be interviewed, 89-90,
202-3
request to have counsel present, 89
witnesses not questioned under oath,
90
Inventory, manipulation of, 111-12
common accounting fraud areas,
108
Investigation
accounting systems, 87, 98-99
audit committee's responsibility for,
56-57, 68
criminal. *See* Investigation, criminal
database information, 86
documents procured for, 85-86
employment termination issues,
91-92
forensic. *See* Investigation, forensic
forensic accountant's role in, 97-102
by the government, 85
implementation checklist, 53
interviewing witnesses. *See*
Interviews of witnesses
lack of subpoena power, 87-90
manpower for, 99
outside counsel retained for, 83
preliminary, 45-46
pretrial (discovery), 131, 132
prior to issuing restated financial
statements, 63
privileged work product, 95-96
privileged written reports, 94-95
purposes of, 81-83
report, 87, 92-94
special committee created for, 57,
68
tasks to perform, 85-87
time frame, 84-85
time pressure, 50, 51-53
unresolved issues, 91-92
written vs. oral report, 92-94
Investigation, criminal, 191-95
accuracy in interview process, 203
cooperation vs. antagonistic stance,
197-98
corporate liability, 213-17
document presentation, 198-200

employee contact with counsel,
200-2
employee interviews, 202-5
Fifth Amendment. *See* Fifth
Amendment privilege
grand jury phase. *See* Grand jury
phase of criminal investigation
grand jury subpoena. *See* Subpoena
duces tecum
indictment of company, 222
joint defense. *See* Joint defense
parallel proceedings, 224-24
phases, 195
plea discussions, 217-19
responsibilities of counsel for target
company, 221-24
risk of disclosure in civil case, 201-2
search of files, 202
sentences imposed, 194
sentencing guidelines. *See* Federal
Sentencing Guidelines
targets and subjects, 210, 214-17
testimonial grand jury phase, 205-12
witness identification, 201
Investigation, forensic
difference between normal GAAS
audit and forensic investigation,
102-5
disruptive to company's operations,
84, 106, 115
documentary evidence, 104
ending the investigation, 118
evidence gathering, 104
framing the issues, 107-8, 113
general ledger information, 113-14
independent forensic accounting
team, 68
interview process, 115-16
lawyer participation, 114-16
new audit system installed as, 251
outside auditor's role, 68, 116-18
preservation of evidence, 106
purpose of, 104
scope and materiality, 104
suspicious documents, 103-4, 106,
114
urgency of, 105
Investigative report to SEC, 177-78
Investment returns in new industry,
297-98

Investors
 identifying vulnerable companies,
   281
 interest in audit committee membership, 295
 interest in objective investigation,
   101
 plaintiff shareholders in class-action
   lawsuit, 138
Irregularity. *See* Accounting irregularities
ISB. *See* Independence Standards
   Board (ISB)
Issuers, 168-69
 Formal Order of Investigation,
   171-72

J

Joint defense
 agreement for reluctant employees,
   203
 in grand jury testimony, 209-10
 multiple counsel, 177
 waiver of privilege, 209-10
 witnesses in criminal investigation,
   201
Joint-defense privilege, 209-10
Joint representations, 177

L

Lawsuits. *See also* Litigation
 civil party, 85, 201
 class-action. *See* Lawsuits,
   class-action
 cross-claims, 79
 effect on auditor's independence,
   78-79
Lawsuits, class-action, 119-20
 commencement of litigation, 120-21
 consolidated complaint, 124-27,
   129-30
 counsel for plaintiffs and defendants, 123-24
 damages estimates, 137-38
 defendants. *See* Defendants in
   class-action lawsuits
 defined, 119
 discovery process, 132-36
 early settlement, 131-32

handling by board of directors,
   58-59
 insurance coverage. *See* Insurance,
   director and officer (D&O)
 liability implications of press
   release, 127-30
 motion to dismiss, 130-31, 135
 parallel criminal proceedings, 225
 production of documents, 132-34
 settlement, 131-32, 136-38
 shareholders as plaintiffs, 129, 137,
   138
 stages of, 120
Lawyers. *See also* Counsel; Outside
   counsel
 interaction with forensic accountants, 114-16
Learn the business by audit committees,
   274-75
Legal counsel. *See* Counsel; Outside
   counsel
Lenders
 contacting, 53
 effects of doubts about company's
   financial stability, 61, 65
 identifying vulnerable companies,
   281
 interest in objective investigation,
   101
 restoring credibility with, 60
Lending agreement, provisions of, 51
Leslie Fay, 33, 287
Levitt, Arthur, 2
 audit committee meetings, 276
 initiatives, 32-40
 speech at New York University
   (1998), 2, 24, 34, 229
 speeches to stop "accounting
   hocus-pocus," 170-71
 "The Numbers Game," 34, 35
Liability
 claims included in consolidated
   complaint, 125-27
 corporate liability for employee
   actions, 213-17
 corporate officials liable to outside
   auditor, 43
 implications of initial press release,
   127-30

vicarious, 213

Listing requirements, 183-84
    agreement, 183
    criteria, 181-82
    delisting. *See* Delisting of securities
    violations, 187-88

Litigation. *See also* Cross-claims;
    Lawsuits
    crisis, 31
    effect on auditor's independence,
        78-79
    juries' expectation gap, 31
    risk to audit committee members,
        43-44
    use of written investigative report,
        94, 134

Loss
    calculation in sentencing guidelines,
        219
    defined for D&O insurance, 148,
        149

Lucent Technologies, 312

M

Managed earnings, 14-15
    battle for corporate culture, 231

Management. *See also* Senior execu-
    tives
    installing new management, 58
    responsibility for financial report-
        ing, 27, 31, 32, 228
    responsibility for restated financial
        statements, 68-69
    tone at the top, 231

Management representations, 76-78

Materiality
    adjusting journal entry, 256
    assessments, 72-74
    forensic investigation, 104
    nonmaterial PAJEs, 256-58
    SAB 99, 73-74, 256-58
    thresholds of GAAS audit, 18, 19

McKesson-Robbins inventory fraud,
    111

Microsoft financial reports, 317

Misreporting. *See* Financial misreport-
    ing

Mistrust in auditor-management
    relationship, 64-65

Momentum investors, 138, 311

Motion to dismiss, 130-31, 133, 135

Mutual funds as shareholders in
    lawsuit, 138

N

NASD. *See* National Association of
    Securities Dealers (NASD)

Nasdaq, 181. *See also* National
    Association of Securities Dealers
    (NASD)
    delisting of securities, 58
    delisting procedures, 186
    trading practices criticized, 182

National Association of Securities
    Dealers (NASD), 181. *See also*
    Nasdaq
    audit committee charter rules, 242,
        244
    audit committee composition rules,
        236
    audit committee configuration, 17,
        41, 234-35, 241
    audit committee independence
        requirements, 235-36, 239-41,
        293
    Blue Ribbon Committee recommen-
        dations, 36, 184
    delisting of securities, 185-86
    investigation by, 23
    listing requirements, 184-85
    new rules of financial reporting, 24
    restructuring in 1996, 182-83
    rules to combat financial fraud, 2

National Commission on Fraudulent
    Financial Reporting. *See* Treadway
    Commission

Negligent wrongdoer penalties, 179

Negotiated resolution with the SEC,
    178-81

New industry, 297-300

New York Stock Exchange (NYSE),
    181
    audit committee charter rules, 242,
        243
    audit committee composition rules,
        235
    audit committee configuration, 17,
        41, 234-35, 241

New York Stock Exchange (NYSE), *cont.*
  audit committee independence requirements, 236, 238, 240-41, 293
  Blue Ribbon Committee recommendations, 36, 184
  delisting of securities, 58
  delisting procedures, 185
  disclosure requirement, 183
  investigation by, 23
  listing requirements, 181, 184-85
  new rules of financial reporting, 24
  rules to combat financial fraud, 2
Non-audit services, 261-62, 264, 267
Nonmaterial PAJEs, 256-58
Non-prosecution agreement, 218
NYSE. *See* New York Stock Exchange (NYSE)

O

Objectivity of forensic accountant, 101-2
Obstruction-of-justice, 217
Offense level for sentencing, 218-19
Officers
  as defendants in class-action lawsuit, 121-22
  defined, for insurance, 146
  indemnification of, 59-60
  insurance coverage, D&O policy. *See* Insurance, director and officer (D&O)
Off-the-record discussion, 218
O'Malley Panel on Audit Effectiveness, 24
  factors in evaluating non-audit services, 267-68
  recommendations of, 39-40
Operational inefficiencies, 312-13, 315
Outside auditor, 18-19. *See also* Auditor
  allocation of responsibility for financial reporting, 31-32
  audit committee's information from. *See* Audit committee information from the outside auditor
  audit committee's interaction with, 17, 40, 249

  blame for financial misreporting, 23-25
  coordination with forensic accountant, 116-18
  as defendant in class-action lawsuit, 123, 134-35
  early involvement in press release, 54
  evolving perceptions of auditor responsibility, 33
  failure to detect fraud, 18-19, 283-85
  forensic accountants' interaction with, 68, 116-17
  impediments to detection of fraud, 250-51
  independence of. *See* Auditor independence
  involvement in finding irregularities, 61-62
  liability of corporate officials to, 43
  outsource of internal audit, 270
  report of investigation to, 95
  retaining regular outside auditor, 57
  SAS-71 review, 38, 249-50
  secondary role in fraud prevention, 30, 31
  upper hand in audit report, 60
  watchdog function, 33
  working papers of, 117
Outside counsel
  investigation conducted by, 83-84
  need for independent counsel, 57, 83
  responding to SEC subpoenas, 176-77
Outsource of internal audit function, 270

P

Pacific Stock Exchange, 181
PAJE (proposed adjusting journal entry), 256
Panel on Audit Effectiveness. *See* O'Malley Panel on Audit Effectiveness
Parallel proceedings, 224-24
Penalties by the SEC, 172-73, 179-80
Periodic financial reporting, 307-8

inefficiencies of, 311-14
Petri dish for accounting irregularities, 303
Philadelphia Stock Exchange, 181
Plea agreement, 217-19
Preannouncements, 317
Preliminary investigation, 45-46
Press inquiries, response by counsel, 221-22
Press release
  in aftermath of discovery, 54-56
  call to SEC prior to, 175
  commencement of class-action litigation, 120-21
  "irregularity" absent from, 56
  liability implications of, 127-30
Pressure for performance, 40-41, 228-29
  CEO's unreasonable demands, 291
  corporate environment, 11, 27, 286-88
  in new industry, 300
  sensitivity to, 232, 291
  unsustainable growth curve, 302
Pressure to misrepresent financial results, 11-12
  CFOs subjected to, 1-2
  Treadway Commission's findings, 26-27
Pretrial investigation, 131, 132
PricewaterhouseCoopers, survey of claims based on accounting irregularities, 1
Prison sentences, 194, 219
Private Securities Litigation Reform Act (1995), 24
Privilege
  attorney-client. *See* Attorney-client privilege
  confidentiality of final investigative report, 177-78
  Fifth Amendment. *See* Fifth Amendment privilege
  witness documents in criminal investigation, 201
  work product, 84, 95-96, 208-9
  written reports, 94-95
Professional skepticism of auditor, 68, 75, 103

abandonment of approach, 251
Proffer discussion, 218
Proposed adjusting journal entry (PAJE), 256
Prospectus
  inclusion in registration statement, 169
  liability for misleading information, 126-27
Proxy statement
  disclosures, 240, 295
  report filed with, 244-46
  SEC rules, 264
Public offering, 123, 126-27
Public Oversight Board, 2, 39

Q

Qualitative listing requirements, 183
Quantitative listing requirements, 183, 188
Quarter-end revenue manipulations, 110, 312-13
Quarterly information
  auditor's level of scrutiny, 18, 249-50
  discussion with audit committee, 260
  market effect of quarterly statements, 309
  preoccupation with quarterly results, 316

R

Real-time demands of financial markets, 306-7, 311, 317
Real-time financial reporting, 315-16
Reckless fraud, 129, 157-58
Records. *See* Books and Records; Document(s)
Regulation FD, SEC, 317
Regulators. *See also* Securities and Exchange Commission (SEC); Self-Regulatory Organization (SRO)
  halt of trading company stock, 61
  notification of, 54, 63
  restoring credibility with, 60
  written report of investigation to, 94
Remedial order, 219

Report(s). *See also* Document(s)
   audit committee report to SEC, 235,
      244-46
   final investigative report to SEC,
      177-78
   forensic investigation, 117
   Forms 8-K, 10-K and 10-Q filed
      with SEC, 169
   internal investigation, 92-94, 134
   investigative tasks, 87
   privileged, 94-95
   use of investigative report in
      litigation, 94, 134
   written vs. oral, 92-94
Representation letters by management,
   76-78
Reserves, 110-11
   common accounting fraud areas,
      108
   cookie-jar reserves, 15
   defined, 110
   reporting unusual activity to audit
      committee, 255-56
   restructuring charges, 111
   for returns, 8
Restated financial statements. *See*
   Financial statements, restated
Restitution by the company, 219
Restructuring charges, 111
Revenue recognition, 109-10
   accelerated shipments, 8, 109
   barter transactions, 110
   bill-and-hold transactions, 109
   common accounting fraud areas,
      108
   consignment sales, 109
   discounting, 110
   looking for unusual patterns, 255-56
Rule 10b-5, SEC, 125
Rule 102(e), SEC, 179

S

SAB 99 (SEC Staff Accounting
   Bulletin Number 99), 73-74,
   256-58
Sampling. *See* Audit sampling
SAS-53 (The Auditor's Responsibility
   to Detect and Report Errors and
   Irregularities)

   errors, defined, 5
   irregularities, defined, 4, 5
SAS-61 (Communication with Audit
   Committees), 254
   audit committee's report to SEC,
      246
   items to be discussed, 259-60
   materiality of uncorrected misstate-
      ments, 258
SAS-71 (Interim Financial Review), 38,
   249-50, 255
SAS-82 (Consideration of Fraud in a
   Financial Statement Audit),
   auditor's responsibility for
   detecting fraud, 4
Scienter, 125, 130
SEC. *See* Securities and Exchange
   Commission (SEC)
Section 10(b), 125-26, 130, 138, 170
Section 11, 127
Section 12(2), 126-27
Section 12(a)(2), 126-27
Section 13, 169
Section 15, 127
Section 20, 126
Section 24, 192
Section 32(a), 192
Securities. *See also* Stock
   delisting. *See* Delisting of securities
   trading based on false financial
      information, 46
Securities Act of 1933
   registration requirement, 168-69
   Section 11, 127
   Section 12(2), 126
   Section 12(a)(2), 126-27
   Section 15, 127
   Section 24 (criminal violations), 192
Securities and Exchange Commission
   (SEC), 167. *See also specific Form*
   administrative and judicial proceed-
      ings, 172-73
   assessment of materiality, 73-74
   audit committee's report to, 235,
      244-46
   auditor independence issue, 261-62
   auditor independence rules, 263,
      264, 266

Blue Ribbon Committee recommendations for new rules, 36, 37-38
comparability of reporting system, 170
confidentiality of investigative report, 177-78
cooperation with, 174-75
corporate disclosure requirements, 168-70
demand for corrected financial information, 61
early communication with, 175-76
Edgar system of electronic filing, 308
effect of no audited financial statements, 65
Enforcement Division. *See* Division of Enforcement of the SEC
filing of audit committee charter, 235, 242
filing of audited financial statements, 235. *See also* SAS-61
hearings on delisting, 189
heightened scrutiny of reporting practices, 2
initial contact, 175
interest in investigation, 83
interest in objective investigation, 101
investigation by, 23
investigative power of, 182
investigative report to, 177-78
Nasdaq trading practices criticized, 182
negotiated resolution, 178-81
new rules of financial reporting, 24, 39
notification of, 54, 63
objectives, 168
penalties, 172-73, 179-80
prohibition on non-audit services, 262
regaining credibility with. *See* Credibility with SEC
registration statement, 169
Regulation FD, 317
regulatory powers of, 167-68
reports filed under Section 13, 169
Rule 10b-5, 125
Rule 102(e), 179

rule for books and records, 253
rules to implement recommendations for audit committees, 234-35, 245
SROs registered, 181
SROs under SEC oversight, 182-83
Staff Accounting Bulletin No. 99 (SAB 99), 73-74, 256-58
transparency of reporting system, 170
Securities Exchange Act of 1934
corporate disclosure requirements, 169-68
original public reporting requirements, 308
Section 10(b), 125-26, 130, 138, 170
Section 13, 169
Section 20, 126
Section 32(a) (criminal violations), 192
Securities exchanges. *See also* Stock exchanges
delisting proceedings, 185, 186, 188-89
halt on trading stock, 52-53
interest in objective investigation, 101
investigation by SEC, 182-83
listing requirements, 183-85
restoring of credibility with, 60
self-regulatory organization. *See* Self-Regulatory Organization (SRO)
suspension of trading, 187
violations of listing requirements, 187-88
Securities law tort reform, 122, 123, 131
Securities Litigation Uniform Standards Act (1998), 24
Self-insurance, 156
Self-Regulatory Organization (SRO), 181-82
corrective measures, 188
creation of, 182
delisting. *See* Delisting of securities
investigation by the SEC, 182-83
listing requirements, 183-84
listing violations, 187-88

Self-Regulatory Organization (SRO), *cont.*
  registration with the SEC, 181, 182
  SEC oversight, 182-83
  suspension of trading, 187
Senior executives
  audit committee's information from, 248-49
  audit committee's relationship with, 272-73
  individual integrity of, 3
  pressure for performance by, 40-41
  SEC penalties, 179
  subject to pressure for performance, 232
  tone at the top, 231
Sentences, criminal, 194
Sentencing guidelines. *See* Federal Sentencing Guidelines
Settlement of class-action lawsuits
  agreement, 139-40
  conference, 137
  early, 131-32
  judge as catalyst for, 137
  negotiated resolution, 131, 136
Shareholders
  buyers in public offering, 126
  class-action litigation, 119-20, 121
  as defendants in class-action lawsuit, 123
  interest in objective investigation, 101
  as plaintiffs in class-action lawsuit, 129, 137, 138
  sellers in public offering, 123
  trading on basis of misinformation, 54
Shipment acceleration, 109
  example of, 8
Shipment timing at quarter-end, 313
SRO. *See* Self-Regulatory Organization (SRO)
Staff Accounting Bulletin No. 99 (Materiality), 73-74, 256-58
Statement on Auditing Standards. *See* SAS-53; SAS-61; SAS-71; SAS-82
Statements on Auditing Standards, Expectation Gap revision of (1989), 24

Stock. *See also* Securities
  delisting of. *See* Delisting of securities
  disruptions in trading of, 54-55
  halt of trading pending new financial information, 52-53, 61
  price after fraud disclosure, 58
Stock exchanges, 61. *See also* Securities exchanges
  notification of, 63
  regulatory powers of, 167, 181
  self-regulatory organization. *See* Self-Regulatory Organization (SRO)
Stock market, volatility of, 14, 311-12, 315
Subpoena
  by grand jury. *See* Subpoena *duces tecum*
  lack of subpoena power in internal investigation, 87-90
  response to subpoena for documents, 198-200, 222
  by SEC Division of Enforcement, 171-72, 176-77
Subpoena *duces tecum*, 195, 202, 208
  documents produced in response, 199-200
Suppliers
  contacting, 53
  interest in objective investigation, 101
  lack of confidence in company, 65
  restoring credibility with, 60

T

Telecommunications industry, 300
Testimonial quality knowledge, 203
Timeliness of audit approach, 251
Time pressure for thorough investigation, 50, 51-53, 84-85
Tone at the top, 27
  corporate environment, 286
  created by CEO and CFO, 291
  established by the audit committee, 231-33, 271-73
Tort reform legislation, 122, 123, 131
Treadmill effect, 10
  example of, 9

in industry downturn, 303
in managed earnings, 15
Treadway, James, 25
Treadway Commission. *See also*
    Committee of Sponsoring
    Organizations of the Treadway
    Commission (COSO)
    consequences of report, 28-30
    formation of, 25
    further developments, 30-32
    Levitt initiatives, 34, 36, 40
    recommendations for public
        companies, 28, 29
    report (1987), 24, 26-28
    study of financial fraud, 25-26

U

Underwriters
    as defendants in class-action lawsuit,
        122-23
    liability for shares purchased in
        public offering, 126-27

V

Venture capitalists
    identifying vulnerable companies,
        281
    interest in objective investigation,
        101

W

Waivers
    attorney-client privilege, 89, 94-95,
        208
    conflict of interest, 216-17
    Fifth Amendment privilege, 207-8
    joint-defense privilege, 209-10
Wall Street analysts. *See* Financial
        analysts
Waste management industry, 300
Web site
    available data, 317
    display of Form 10-K and 10-Q, 308
Wells Submission, 172
Whistleblower, 20
    assistance in preparing restated
        financial statements, 49
    preliminary investigation, 45-46
Whitney, John O., 272

Witnesses
    debriefing of, 221
    defined, 210-11
    Fifth Amendment privilege, 206-8,
        211
    identity in criminal investigation,
        201
    immunity of, 210-12, 217-18
    inaccuracies in recollections of,
        203-4
    interviewing of. *See* Interviews of
        witnesses
    privileges before grand jury, 206-10
    representation of, 176-77
    target or subject, 210, 214-17
Working papers of auditor, 66-67, 117
Work product as privileged informa-
        tion, 84, 95-96, 208-9
Written reports, 92-94, 117, 134
Wrongful act
    claim for, 147-50
    defined, 147
    interrelated, 149